Collins

WJEC Eduqas GCSE 9-1

Food Preparation and Nutrition

Revision Guide

Kath Callaghan, Fiona Balding, Jacqui Keepin, Barbara Monks, Barbara Rathmill and Suzanne Gray with Louise T. Davies

About this Revision & Practice book

Revise

These pages provide a recap of everything you need to know for each topic.

You should read through all the information before taking the Quick Test at the end. This will test whether you can recall the key facts.

> **Quick Test**
>
> 1. Name two main groups of fruits.
> 2. Name two main groups of vegetables.
> 3. Why it is more beneficial to buy and eat fruit and vegetables that are in season?

Practise

These topic-based questions appear shortly after the revision pages for each topic and will test whether you have understood the topic. If you get any of the questions wrong, make sure you read the correct answer carefully.

Review

These topic-based questions appear later in the book, allowing you to revisit the topic and test how well you have remembered the information. If you get any of the questions wrong, make sure you read the correct answer carefully.

Mix it Up

These pages feature a mix of questions for all the different topics, just like you would get in an exam. They will make sure you can recall the relevant information to answer a question without being told which topic it relates to.

Test Yourself on the Go

Visit our website at **collins.co.uk/collinsGCSErevision** and print off a set of flashcards. These pocket-sized cards feature questions and answers so that you can test yourself on all the key facts anytime and anywhere. You will also find lots more information about the advantages of spaced practice and how to plan for it.

Workbook

This section features even more topic-based questions as well as practice exam papers, providing two further practice opportunities for each topic to guarantee the best results.

ebook

To access the ebook revision guide visit

collins.co.uk/ebooks

and follow the step-by-step instructions.

Contents

Contents

Bread, Cereals, Flour and Oats

You must be able to:

- Know and understand the value of different commodities in the diet
- Know how to store commodities such as bread, cereals, flour and oats correctly
- Know the origins of these different commodities.

Bread

- Bread is a popular staple food eaten on a daily basis. It is used to make many light meals such as lunchtime sandwiches.
- Bread styles and types vary greatly and include white bloomers, sliced wholemeal loaves, crusty rolls and pitta bread.
- Bread is made by mixing strong flour (which is high in gluten) with liquid (water or milk) and a raising agent such as yeast. Salt is added and a small amount of sugar and fat can also be used. The ingredients are mixed until a dough is formed, which is then kneaded and shaped. Bread dough must be proved before baking.

Nutritional Content	Storage Information
• Bread provides the nutrients carbohydrates, protein, some B group vitamins, calcium and iron. Wholemeal varieties will provide dietary fibre (NSP).	• Bread storage depends on the type of bread. It can be well wrapped and frozen for longer storage; stored in a sealed paper bag or bread bin for short term storage if purchased fresh from a baker's; or kept in its plastic wrapper, if purchased from a supermarket, and in a cool, dry place. • Bread should not be refrigerated as it can affect the texture and flavour.

Cereals

- Wheat, oats, rye and barley are some of the cereals grown in the UK.
- A cereal is referred to as a grass with starchy edible grains or seeds used as food.
- Cereals are processed into other raw ingredients or foods before we eat or use them.
- Wheat is a common cereal used in many popular foods such as bread and breakfast cereals, e.g. Weetabix.

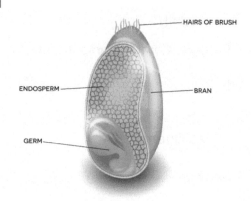

A grain of wheat

Nutritional Content	Storage Information
• Cereals are a good source of dietary fibre (NSP) and carbohydrates, providing energy in the diet. • Other nutrients provided by cereals include protein (Low Biological Value), B vitamins and vitamin E, some iron and fat.	• Cereals should be stored in an airtight container to prevent them becoming stale and in a cool, dry place. • Always use older cereals first and do not combine old and new together. • Incorrect storage can lead to a release of odours, mould developing and bacteria contamination, which could lead to food poisoning.

Flour

- Wheat is the main cereal processed to produce a variety of flours.
- Wheat flour can be of different strengths: strong flour is high in gluten and used in bread making; weak flour is used for baked goods, e.g. cakes and biscuits.
- Wholemeal, self-raising and brown are examples of different wheat flour types.
- Different flour types have different extraction rates, which states how much of the wholegrain of wheat has been used in the milling of the flour. White flour has an extraction rate of 70–75% as the germ and bran are removed during the milling process.

> ## Key Point
>
> **Processed** is when a raw material is changed to make it more suitable for making other food products, or to make it more edible.

Nutritional Content	Storage Information
• Wholemeal flour is a good source of dietary fibre (NSP) and starchy carbohydrates. • Strong flour has a high protein content. • White flour is fortified in the UK with B vitamins thiamine and niacin as well as minerals, calcium and iron.	• Flour must be stored in its original packaging in an airtight container in a cool, dry place. This should prevent the presence of weevils, which are known to live and breed in flour. • Always use flour within its use-by date. • Do not mix old and new flour together.

Oats

- Oats are grains from the cereal plant.
- A protective husk covers the oat grain, which is removed before the oats can be used as a food.
- Oats can be ground to produce a fine flour. They are also rolled or crushed to produce oatmeal. Rolled oats are used to make porridge.

> ## Key Point
>
> **Fortified** is when nutrients are replaced in a food as they have been removed or lost during the processing stage.

Nutritional Content	Storage Information
• Oats provide mainly starchy carbohydrates. The energy provided will be a slow-release energy source. Oats also provide soluble dietary fibre (NSP). • Protein, calcium, fat, iron and some B group vitamins are also provided in smaller amounts.	• Oats should be stored in a dry, cool area and in an airtight container once opened.

> ## Key Words
>
> gluten <br> proving <br> dietary fibre (NSP)
 contamination <br> weevils

> ## Quick Test
>
> 1. List two nutrients found in bread.
> 2. Explain why it is important to store cereals correctly.

Rice, Potatoes and Pasta

You must be able to:

- Know and understand the value of different commodities in the diet
- Know how to store commodities such as rice, potatoes and pasta correctly
- Know the origins of these different commodities.

Rice

- Rice grains are covered in a thick outer husk when the crop is harvested. This is removed during the processing stage.
- Rice types can vary in size, e.g. short and long grain, and colour: white, brown and red.
- Short grains can be very starchy. Rice pudding can be made using this type of rice.
- Long grain rice can have a firm, fluffy texture. Examples include Jasmine and Basmati rice.
- Rice can be cooked using various methods e.g. baking, boiling, and steaming.
- It is a staple food and can be served with sweet and savoury foods.

> **Key Point**
>
> A staple food is eaten frequently. It makes a valuable energy contribution to the daily diet.

Nutritional Content	Storage Information
• White rice mainly provides starchy carbohydrates; brown rice can provide some dietary fibre (NSP).	• Rice should be stored in a cool, dry cupboard or area. • Rice should be stored in an airtight container once opened. • Cooked rice is a high-risk food. If storing hot, it must not be stored for longer than two hours, and must be kept above 65°C. If storing cold, it must be rinsed in cold water, chilled and refrigerated.

Potatoes

- A potato has a skin on the outside, a fleshy section under the skin and a watery core in the centre called the pith.
- Potatoes are grown in the UK; some types include King Edward, Maris Piper and sweet potatoes.
- Potatoes are a staple food. They form a main part of many meals and can be cooked by roasting, baking, boiling, boiling and then mashing, or shallow and deep frying.

Nutritional Content	Storage Information
• Potatoes provide starchy carbohydrates, Vitamin C and some B group vitamins. • Potatoes have a high water content. • The skin, if eaten, provides dietary fibre (NSP).	• Potatoes should be stored in a dark, cool, airy place. If stored in a light environment they can turn green and become toxic. • Potatoes can be stored in vegetable racks, paper or hessian bags. If stored in plastic bags they can sweat and eventually rot.

Pasta

High protein content
— Requires little water to make dough
— easier to dig

- Pasta is made from a strong wheat called durum wheat.
- Egg can be added to make a paste, which can be rolled and shaped to make a variety of pastas.
- Pasta can be sold either fresh or dried. Types include lasagne sheets, filled tortellini, and cannelloni tubes.
- Pasta can be flavoured, e.g. with herbs and garlic. Coloured varieties include green, which is made using spinach, and red, which is made using tomato paste.
- Dried pasta is considered a good store cupboard ingredient as it has a long shelf life.

• Boiled to remove starch & prevent too sticky
• Xanthan gum is added to stabilise, give elasticity.
• Al dente – perfectly cooked.

Convenience food.

Nutritional Content	Storage Information
• Pasta provides the body with starchy carbohydrates, some protein and iron. • Whole wheat pasta contains more dietary fibre (NSP).	• Fresh pasta should be stored in a refrigerator. It can also be stored in a freezer. • Dried pasta (uncooked) should be stored in its packaging in a dry environment, and in an airtight container once opened. • Cooked pasta should be rinsed with cold water and stored in the refrigerator in an airtight container.

Quick Test		**Key Word**
1. Name two methods used to store fresh pasta. 2. Name two suitable cooking methods for potatoes.		dietary fibre (NSP) toxic

Fruit and Vegetables

You must be able to:

- Know and understand the value of fruits and vegetables in the diet
- Know how to store fruits and vegetables correctly
- Know the origins of different fruits and vegetables.

Fruit

- There are four main groups of fruits:
  - hard fruits, e.g. apples
  - soft/berry fruits, e.g. raspberries
  - citrus fruits, e.g. lemons
  - stone fruits, e.g. peaches.
- Other fruits, referred to as exotic or tropical, can include papaya and mango.
- Many fruits grown in the UK can be from a particular region of the country.
- Fruits that are not grown in the UK are imported from other countries to sell in shops.
- Many types of fruits are seasonal, which means they are only grown at certain times of the year.
- Fruits are very different in their colour, shape, size, flavour and texture.
- Fruits can be bought dried, fresh, canned, bottled and frozen.
- Healthy diet guidelines recommend that 5–7 portions of fruit and vegetables are eaten per day.

Nutritional Content	Storage Information
• Various nutrients can be supplied by eating a range of different fruits. Cooking some fruits can reduce their nutritional value, particularly vitamin C. • Key vitamins A, C and E can be obtained by eating mangoes, oranges and avocados. • Carbohydrates and the minerals potassium and magnesium are found in bananas. • Fruits provide dietary fibre (NSP).	• Hard fruits can be stored in the refrigerator or kept at room temperature. • Soft/berry fruits, e.g. strawberries, should be stored in the refrigerator. • Stone fruits, e.g. plums, can be stored in a refrigerator or in a fruit bowl, which will assist ripening. • Citrus fruits can be stored in a cool, dry place or refrigerated.

Key Point

Many fruits and vegetables are imported from other countries because the UK does not grow them. They are imported in order to meet demands made by shop customers who want to buy them all year round.

Vegetables

- Vegetables are grown above and below the ground depending on the type.
- Vegetables are grouped according to the different part of the plant they come from. Examples are shown in the table below.

Vegetable Group	Examples
Fruits and seeds	Peppers, sweetcorn, peas
Flowers	Broccoli, cauliflower
Leaves	Spinach, cabbage
Stems	Celery, asparagus
Shoots	Bamboo shoots, pea shoots
Tubers	Potatoes, sweet potatoes
Roots	Parsnips, swede, carrots
Bulbs	Leeks, onions

- Vegetables are very versatile; they can be eaten raw and juiced, and they can be cooked using various methods, e.g. steaming, roasting, boiling and stir frying.
- Vegetables that are frozen and canned still count towards the recommended 5–7 portions per day.

Nutritional Content	Storage Information
<ul><li>Eating a range of different vegetables on a daily basis will provide the body with nutrients such as carbohydrates, protein, vitamins A, C and E, dietary fibre (NSP), calcium and iron.</li><li>Vegetables have a high water content.</li><li>Fresh, raw, green vegetables can have a higher vitamin C value. Cooking them can reduce this.</li></ul>	<ul><li>Chilled storage for short term is best for many fresh, green types of vegetables to help reduce the loss of nutrients. The longer they are stored, the more their nutritional value will decrease.</li><li>Root and bulb vegetables can be stored in dry, well ventilated, cooler areas.</li></ul>

> ## Key Point
>
> Fruits and vegetables in season will be at their best in terms of flavour, ripeness and sweetness. This can mean a higher nutritional value.

> ## Quick Test
>
> 1. Name two main groups of fruits.
> 2. Name two main groups of vegetables.
> 3. Why it is more beneficial to buy and eat fruits and vegetables that are in season?

> ## Key Words
>
> seasonal

Milk, Cheese and Yoghurt

You must be able to:

- Understand how milk and milk products can be processed to produce different products
- Know and understand the value of milk and milk products in the diet
- Know how to store milk and milk products correctly.

Milk

- Milk comes from a variety of animals; in Britain we drink mainly cow's milk.
- Fresh milk has a layer of cream on top.
- Homogenised milk is forced through tiny holes in a machine. This breaks up the fat and disperses it, so it doesn't reform as a layer.
- Lactose-intolerant people can substitute animal milk in their diet with milk made from soya, rice, coconut, almond or oats.
- These milks don't contain lactose.
- To make milk safe to consume it is heat-treated to kill any harmful bacteria.

Types of Milk

- Using primary processing, milk is processed to produce a variety of different types:
  - Pasteurised – this extends shelf life.
  - Skimmed – this is pasteurised but has had all or most of the fat removed.
  - Semi-skimmed – this is pasteurised but has had some of the fat removed.
  - Ultra-Heat Treated (UHT) – also known as 'long life', this has a shelf life of up to six months.
  - Sterilised – this has a longer shelf life, is homogenised and has a slightly caramel flavour.
  - Dried – does not need refrigeration until reconstituted; it's made by evaporating the water from the milk, which leaves a fine powder; it's non bulky to store.
  - Canned:
    - o evaporated – milk that has had water evaporated off; it's sweet and concentrated, homogenised and is sealed in cans and sterilised
    - o condensed – evaporated milk that hasn't been sterilised; it has added sugar and is very thick.
- See table on page 13 for nutritional content and storage information for milk.

> ### Key Point
>
> Primary processing is the initial process that the food product goes through for us to be able to use it.

Cheese

- Cheese is milk in its solid form.
- There are many regional and international varieties of cheese, depending on the methods or animal milks used to produce them. Examples include camembert, mozzarella, and stilton.
- Different types of cheeses can be used to make both sweet and savoury dishes, e.g. cheesecake made using a cream cheese, and leek and cheese quiche made using a cheddar cheese.
- Cheese has many different characteristics and functions:
  - It can add colour as it can go golden brown when heated.
  - It can provide a subtle flavour if a mild cheese is used or a sharp/mature flavour if strong cheese is used.
  - It can add a different texture as it becomes very soft and moist when heated and melted.

> **Key Point**
>
> Pasteurisation is a heat treatment. Milk is heated to a high temperature of 72°C for a short time (15 seconds) and then cooled rapidly. This is known as HTST.

Nutritional Content	Storage Information
• Contains protein of high biological value (HBV). • Can have a high fat content. • Good source of calcium, and will provide some phosphorous and sodium. • Contains vitamin A and some B-group vitamins and vitamin D; this will vary depending on the cheese type.	• Cheese must be stored in a refrigerator between 0 and 5°C. • Soft cheeses can have a short shelf life so should be consumed quickly. • Hard-pressed types, e.g. cheddar, can be stored for longer. Cheese should be wrapped to prevent it drying out.

Yoghurt

- Yoghurt is made from milk that has a friendly bacteria culture added to it. Different types of milk can be used to make yoghurt.
- Flavourings, such as vanilla, fruits and sometimes sugar, are added to yoghurts.
- Examples of different types of yoghurts include Greek, set and live yoghurts.

Milk and Yoghurt

Nutritional Content	Storage Information
• Milk and yoghurt have a very similar nutritional content. • They contain protein of high biological value (HBV). The amount of fat will vary depending on the milk type. • Both milk and yoghurt contain carbohydrates as lactose (sugar). • Both milk and yoghurt provide vitamin A and some of the B group vitamins. Some milk is fortified with Vitamin D in the UK and can contain a small amount of vitamin C. Vitamin E can be found in whole-milk yoghurt.	• Fresh milk must be stored in the refrigerator. It should not be consumed past the use-by date. • Long life milks, e.g. UHT, can be stored in a cool, dry place until opened, then must be refrigerated and stored as fresh milk. • Yoghurt must be stored in the refrigerator and used within the use-by date.

> **Key Words**
>
> homogenised
> primary
>   processing
> pasteurised
> skimmed
> semi-skimmed
>
> Ultra-Heat
> Treated (UHT)
> sterilised
> dried
> evaporated
> condensed

> **Quick Test**
>
> 1. State the meaning of the letters HBV.
> 2. Describe two different functions of cheese.
> 3. What is pasteurisation?

Meat

You must be able to:

- Know the main sources of meat and how they are prepared
- Understand the structure of meat and how this affects the cooking method used.

Classifications of Meat

- Meat is classified as the muscle tissue of dead animals and birds.
- There are four main meat sources:
  - Animals: pork (pigs), beef (cattle), lamb (sheep).
  - Poultry: chicken, turkey, duck, goose.
  - Game: feathered or furred; venison, rabbit, pheasant.
  - Offal: liver, tongue, tripe, kidney, heart, brain, trotters.

The Structure of Meat

- Meat is a muscle made of cells, which consist of fibres held together by connective tissue. Long fibres are associated with tough meat – the older an animal is, the tougher the meat.
- Muscles that work a lot, such as the thighs and shoulders of animals, provide tough meat, e.g. shin beef, brisket. Small fibres are associated with tender cuts.

Meat Cuts and Cooking

- Cuts of meat from muscle areas that do a lot of work will need longer, slower cooking methods in wet heat, e.g. stewing, braising, pot roasting and casseroling.
- Meat from tougher cuts can be ground or minced to break up the connective tissues so that it cooks more quickly.
- Cuts of meat from muscle areas not so heavily used by the animal, e.g. the back and the rump, can be cooked much more quickly in dry heat, e.g. grilling, stir-frying.

Marinating and Tenderising

- Marinades are added to meat before cooking to add flavour, and the acid content (e.g. lemon juice, yoghurt, wine) breaks down the protein.
- Meat is tenderised by using a marinade, mincing or using a steak hammer.

The Effects of Cooking Meat

- The browning of meat is caused by a reaction with natural sugars and proteins to produce a dark colour. This is called the Maillard reaction or non-enzymic browning.

> **Key Point**
>
> The length and type of cooking method depends on the type of **muscle fibre**.

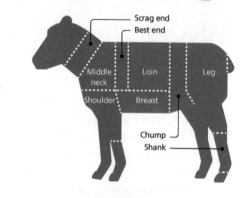

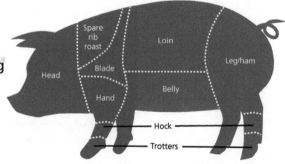

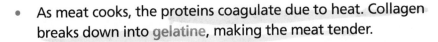
- As meat cooks, the proteins coagulate due to heat. Collagen breaks down into **gelatine**, making the meat tender.

Checking for Readiness

- You should know the safety rules for cooking different meat.
- Meat joints can be tested using a meat probe or temperature probe. To determine if a steak is rare, medium or well done the 'poke' test can be learned and used.
- The following foods should not be eaten if undercooked: chicken (80 °C), pork (75 °C), offal and game, burgers, sausages, kebabs.

Cooking Different Meat Joints

Meat	Temperature	Time per 500 g
Pork	75–80 °C	30 mins + 15 mins
Poultry	75–80 °C	20 mins + 20 mins
Beef	Rare: 52 °C	20 mins
Lamb	Well done: 75–80 °C	30 mins

Nutritional Content and Storage Information

Nutritional Content

- Meat contains:
  - Protein, including **collagen**, **elastin** and **myoglobin**, which makes the meat red in colour.
  - Fat (saturated) – provides warmth and protection of the animal's internal organs.
  - Minerals, e.g. iron, calcium and phosphorus – needed to form red blood cells, bones and teeth, and for energy metabolism.
  - Vitamins B6 and B12 – needed to release energy from foods.
  - Cholesterol.

Storage Information

- Raw meat should be kept separate from cooked meat to avoid **cross-contamination**.
- Raw meat should be stored covered at the bottom of the fridge so meat juices cannot drip onto other foods.
- Cooked meat should be kept chilled and covered and treated as a high-risk food.
- Chilled meat should be stored at between 0 °C and 5 °C.
- Frozen meat should be stored at between –18 °C and –22 °C.

Key Words

Maillard reaction
non-enzymic browning
gelatine
collagen
elastin
myoglobin
muscle fibre
cross-contamination

Quick Test

1. Where would you store meat when not preparing it?
2. Name the four main sources of meat.
3. Why are marinades added to meat?

Fish

You must be able to:

- Know how to classify different types of fish
- Explain how to choose, handle and prepare different types of fish.

Classifications of Fish

- There are three main classifications of fish:
  - **White fish** has flesh that is white in colour and contains less fat. White fish can be round or flat, e.g. cod, haddock.
  - **Flat fish** – examples include plaice, sole and halibut.
  - **Oily fish** has flesh that is coloured and contains more fat than white fish but this is healthy fat with fish oils. Examples include salmon, sardines, mackerel and tuna.
- There are two main classifications of **shellfish**:
  - Crustaceans – crabs, lobsters, prawns, crayfish, shrimp and squid (which has a hard backbone that must be removed during preparation).
  - Molluscs – oysters, mussels, scallops, winkles and cockles.

Buying Quality Fish

- To ensure you are buying quality fish, you need to make sure that: eyes are bright, not dull; scales are in place; gills are bright red; it has a slightly salty, fresh smell of the sea (fish smells bad as it deteriorates); it has a thin layer of slime; the flesh is firm.

Preserving Fish

- There are a number of ways of preserving fish:
  - **Canning** – cans are heated to 121 °C to kill bacteria; this heating creates a vacuum inside the can. Any blown or dented cans can cause food poisoning as the vacuum is broken and clostridium botulinum food poisoning can occur.
  - **Freezing** – sea fish are frozen within 90 minutes of capture to a minimum temperature of −18 °C. This stops food-poisoning bacteria from reproducing and forces the bacteria to become dormant – it does not kill the bacteria.
  - Smoking – to 76 °C or above, removes moisture from the fish and gives a distinctive flavour, e.g. smoked salmon.
  - Salting – salt is added to fish to remove its moisture. Food-poisoning bacteria cannot survive without moisture.

Preparing and Cooking Raw Fish

To Prepare
• Use a blue chopping board (sanitized).
• Use a filleting knife (sharp and sanitized).
• Check for freshness.

> **Key Point**
>
> It is important to wash your hands after handling fish to prevent cross-contamination.

To Cook

- Fish cooks quickly because the muscle is short and the connective tissue is thin. The connective tissue is made up of collagen and will change into gelatine and coagulate at 75 °C.
- Fish can be grilled, baked or fried. Often fish is enrobed in breadcrumbs/batter to protect it when using high heat.
- Fish can also be cooked gently by steaming or poaching without coating the flesh.

Filleting a Flat Fish

 Use a filleting knife to descale and remove the fins. Cut off the head just behind the gills.

 Cut from head to tail down to the bone, to one side of the centre line.

 Turn the knife almost parallel to the table. Cut horizontally against the backbone towards the outer edge. Separate the fillet from the bone and remove it.

Filleting a Round Fish

 Descale and remove the fins. Cut into the top of the fish on one side of the tail; detach the backbone from head to tail.

 Cut under the flesh towards the tail and detach the cut piece.

 Cut along the curved rib bones and finish detaching the fillet at the head. Turn over and repeat to remove the second fillet.

Nutritional Content and Storage Information

Nutritional Content

- Nutrients in fish include:
  - Protein – for growth and repair.
  - Minerals – iron, zinc and iodine – for red blood cells, metabolism and to regulate blood sugar.
  - Vitamins A and D – for vision, body linings, the immune system, bone health, and to help with mineral absorption.
- Oily fish contains Omega 3 fatty acids for brain development, healthy bones and joints.

Storage Information

- Most fresh fish is best eaten on the day it has been bought as it can spoil very quickly and be unsafe to eat.
- Shellfish must be prepared and eaten within two days of purchase.
- Fresh fish must be stored in the refrigerator. Ice is often used to store fish on boats and in supermarkets to keep it fresh.
- Fresh fish can be frozen on the day it has been bought and stored for several months; it must be defrosted before use.

> **Key Point**
>
> White fish carry oil in the liver; oily fish carry oil throughout the flesh.

Quick Test

1. State which type of fish contains the most Omega 3 fatty acids.
2. List the equipment needed when preparing raw fish.

> **Key Words**
>
> crustacean   connective
> mollusc   tissue
> smoking   coagulate
> salting   enrobed

Eggs and Poultry

You must be able to:

- Know and understand the value of eggs in the diet and recognise different egg types
- Know about the different characteristics and functional properties of eggs
- Know the nutritional information of poultry and how to store poultry safely.

Eggs

- Eggs are regarded as one of the most versatile and useful foods. They can be used to make meals suitable for breakfast or a light snack/lunch, e.g. scrambled eggs or a cheese omelette.
- They have many working characteristics and functional properties that are needed in the making of products:
  - Quiches – eggs are used to set the quiche.
  - Bread products – eggs will enrich the dough or mixture by providing additional nutrients and a deeper dough colour.
  - Pastry – beaten eggs can be used to glaze the pastry and give it a shiny golden colour.
  - Burgers – eggs are used to bind the ingredients together.
- In this country, we can eat and cook with eggs from hens, ducks, geese and quails. Hen eggs are most commonly used.

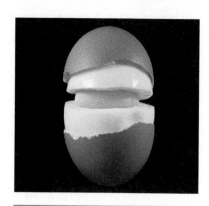

Egg Structure and Size

- The shell is the outer casing; it can be white or brown in colour.
- An egg has three sections: the shell is 10%, the egg white is 60% and the yolk is 30%.
- Eggs can be bought in a range of sizes from supermarkets. Sometimes boxes of eggs can have mixed sizes (see alongside).

Egg sizes

Very large – the weight of the egg is 73g and over.

Large – the weight of the egg is between 63g and 73g.

Medium – the weight of the egg is between 53g and 63g.

Small – the weight of the egg is 53g or under.

Egg Types

Type of Eggs	Description	Example
Enriched cage/colony cage farm eggs (previously battery cages)	Hens are housed indoors in a cage to promote egg laying. The cage includes a limited scratch area, perch and nest box.	
Barn eggs	Hens are in a barn and are given freedom to move around. Perches and nest boxes are provided. Some are provided with foraging materials.	
Free range eggs	The hens can live in buildings on farms with the option to walk around outside. They can scratch and peck the ground for food and lay their eggs in nests.	

Nutritional Content	Storage Information
• Protein is found in both the egg white and the yolk. • The egg yolk provides iron and some fat, as well as Vitamins A, D and E. • The egg white has some B vitamins. • Water is found in both the white and yolk.	• Eggs should not be stored near strong smelling foods as they will absorb the flavours. • Eggs should be stored in a refrigerator, placed with the pointed end downwards. • Eggs are best used when they are fresh. Best before dates should be noted.

Poultry

- Poultry is chicken, turkey, duck and goose; they are all birds.
- Poultry resembles other meats in structure; it has muscle fibres and connective tissue. The muscle fibres in poultry are usually shorter than the fibres in beef and lamb. This can make the meat more tender when eaten.
- The breast of poultry is always more tender than the legs.
- Chicken is the most favoured form of poultry eaten in the UK.
- Ducks are richer in taste as the flesh is fattier than a chicken.

Nutritional Content	Storage Information
• Poultry, like other meats, contains protein (HBV). • Saturated fat content will vary depending on the type of poultry, which parts of the bird are eaten and the method of cooking used, but it is less than other meats. • Poultry provides some B-group vitamins. Chicken provides the minerals magnesium and phosphorus.	• Raw poultry should be stored covered at the bottom of the refrigerator so juices cannot drip onto other foods. • Raw poultry must be kept away from cooked meat and poultry to avoid any cross contamination. • Poultry must be used within its use by date. • If poultry has been frozen it must be defrosted thoroughly before being cooked.

Boning a Chicken

- Do not wash the chicken as this can increase risk of food poisoning through spreading bacteria.
- Place **whole chicken** on a red board.
- Remove the legs. Cut down through the skin and between the joints. Turn the chicken over and break the legs.
- Find the knuckle and cut through the leg to separate the **drumstick** and the **thigh**.
- Cut through the joints to remove the **wings**.
- Find the wishbone at the front of the bird. Cut a V-shape on either side of the bird to release the wishbone, then cut through the knuckle at the base. Carefully remove the **breasts** from the carcass.

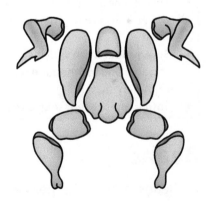

Quick Test

1. State the three sections of an egg.
2. Explain the difference between a very large egg and a small egg.
3. Name three different types of eggs.

Key Words

glaze
muscle fibres
saturated fat

Soya, Tofu, Beans, Nuts and Seeds

You must be able to:

- Know about the different uses of soya, tofu, beans, nuts and seeds
- Understand the origins of these commodities
- Understand the nutritional contribution made by these commodities.

Soya and Tofu

- Soya beans grow in pods – they are normally green in colour.
- They are available in cans, as a **dried form**, and **fresh from pods** (also known as **edamame beans**).
- Soya beans are transformed into many different foods, e.g.
  - Soya milk – a plant-based milk
  - Miso – a fermented soya bean paste used in Asian cuisine that provides flavouring
  - Tempeh – cooked soya beans that are gently fermented then formed into a solid textured block or cake
  - Soya flour – whole dry beans finely ground to form flour.
- Tofu is made from soya milk – it is made by curdling the fresh milk, then removing any liquid which leaves curds. The remaining curds are then pressed, forming a set block.
- Tofu is also known as **bean curd**. It can be quite spongy and springy in texture. Cooking it can make it more crispy.
- Tofu is bland in flavour and must be cooked or marinated with stronger flavoured foods to improve it.

Soya beans

Sliced fresh raw tempeh

Nutritional Content	Storage Information
<ul><li>Soya beans and tofu provide a <u>rich source of protein</u> (HBV). They are regarded as an excellent alternative to meat.</li><li>Soya products can provide B vitamins and minerals (calcium and magnesium). They can be a good source of dietary fibre (NSP).</li><li>Tofu is an excellent source of iron and calcium.</li></ul>	<ul><li>Fresh edamame beans and other products, e.g. tempeh, should be stored in the refrigerator.</li><li>Canned soya goods and dried products should be kept in a cool, dry place.</li><li>Chilled tofu must be kept in the refrigerator.</li><li>Tofu can be stored in the freezer.</li></ul>

Beans

- Beans, along with peas and lentils, are known as **legumes**. They are also referred to as **pulses**. Examples include butter beans, haricot beans and black-eyed beans.
- Beans are an excellent source of protein for a person who does not consume any meat or fish.
- Dried beans (pulse vegetables) have been used as a staple food for many years in some countries.
- Pulse vegetables are sold fresh, dried, canned and frozen.

Mixed pulses

- Canned beans are a good store cupboard food as they can be used in the making of dishes such as chilli and curry or served as a nutritious snack, e.g. beans on toast. Canned beans do not require any preparation whereas dried beans require soaking before they can be used.

Nutritional Content	Storage Information
• Beans provide an excellent amount of protein and are a good source of dietary fibre (NSP). • They provide some B group vitamins and iron and calcium.	• Canned beans (pulses) are stored in a cool, dry place until opened and then stored in the refrigerator in an airtight container. • Fresh beans must be stored in the refrigerator. • Dried beans are best stored in airtight containers. Once they have been soaked they must be covered and refrigerated.

Nuts and Seeds

- Many different varieties of nuts are available, e.g. walnuts, hazelnuts, almonds, pecans, chestnuts and pistachios.
- Nuts can be eaten on their own as a snack, or can be used in the cooking of savoury foods, e.g. chestnut, mushroom and shallot pie, or added to sweet baked goods, e.g. cakes.
- Some people are allergic to nuts and a severe reaction could be life threatening.
- Some nuts are described as edible kernels (e.g. almonds), some are referred to as seeds (e.g. pine nuts) and some are regarded as fruits inside a dry shell (e.g. cashews).
- Edible seeds are a significant part of a plant. Popular seeds used in food preparation and eating include pumpkin, sunflower, chia, poppy and sesame. They can be sprinkled on bread dough and baked, or added to salads for extra crunch. Sunflower seeds are used for making oil.

Nutritional Content	Storage Information
• Nuts and seeds provide protein and dietary fibre (NSP). • Nuts provide B-group vitamins, calcium and iron – this can vary with different nut types. Seeds provide vitamins B and E, iron and zinc. • Some nuts can be quite high in fat, so are high in calories. Seeds can be a source of essential fatty acids, e.g. flax seeds.	• Nuts must be stored in an airtight container to avoid contact with moisture and strong smells. Nuts can become rancid due to their fat content. • Once opened seeds should be stored in an airtight container.

Key Point

A pulse vegetable is an edible seed that grows in a pod.

Key Point

Anaphylaxis is when a person has a severe allergic reaction to nuts. Symptoms can include swelling of the throat or tongue and shortness of breath.

Sunflower seeds and sunflower oil

Quick Test

1. State the name of fresh soya beans in a pod.
2. List three examples of nuts.
3. Explain why nuts are high in calories.
4. Why are canned beans a good store cupboard ingredient?

Key Words

curdling
bland
rancid

Butter, Oils, Margarine, Sugar and Syrup

You must be able to:

- Know about the different uses of butter, oils, margarine, sugar and syrup
- Understand the origins of these commodities.

Butter

- Butter is a dairy product. It is made by churning or stirring cream or milk until the butterfat sticks together and separates from the buttermilk.
- It is a solid block when stored chilled; when heated it will melt.
- Butter has a rich flavour and a high saturated fat value.
- Butter is used in food preparation to:
  - aerate – when making cakes, butter is creamed with sugar to add air and help the cake rise
  - shorten – butter is rubbed into flour for a short, crumbly feel when making pastry
  - spread or brush on food to provide moistness and a buttery flavour, e.g. butter is spread on the top of filo pastry to stop it drying out.

Oils

- Vegetable oils are used in food preparation and cooking to:
  - marinade foods
  - fry foods
  - baste foods during the cooking process
  - make dressings to combine with other foods.
- Vegetable oils are naturally found in seeds (e.g. sunflower oil) and nuts (e.g. walnut oil).
- Many different types of vegetable oils are available, such as olive oil, rapeseed oil and corn oil.

Margarine

- Margarine is made from vegetable oils or a combination of oils and some water.
- It is considered to be a cheaper alternative to butter.
- Margarine can be a block form – this type is recommended for pastry making, or a tub form – this type is recommended for cake making. Some low-fat spreads and tub margarines have a low fat, high water content, which makes them unsuitable for baking.

Nutritional Content	Storage Information
• Butter provides vitamins A and D. Salted varieties will provide some sodium. • Oils and margarine provide unsaturated fat. • Margarine has vitamins A and D added to it by law.	• Butter and margarine must be stored in a refrigerator. Both fats are suitable for freezing to extend their shelf life. • Butter should be covered when stored to prevent it from going rancid. • Oils should be stored away from direct sunlight, in a cool, dark place.

Sugar and Syrup

- Sugar comes from either sugar beet, which is a root crop, or sugar cane, which is a large bamboo-type grass.
- There are many different types of sugar available:
  - Granulated white sugar – a coarse ground sugar
  - Caster – a finer crystal sugar
  - Icing – a powder sugar
  - Brown sugar – soft brown and dark brown, these contain molasses, which is a dark syrup
  - Demerara – coarse brown crystals made from raw sugar.
- Sugar has many uses:
  - To provide colour to food products – when it is heated, sugar caramelises and gives a golden colour.
  - To provide aeration to a cake mixture – it traps air when creamed with butter or margarine.
  - To act as a preservative in jams – the high sugar content prevents the growth of microorganisms.
- Golden syrup is the most popular sweet syrup. It is used in the making of syrup sponge pudding and flapjacks, and can be used in meat marinades.
- Black treacle is classed as syrup. It has a thicker consistency than golden syrup, and a more intense flavour and darker colour. It can be used in seasonal goods, e.g. Christmas puddings and cakes.

Sugar cane

Nutritional Content	Storage Information
• Sugars and syrups are pure carbohydrates; they provide energy. They do not provide any other nutrients.	• Sugars and syrups should be stored in a cool dry place. • Sugar should be kept away from moisture and strong odours.

 Quick Test

1. State two uses of vegetable oils.
2. Explain why some low-fat spreads and tub margarines are unsuitable for baking.

 Key Words

aerate
baste
microorganisms

Practice Questions

Bread, Cereals, Flour and Oats

1 Which two ingredients shown below would be used in bread making? Place a tick (✓) in **two** boxes. [2]

Cornflour ☐   Yeast ☑   Baking powder ☐   Water ☑

2 Explain why bread must be proved before being baked. [3]

Bread is proved before baking to allow the yeast to help the dough rise. It ~~was~~ produces CO_2.

3 Suggest a suitable storage method for each type of bread listed below. [2]

a) Fresh bread from the bakers that is not going to be needed until two weeks later.

Storage method: *freezer.*

b) Sliced bread purchased at the supermarket.

Storage method: *Plastic bag, cool dry place.*

4 Tick (✓) **one** box for each statement listed below to show if each one is **true** or **false**. [2]

Statement	True	False
a) Oats are pods that come from the cereal plant.		✓
b) The energy provided by oats is slow-release energy.	✓	

Rice, Potatoes and Pasta

1 Name **two** long grain rice examples. [2]

I: *Basmati*

II: *Jasmine*

2 Name the **three** sections that make up a potato. [3]

I: _Potato skin_

II: _Potato flesh_

III: _Potato core (Pith)_

3 Explain why potatoes should not be stored in a plastic bags. [2]

It causes them to sweat and get spoilt

Fruit and Vegetables

1 Name **two** different vitamins obtained from eating mangos and oranges. [2]

I: _Vitamin C_   II: _Vitamin A_

2 State **two** different forms of fruits sold in supermarkets. [2]

I: _Canned_   II: _Fresh_

3 Plums are an example of a stone fruit. Name **two** other examples. [2]

I: _Cherry_   II: _Peaches_

4 Name **two** different examples of vegetables that are classed as leaves. [2]

I: _Lettuce_   II: _Cabbage_

Milk, Cheese and Yoghurt

1 What is the difference between fresh milk and homogenised milk? [2]

Fresh milk forms cream on the top.
while, Homogenised milk is forced through tiny holes
in a machine to break up & disperse the fat so that it

2 What does UHT stand for? _doesnt reform as a layer._ [1]

Ultra Heat Treated

3 A cheese and tomato quiche is being made. Describe **two** functions of the cheese.   [4]

Function I: _The cheese adds flavour to the quiche. Mild cheese – subtle flavour, mature cheese – sharp flavour_

Function II: _It also adds texture as the cheese melts. It makes it more appetising_

Meat

1 Which term best describes the structure of meat? Tick (✓) **one** answer.   [1]

a) Meat is the flesh of animals.   ☐

b) Meat is muscle composed of fibres held together by connective tissue.   ☑

c) Meat is a combination of flesh and fat held together by connective tissue.   ☐

d) Meat is a combination of tender and tough muscle fibres.   ☐

2 Which of the statements is **not** true? Tick (✓) **one** answer.   [1]

a) Tender meat comes from younger animals.   ☐

b) Tender meat has shorter muscle fibres.   ☐

c) Tougher meat cuts can be minced to break up connective tissue.   ☐

d) Tougher meat comes from parts of the animal that do the least work.   ☑

3 This question is about cooking meat. Name **two** methods suitable for cooking each of the following types of meat:

a) Shin beef

I: _Stewing_   II: _Braising_   [2]

b) Rump steak

I: _Grilling_   II: _Baking_   [2]

c) Beefburger

I: _Grilling_   II: _Frying_   [2]

Fish

1 Which of the following fish would you expect to find preserved in a can? Tick (✓)
   one answer. [1]

   a) Cod ☐

   b) Plaice ☐

   c) Sardine ☑

   d) Halibut ☐

2 Which choice would **not** be suitable when enrobing a fish fillet before cooking?
   Tick (✓) **one** answer. [1]

   a) Breadcrumbs ☐

   b) Polenta ☐

   c) Batter ☐

   d) Chocolate ☑

3 Give **one** example of each of the following classifications of fish:

   a) White fish _Haddock_ [1]

   b) Flat fish _Halibut_ [1]

   c) Oily fish _Mackerel_ [1]

4 Explain how you would select a quality fish when buying from a fresh fish counter. [5]

   To assess freshness — fresh smell bright eyes,
   firm flesh, scales in place, thin layer of
   slime, gills are red.

Practice Questions

Eggs and Poultry

1 Name **two** different birds that are classed as poultry. [2]

I: Hens

II: Ducks

2 Explain why poultry can be more tender when eaten, compared to meat such as beef or lamb. [1]

Poultry meat usually has shorter fibres.

Soya, Tofu, Beans, Nuts and Seeds

1 Name **three** different foods made from soya beans. [3]

I: Soya milk

II: Tempeh

III: Miso

2 Explain how tofu is made. [3]

soya milk is curdled. Excess liquid is removed. The curds are pressed together in the shape of a block.

3 Tick (✓) the correct term that describes beans, peas and lentils. [1]

Soya ☐

Tempeh ☐

Legumes ☑

4 Explain what a pulse vegetable is.　　　　　　　　　　　　　　　　　　[1]

A Pulse vegetable is a dried bean that is an edible seed in a pod. Staple food that can be dried fresh, frozen or canned.

Butter, Oils, Margarine, Sugar and Syrup

1 Butter has many uses in food preparation. Complete the chart by explaining each use.　[4]

Uses of butter in food preparation	Explanation
Shorten	Butter can be rubbed with flour to give a short, crumbly texture in pastry
Aerate	Butter can be creamed with sugar which helps trap air & make the food rise

2 Butter is a dairy product. List **two** key characteristics of butter.　　　　　　[2]

I: High in saturated fat

II: Rich flavour

3 List **two** advantages of using margarine instead of butter when baking.　　[2]

Advantage I: It is cheaper than butter

Advantage II: how fat means healthier. unsaturated fat.

Protein and Fat

You must be able to:

- Demonstrate knowledge and understanding of the functions, structures and main sources of protein and fat
- Know the biological value of protein
- Understand the consequences of excess and deficiencies of both protein and fat.

Protein

- Protein is a **macronutrient**. A macronutrient is needed by the body in large amounts.
- Protein is formed from chains of simpler units called amino acids.
- Amino acids that need to be provided by the diet are called essential amino acids. The essential amino acids needed by our bodies are shown in the table alongside.
- Non-essential amino acids can be made by our bodies from the protein we eat. Examples of these include Alanine, Asparagine, Aspartic acid and Glutamic acid.

Sources of Protein

- **Animal sources** – meat, fish, poultry, milk, eggs, cheese, insects.
- **Plant sources** – soya, nuts, seeds, pulses (e.g. lentils), mycoprotein (Quorn), TVP (Texturised Vegetable Protein).

The Biological Value of Proteins

- The biological value of protein means the amount of essential amino acids present.
- Animal protein sources contain all the essential amino acids required by the body; they are of High Biological Value (HBV).
- Mycoprotein (Quorn) and Texturised Vegetable Protein (TVP) are of HBV too.
- Proteins from plant sources are of Low Biological Value (LBV) and lack some essential amino acids. The exception is soya, which is a plant protein of HBV.

Protein Complementation

- Proteins of LBV can be eaten together to provide all the essential amino acids, e.g. beans on toast. This is protein complementation, and is important for vegetarians and vegans.

Protein Excess and Deficiencies

- Excess protein in the diet is used as energy.
- Protein deficiencies are rare but in developing countries kwashiorkor is a severe form of protein malnutrition.
- Some groups of people have a higher need for protein: babies and children – for growth; adolescents – for growth spurts; pregnant women – for the growing baby; and nursing mothers – for lactation (milk production).

Key Point

Protein is required by the body for growth, maintenance and repair. Proteins are built up of units of amino acids.

Essential Amino Acids
Histidine
Isoleucine
Lysine
Leucine
Methionine
Phenylalanine
Threonine
Tryptophan
Valine

Fat

- Fat is a macronutrient. It can be solid or liquid.
- Fat is made up of fatty acids and glycerol.
- Fatty acids can be described as:
  - saturated fats – solid at room temperature, e.g. butter
  - unsaturated fats – further described as monounsaturated and polyunsaturated. These fats are considered to be the 'healthier' fats.
- The structure of fatty acids influences their effect on our health.
- The characteristics of fatty acids influence cooking choice.

Revise

Functions of Fat in the Diet

- Fat provides concentrated energy.
- Fat is a source of fat-soluble vitamins A, D, E and K.
- Fat provides protection for the major organs in the body.
- Fat is a component of hormones.

Sources of Fat in the Diet

- Saturated fats can increase the cholesterol level in the blood. Too much bad cholesterol can lead to health problems. Sources include butter, ghee, lard, cream, hard cheese, meat pies, coconut oil and palm oil.
- Unsaturated fats can help reduce cholesterol in the blood. Sources include oily fish, nuts, seeds, avocados, vegetable oils, soya beans, and some functional foods, such as cholesterol-lowering spreads. Functional foods are foods specially developed to improve health.

Hydrogenated Fat and Trans Fats

- Making solid fat from a liquid oil is called hydrogenation.
- Trans fats can be formed when oil goes through the process of hydrogenation to form a solid. This process occurs as the molecules flip and rotate.

Fat Excess and Deficiencies

- Fat is only needed in small amounts and excess fat in the diet can lead to weight gain.
- Excess saturated fat raises blood cholesterol levels.
- Trans fats have been linked to health problems including heart disease and some cancers.
- Fat deficiency in babies and children could affect normal growth.
- Fat deficiency could result in a poor supply of fat-soluble vitamins.

> ### Key Point
>
> Fats can be classified as either saturated or unsaturated. Saturated fats are considered to be more harmful to health because they raise levels of cholesterol.

> ### Key Words
>
> amino acids
> essential amino acids
> High Biological Value (HBV)
> Low Biological Value (LBV)
> protein complementation
> kwashiorkor
> fatty acids
> glycerol
> saturated fats
> unsaturated fats
> fat-soluble vitamins
> cholesterol
> hydrogenation
> trans fats

> ### Quick Test
>
> 1. What are the functions of fat in the diet?
> 2. What are the simple units of protein called?
> 3. Give an example of protein complementation.

Carbohydrates

You must be able to:

- Know and understand the functions, structures and main sources of carbohydrate
- Understand an individual's need for carbohydrate
- Demonstrate a knowledge and understanding of the consequences of consumption of excess carbohydrate and of deficiencies in carbohydrate.

Carbohydrate

- The body's cells require a constant supply of glucose, which is used as fuel to provide energy.
- Sugars and starches are types of carbohydrate.
- Dietary fibre is also a type of carbohydrate but it cannot be digested to provide energy.
- Carbohydrates are produced mainly by plants during the process of photosynthesis.
- Carbohydrates can be classified according to their structure: monosaccharides, disaccharides, polysaccharides.

> **Key Point**
>
> Carbohydrate provides the body with energy. Most of our energy should come from starchy foods.

Monosaccharides	Disaccharides	Polysaccharides
Monosaccharides are the simplest form of carbohydrate structure. They include: – glucose – all other carbohydrate is converted into this in the body – galactose – found in the milk of mammals – fructose – found in fruit.	Disaccharides are more complex sugars that are formed when two monosaccharides join together. They include: – sucrose – 1 unit of glucose plus 1 unit of fructose – maltose – 2 units of glucose linked – lactose – 1 unit of glucose plus 1 unit of galactose.	Polysaccharides are made up of many monosaccharides units joined together. They include: – starch – many glucose units formed together – glycogen – formed after digestion – dietary fibre – dextrin – toasted crust on bread; sugars caramelise on the surface – cellulose – formed by plants from glucose – pectin – found in fruit, forms a gel on cooking.

Function and Sources of Carbohydrate

- Sugars are digested quickly in the body, providing instant energy.
- Starches have to be digested into sugars before absorption – this is slow energy release.
- Eating foods high in dietary fibre can be beneficial to people trying to lose or control weight as they are filling, and can make you feel fuller for longer. This helps prevent snacking between meals.
- Eating starchy carbohydrates rather than sugary foods is the healthier way to provide the body with energy. Starch (a polysaccharide) is found in bread, pasta, rice, breakfast cereals and potatoes.
- Sugars are found in a variety of sources including table sugar (sucrose), honey and jam, fruit juice, sweets and chocolate, fruit and vegetables.

Excess and Deficiencies of Carbohydrate

- Excess carbohydrate is converted to fat and is stored under the skin; this is the main cause of obesity.
- Excess sugar in the diet is linked to dental decay.
- There is evidence to suggest that the rise in Type 2 diabetes is linked to diets high in sugar.
- If insufficient carbohydrate is eaten, the body will firstly start to use protein and fat as an energy source.

Dietary Fibre

- The scientific name for fibre is Non–Starch Polysaccharide (NSP).
- Soluble NSP absorbs water, forming a gel-like substance. It can inhibit the absorption of cholesterol.
- Insoluble NSP is not absorbed by the body. It passes through the body as waste, which helps prevent bowel diseases.

Function and Sources of Dietary Fibre

- Dietary fibre makes food matter passing through the intestines soft and bulky.
- Dietary fibre can be found in wholemeal bread, wholegrain breakfast cereals (e.g. bran flakes, shredded wheat, porridge oats), wholemeal pasta and wholemeal flour; fruit and vegetables; potato skins; dried fruit, nuts and seeds, beans, peas and lentils.
- Adults should consume at least 18 g of fibre per day.
- Young children must gradually add high fibre foods to their diets.
- Fibre deficiency can lead to:
  - Constipation – this is when faeces become difficult to expel from the body because they are hard and small.
  - Diverticular disease – pouches form in the intestines, which become infected with bacteria.
- A low-fibre diet can be linked to cancer, particularly bowel cancer.

Key Words

dietary fibre
monosaccharides
disaccharides
polysaccharides
Non–Starch
 Polysaccharide (NSP)
constipation
diverticular disease

Quick Test

1. What is the function of carbohydrate in the body?
2. What happens if too much carbohydrate is eaten?
3. What does NSP stand for?

Vitamins

You must be able to:

- Demonstrate knowledge and understanding of the sources and functions of both fat-soluble and water-soluble vitamins
- Know and understand the consequences of excess and deficiencies of fat-soluble and water-soluble vitamins
- Understand the retention of water-soluble vitamins during cooking.

Fat-soluble Vitamins

Vitamin	Function in the Body	Sources	Deficiency/Excess
Vitamin A (Retinol, Beta carotene)	• Normal iron metabolism • Maintenance of normal vision • Maintenance of skin and the mucus membranes • Essential for maintaining healthy immune function	• Animal sources – liver and whole milk (retinol) • Plant sources – green leafy vegetables, carrots, and orange-coloured fruits (carotenoids) • Margarine, which is fortified by law	• Excess can be toxic, causing liver and bone damage • Excess retinol can lead to birth defects • Deficiency can cause night blindness
Vitamin D (Cholecalciferol)	• Absorption and use of calcium and phosphorus • Maintenance and strength of bones and teeth	• Dietary sources – oily fish, meat, eggs and fortified breakfast cereals and margarines (vitamin D added by law) • Sunlight on the skin (Cholecalciferol)	Deficiencies: • Bones that become weak and bend • Rickets in children • Osteomalacia in adults • Weak teeth
Vitamin E (Tocopherol)	• Antioxidant that helps protect cell membranes • Maintains healthy skin and eyes	• Polyunsaturated fats, e.g. sunflower oils • Nuts, seeds and wheatgerm	• Very rare
Vitamin K (Phytomenadione)	• Normal clotting of blood	• Green leafy vegetables, cheese, bacon and liver	• A deficiency is rare • Newborn babies are given a dose of vitamin K

Water-soluble Vitamins

Vitamin	Function in the body	Sources	Deficiency
Vitamin B1 (thiamin)	• Release of energy from carbohydrates • Nervous system function • Normal growth of children	• Wholegrain products • Meat • Milk and dairy • Nuts • Marmite • Fortified breakfast cereals • Fortified white and brown flour	• Beri-beri, which affects the nervous system

Vitamin B2 (riboflavin)	• Energy release from foods • Healthy nervous system	• Same as vitamin B1 thiamin	• Cracking skin around the mouth • Swollen tongue • Failure to grow
Vitamin B3 (niacin)	• Energy release from carbohydrate foods • Healthy nervous system and skin	• Dairy products • Meat and poultry • Cereals and wholegrain products	• Very rare • Pellagra could develop – diarrhoea, dermatitis, dementia
Vitamin B9 (Folate/Folic acid)	• Neural tube development in unborn babies	• Green leafy vegetables • Potatoes, asparagus, bananas • Beans, seeds and nuts • Wholegrain products • Breakfast cereals	• Spina bifida in unborn babies. Pre conception and pregnant women need a good supply
Vitamin B12 (cobalamin)	• Supports production of energy • Protective coating around nerve cells	• Meat and fish • Cheese, eggs and milk • Marmite • Fortified breakfast cereals	• Pernicious anaemia
Vitamin C – (ascorbic acid)	• Absorption of iron • Production of collagen that binds connective tissue • Antioxidant – protects from pollutants in the environment	• Citrus fruits • Kiwi fruit • Blackcurrants • Potatoes • Salad and green vegetables, e.g. broccoli, kale	• Weak connective tissue and blood vessels • Bleeding gums and loose teeth • Anaemia • Severe cases – scurvy

Vitamins and Food Preparation

- Vitamins B and C are water-soluble so will dissolve into water during cooking. Vitamins B1 and C are destroyed by heat. Vitamin C is destroyed on exposure to oxygen.
- To maximise vitamin retention:
  - prepare foods quickly just before serving
  - use small amounts of boiling water to cook
  - use cooking liquid to make sauces
  - avoid lots of cutting of vegetables
  - water soluble vitamins – avoid cooking in water as they are easily destroyed, instead steam, roast, fry or grill
  - fat-soluble vitamins – avoid cooking in fat, instead boil, steam or grill.
- Vitamins A, C and E contain antioxidants that work together to protect cells against oxidative damage from free radicals.

> **Key Point**
>
> Vitamins are **micronutrients**, required to do essential jobs in the body.

> **Key Words**
>
> fortified
> rickets
> osteomalacia
> antioxidant
> thiamin
> riboflavin
> niacin
> folate/folic acid
> spina bifida
> cobalamin
> ascorbic acid

> **Quick Test**
>
> 1. What are the fat-soluble vitamins?
> 2. Give **three** good sources of vitamin C.
> 3. Which vitamin is connected with the healthy development of the spine in unborn babies?

Minerals and Water

You must be able to:

- Demonstrate knowledge and understanding of the functions and main sources of calcium, iron, fluoride, magnesium, sodium and iodine
- Show knowledge and understanding of the consequences of deficiencies of calcium, iron, fluoride, magnesium, sodium and iodine in the diet
- Know and understand the function of water in the diet.

Minerals

- Minerals are **micronutrients**. They are required in small amounts.
- Minerals include calcium, iron, fluoride, magnesium, sodium and iodine.

> **Key Point**
>
> Minerals have essential functions in the body.

Calcium

Function	Sources	Deficiency
<ul><li>Strengthens bones and teeth – with Vitamin D</li><li>Bones are able to reach peak bone mass – maximum strength</li><li>Growth of children</li><li>Clots blood after injury</li><li>Promotes nerves and muscles to work properly</li></ul>	<ul><li>Milk and dairy foods</li><li>Green leafy vegetables</li><li>White bread – calcium is added by law</li><li>Soya products</li><li>Fish eaten with the bones, e.g. sardines</li></ul>	<ul><li>Bones don't reach peak bone mass and become weak and break easily – common in older people (osteoporosis)</li><li>During pregnancy, a woman's teeth and bones weaken</li><li>Poor clotting of the blood</li></ul>

Iron

Function	Sources	Deficiency
<ul><li>Supports the production of haemoglobin in red blood cells; this transports oxygen around the body</li><li>Vitamin C is required to absorb iron</li></ul>	<ul><li>Red meat – liver</li><li>Lentils, dried apricots, cocoa, chocolate, corned beef and curry spices</li><li>Green leafy vegetables, e.g. spinach</li><li>Breakfast cereals fortified with iron</li></ul>	<ul><li>Iron deficiency is called anaemia; symptoms include tiredness</li><li>Low intake of dietary iron, particularly in young women (due to supplies lost through blood during periods), can cause iron deficiency anaemia</li><li>Pregnant women may become deficient due to additional blood needed to support the growing baby</li></ul>

Fluoride

Function	Sources	Deficiency
<ul><li>To strengthen the enamel layer of teeth</li></ul>	<ul><li>Saltwater fish, tea</li><li>Some water authorities fortify their water supply with fluoride</li></ul>	<ul><li>Teeth may develop cavities and require filling</li></ul>

Magnesium

Function	Sources	Deficiency
<ul><li>Enables body to function well</li><li>Supports a healthy immune system</li><li>Normal bone and teeth growth</li></ul>	<ul><li>Spinach</li><li>Brown rice</li><li>Pumpkin seeds</li><li>Mackerel</li></ul>	<ul><li>Cramps and muscle spasms, which can progress into muscle weakness</li><li>Can be associated with headaches and migraines</li></ul>

Sodium

Function	Sources	Excess and Deficiency
• Needed by the body to regulate the amount of water in the body • Needed to assist the body in the use of energy • Required to help control muscles and nerves	• Processed foods – for flavour and as a preservative • Salt added to food in home cooking for flavour • Salt added at the table	• A deficiency is rare, but can lead to muscle cramps after exercise in hot conditions • People suffering with sickness and diarrhoea can lose salt • Excess salt in the diet is linked to high blood pressure, heart disease and strokes

Iodine

Function	Sources	Deficiency
• Regulates hormones in the thyroid, which controls the body's metabolic rate	• Seafood • Foods grown in iodine-rich soils	• Poor functioning of the thyroid gland, resulting in feeling tired and lethargic • A goitre (swelling) in the thyroid gland

Water

- The body is nearly two-thirds water. The functions of water are:
  - For normal brain function
  - To decrease risk of kidney problems
  - For normal blood pressure
  - To help bowel movements
  - To regulate temperature and maintain hydration
  - To make body fluids – blood, saliva, mucus membranes.
- The main sources of water are drinking water, milk, tea, coffee and fruit juices.
- The remaining 20% of water needed comes from foods such as soup, yoghurt, fruit and vegetables.
- Water should be drunk every day. 6–8 glasses daily is recommended.
- People with increased water needs are:
  - Those with an active lifestyle during hot weather – water needs increase due to perspiration.
  - Anyone suffering from vomiting or diarrhoea, to avoid dehydration.
  - Lactating mothers (breast feeding), for milk production.
  - Elderly people, to help prevent kidney problems and infections.
  - During hot weather, water needs increase due to perspiration.

Key Point

Water makes up two thirds of the body so it is vital to drink regularly to stay hydrated.

Key Words

peak bone mass
haemoglobin
anaemia
thyroid
dehydration
lactating

Quick Test

1. Why do teenage girls need an increased supply of iron?
2. What is peak bone mass?
3. Which hormones in the body are affected by a lack of iodine?
4. Name **two** good sources of calcium in the diet.

Review Questions

Bread, Cereals, Flour and Oats

1 Cereals are used to produce different food products after they have been processed.
Define what a cereal is. [2]

A cereal is a cultivated grass with starchy edible grain.
Ex: Wheat, rice, barley.

2 Name **two** cereals that are grown in the UK. [2]

I: *Oats*   II: *Wheat*

3 Plain flour is an example of wheat flour. Name **two** other types of flour. [2]

I: *self raising*   II: *Brown flour.*

Rice, Potatoes and Pasta

1 Tick (✓) the correct type of wheat used to make pasta. [1]

Gluten ☐   Arborio ☐   Durum ☑   Wholemeal ☐

2 Explain why dried pasta is a good store cupboard ingredient. [2]

It has a long shelf life and can be cooked by boiling for a few minutes. It will not go off for a long period of time.

Fruit and Vegetables

1 Explain the benefits of eating raw green vegetables rather than cooking them. [2]

Raw green vegetables are richer in nutrients as vitamins tend to get destroyed on cooking. (water soluble like vit C)

2 State **two** suitable methods for cooking cauliflower. [2]

I: *Boiling*   II: *Roasting*

3 Explain why many fruits and vegetables are imported from other countries. [3]

Fruits & vegetables are seasonal. Therefore, they have to be imported from other countries to meet the all-year round demand & if they are not grown in the UK.

Milk, Cheese and Yoghurt

1 Which type of milk is the thickest? Circle the correct answer. [1]

evaporated milk   **condensed milk** *(circled)*   **sterilised milk**

2 Name the value of the protein found in yoghurt. [1]

High biological value.

Meat

1 What temperature should pork be cooked to in order for it to be safe to eat? Tick (✓) **one** answer. [1]

a) 63 °C ☐   **b)** 72 °C ☐   **c)** 74 °C ☐   **d)** 75 °C ☑

2 What causes meat to become firm when cooked? Tick (✓) **one** answer. [1]

a) Non-enzymic browning ☐   **b)** Coagulation ☑

c) Maillard reaction ☐   **d)** Gelatinisation ☐

3 State which type of meat comes from these animals:

a) Pig *Pork* [1]

b) Cattle *Beef* [1]

c) Sheep *Lamb* [1]

d) Deer *Venison* [1]

e) Poultry *Chicken* [1]

Review Questions

Fish

1. What sign would indicate that a fish is **not** good quality? Tick (✓) **one** answer. [1]

   a) Bright eyes ☐   b) Thin layer of clear slime ☐

   c) Firm flesh ☐   d) Offensive odour ☑

2. Which of the following statements is **true**? Tick (✓) **one** answer. [1]

   a) Fish takes a long time to cook. ☐

   b) Fresh fish should have red gills. ☑

   c) Fish cannot be fried without using a coating. ☐

   d) Fish contains a lot of carbohydrate. ☐

3. Explain **three** ways in which fish can be preserved commercially and give **one** example of each. [6]

Method	Example
Canning	sardines
smoking	Salmon
salting	Herring

4. Which **two** methods of preserving fish involve removing moisture from the fish? [2]

   I: smoking   II: salting

5. Name **four** nutrients found in oily fish. [4]

   I: Omega 3 Fat (unsaturated)   III: Vitamin D

   II: Protein   IV: Iodine

Eggs and Poultry

1. Explain how eggs should be stored. [2]

   Eggs should be stored in the refrigerator with the pointy end downwards, away from strong smells.

Soya, Tofu, Beans, Nuts and Seeds

1 Name **one** type of seed and explain how it could be used in food preparation and cooking. [2]

Name of seed: _Sesame seeds_

Explanation: _Used to add Texture, on bread rolls and colour to food._

2 The definition of a nut can vary depending on the nut type. Give the definition of a cashew nut. [1]

A fruit inside a dry shell.

3 Name **two** minerals found in seeds. [2]

I: _Iron_   II: _Zinc_

Butter, Oils, Margarine, Sugar and Syrup

1 Explain the differences between sugar beet and sugar cane. [2]

Sugar beet is an underground root
Sugar cane is similar to bamboo-grass

2 Draw a line to match each sugar type with the correct description. [2]

Sugar type	Description
Caster sugar	A powder sugar
Demerara sugar	A finer crystal sugar
Icing sugar	Coarse crystals made from raw sugar

Protein and Fat

1 Which of the following is a good source of High Biological Value protein? Tick (✓) **one** answer. [1]

a) Lentils ☐ b) Cheese ☑

c) Baked beans ☐ d) Bread ☐

2 Give **one** example of how protein foods can be combined to complement each other. [2]

Beans on toast

3 Which of the following is a function of fat in the diet? Tick (✓) **one** answer. [1]

a) Repair of body cells ☐ b) Insulation and warmth ☑

c) Protects enamel on teeth ☐ d) Makes connective tissue ☐

4 Name **two** foods that contain saturated fatty acids. [2]

I: *Butter* II: *Meat*

Carbohydrates

1 What is the name given to the production of carbohydrates by plants? Tick (✓) **one** answer. [1]

a) Cholesterol ☐ b) Hydrogenation ☐

c) Photosynthesis ☑ d) Marinade ☐

2 Explain why the body needs carbohydrates. [2]

The body needs carbohydrates for energy needed for growth carrying out basic functions and staying physically active

3 Dietary fibre is also known as: [1]

N *on* S *tarch* P *olysaccharide*.

4 Give **three** good sources of dietary fibre in the diet. [3]

I: *Fruits* II: *Vegetables* III: *Nuts*

Vitamins

1 Which are the water-soluble vitamins? [2]

B Vitamins (B1, B2, B3, B9, B12) & Vitamin C

2 Which food is a good source of vitamin C? Tick (✓) **one** answer. [1]

a) Bread ☐ **b)** Oily fish ☐ **c)** Oranges ✓ **d)** Butter ☐

3 What type of vitamins are vitamins, A, D, E and K? [1]

Fat-soluble

4 Apart from dietary sources, how else does the body obtain vitamin D? [2]

From sunlight on skin which enables the body to make Vit D.

Minerals and Water

1 Name the condition caused by a lack of iron in the diet. Tick (✓) **one** answer. [1]

a) Scurvy ☐ **b)** Anaemia ✓ **c)** Beri-beri ☐ **d)** Dermatitis ☐

2 What is the function of iron in the body? [2]

Iron helps in the production of Haemoglobin which helps transport oxygen in the body

3 Name **two** good sources of iron in the diet. [2]

I: *Green leafy vegetable* II: *Red meat*

4 Milk contains calcium. Name **two** other good sources of calcium in the diet. [2]

I: *Cheese* II: *Green leafy vegetables*

5 Give **three** reasons why water is an important part of a healthy diet. [3]

I: *It helps regulate body temperature*

II: *It reduces the risk of kidney function*

III: *It improves brain function*

Making Informed Choices

You must be able to:

- Demonstrate knowledge and understanding of the Eatwell Guide and the Healthy Eating Guidelines
- Have knowledge and understanding of the diet requirements throughout life.

The Eatwell Guide

- The Eatwell Guide shows the proportions of food groups that should be eaten daily in a well-balanced diet.

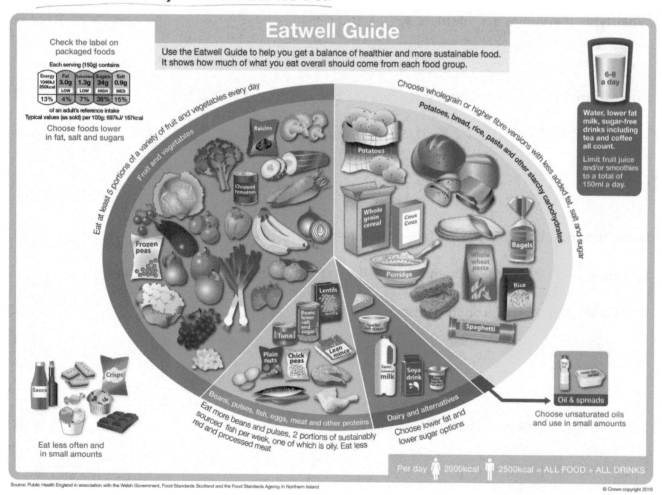

Current Guidelines for a Healthy Diet

- Base your meals on starchy carbohydrates.
- Eat lots of fruit and vegetables (5–7 portions per day).
- Eat plenty of fish, including oily fish.
- Cut down on saturated fat and sugars.
- Eat less salt – no more than 6 g a day for adults.
- Get active and be a healthy weight.
- Don't get thirsty (drink six to eight glasses of water a day).
- Don't skip breakfast.

Nutritional Needs Throughout Life

Babies

- Newborn babies should have only milk for the first 4–6 months of life.
- First milk is called colostrum and it is full of antibodies.
- Human milk provides babies with all their nutritional requirements, except for iron. Babies are born with a supply of iron stored in the liver.
- The introduction of solid foods is called 'weaning'.

Children

- Toddlers aged 1–3 years grow rapidly and so it is essential they get a well-balanced diet to support their physical development.
- Toddlers are physically very active and need a good supply of fat, which also helps the development of the brain and nervous system.
- New healthy foods need to be introduced in an attractive and appealing way.
- Sweets, biscuits, cakes and fizzy drinks must be avoided. Sugary foods cause dental decay and are strongly linked to obesity.

Teenagers

- Adolescence is a period of rapid growth and this is when puberty occurs.
- The need for energy and most nutrients is relatively high.
- After menstruation begins, girls need more iron to replace blood losses. Iron-deficiency anaemia is common in teenage girls.

Pregnancy

- A healthy diet is required in pregnancy to ensure the baby receives the essential nutrients required for development.
- Folate (Folic acid) is needed both before and during early pregnancy for the development of the neural tube of the foetus.
- The baby's bones require a good supply of calcium from the mother's diet.
- A pregnant mother will need a diet rich in iron for the production of additional blood supply and to lay down an iron store in the baby's liver.
- Constipation is common in pregnancy so a diet high in dietary fibre (NSP) is important.

Adults and Older People

- Adults need to maintain a healthy balanced diet to keep the body working properly and prevent diet-related problems from emerging.
- In older people, energy requirements decrease. They will require smaller portions at meal times.
- Older people need to keep hydrated by drinking plenty of fluids.
- Osteoporosis may occur when bones become weak, brittle and break easily.
- Older people are advised to eat calcium-rich foods to help strengthen bones.

 Quick Test

1. Give **three** recommended guidelines to a healthy diet.
2. Why is a good supply of folate needed in early pregnancy?
3. What is colostrum?
4. In babies, what is the introduction of solid foods called?

 Key Words

Eatwell Guide	iron-deficiency
colostrum	anaemia
puberty	foetus
menstruation	osteoporosis

Diet, Nutrition and Health

You must be able to:

- Demonstrate knowledge and understanding of the health conditions linked to food and nutrition
- Demonstrate knowledge and understanding of the terms relating to diet, health and energy needs.

Diet-related Medical Conditions

Bowel Cancer

- Bowel cancer is the second-biggest illness/cause of death in the UK.
- The risk of bowel cancer and diverticular disease can be greatly reduced by increasing fibre/NSP (non-starch polysaccharide) intake.

Obesity, Cardiovascular Disease (CVD) and Coronary Heart Disease (CHD), Type 2 Diabetes and Liver Disease

- **Obesity** is an abnormal accumulation of body fat. Obesity is associated with coronary heart disease, diabetes, types of cancer and high blood pressure.
- Cardiovascular disease (CVD) is a standard term for conditions affecting the heart or blood vessels. There are many types of CVD. Coronary Heart Disease (CHD) is one of the main types.
- **Coronary heart disease** is caused by fatty substances (cholesterol) building up in the walls of the arteries that run to the heart.
- Arteries narrow, reducing the supply of oxygen to the heart.
- Diets high in saturated fats produce cholesterol. Everyone should reduce their intake of saturated fat.
- High blood pressure can lead to an increased risk of stroke. High blood pressure can be linked to increased salt intake. The maximum recommended amount of salt to be consumed per day is 6 grams. Salt can be hidden in processed foods.
- With **Type 2 diabetes**, either too little insulin is produced or the body's cells fail to react to the insulin that is produced. This results in high levels of sugar in the blood.
- Diabetes is controlled by careful management of sugar in the diet, plus insulin medication frequently injected.
- Type 2 diabetes is increasingly linked to obesity.
- There are many different types of **liver disease**. One of the most common is non-alcoholic fatty liver disease (NAFLD). Usually seen in people who are overweight or obese, it is caused by a build-up of fat in the liver.

Iron Deficiency Anaemia

- Anaemia is common in teenage girls due to menstruation.
- Symptoms of anaemia include tiredness, lack of energy, shortness of breath and pale complexion.
- Pregnant women also need increased iron supplies in the diet.
- Anaemia is simply diagnosed with a blood test.

> **Key Point**
>
> Obesity is the main cause of diet-related illness in the UK.

> **Key Point**
>
> Cholesterol is a type of fat found in the blood, which is made in the liver and also obtained from the food you eat.

Dental Health

- Sugar is a major cause of **tooth decay** in children. Sugar increases acids on the teeth, causing irreparable damage. In tooth decay, acids erode the protective white enamel surface of the teeth.

Bone Health

- **Osteoporosis** is common in old age. Bones can become weak, brittle and more likely to break. It also causes the spine to curve forward, making walking difficult. A diet rich in calcium and vitamin D is required to ensure maximum bone strength.

Energy Needs

- Energy is required for us to grow, to keep the basic functions of our body going, and to be physically active.
- Energy requirements depend on your Basal Metabolic Rate (BMR). BMR is the energy needed by the body to power your internal organs when completely at rest.
- BMR depends on a person's age, gender, and body size.
- We use energy for movement of all types, known as Physical Activity Level (PAL). More physically active people require more food to supply their energy needs.
- Nutritionists devise Estimated Average Requirements (EARs) tables that provide guidelines to energy needs at various stages of life.
- Malnutrition is a result of under-consumption of nutrients. Anorexia and bulimia can lead to malnutrition symptoms.

Energy Intake and Expenditure

- The amount of energy **calories (kcal) or kilojoules (kJ)** a food contains per gram is known as its energy density.
  – Fat = 9 kcal/g; Protein = 4 kcal/g; Carbohydrate = 4 kcal/g
- What we weigh depends on the balance between how much energy we consume from our food and how much energy we use up by being physically active.
- Government guidelines state that we need to undertake 60 minutes of aerobic activity every day.
- Reference Intake (RI) is the recommended amount of each nutrient that is required daily. These replaced GDA in some instances.

Body Mass Index

- Body Mass Index (BMI) is a measure that adults can use to see if they are a healthy weight for their height.
- The ideal healthy BMI is between 18.5 and 25.

Key Point

Osteoporosis means 'porous bones' – bones lose their strength and are more likely to break.

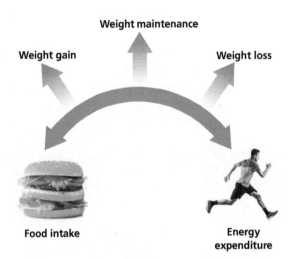

Weight maintenance

Weight gain

Weight loss

Food intake

Energy expenditure

Key Point

Energy balance is the balance of energy consumed through eating and drinking compared to energy burned through physical activity.

Key Words

Basal Metabolic Rate (BMR)
Physical Activity Level (PAL)
Estimated Average Requirements (EARs)
energy density
Reference Intake (RI)
Body Mass Index (BMI)

Quick Test

1. What is osteoporosis?
2. Name **two** symptoms of anaemia.

Food Choices

You must be able to:

- Understand that religions, customs and beliefs influence food choice
- Know about conditions that may be caused by an intolerance or allergy to food.

Religious Diets

- Some religions have their own dietary laws and rules. For example:
  - Jewish people eat kosher food, which means food that has been prepared according to Jewish law.
  - Muslims only eat meat that is halal, where animals are slaughtered in a religiously approved way.

Religion	Dietary Requirements
Judaism	• No shellfish or pork • Only kosher meat • No dairy foods are eaten with meat in a meal
Hinduism	• No beef or beef products • Many Hindus are vegetarian
Islam	• No pork • Only halal meat can be eaten
Sikhism	• No beef • Many Sikhs are vegetarian or ovo-lacto vegetarian
Christianity	• No particular dietary requirements
Buddhism	• Vegetarian
Rastafarianism	• Vegetarian or vegan • White fish sometimes eaten (but no shellfish)

> **Key Point**
>
> A diet consists of the foods that a person chooses to eat.

Vegetarians

- Vegetarians don't eat meat, poultry, fish, or products such as gelatin that have been obtained by killing animals.
- Ovo-lacto vegetarians eat eggs and dairy products (but only cheese made with vegetable rennet).
- Lacto vegetarians eat dairy products and honey, but not eggs.
- Vegans do not eat any food with an animal origin. To make sure that their diet is not deficient in certain nutrients (e.g. iron and vitamins D and B12, which are commonly found in animal products), vegans can get the necessary nutrients in their diet from a variety of sources including peas, beans, lentils, nuts and seeds. Soya and fortified products are also sources of protein.
- The reasons why people become vegetarian include: religious dietary laws; ethical reasons, e.g. meat and fish farming being wasteful of the Earth's resources; moral reasons, e.g. animal cruelty; health reasons, e.g. allergies or because they come from a vegetarian family.

Medical Conditions

- Diabetes is a condition caused because the pancreas doesn't produce any, or enough, insulin to control the amount of sugar in the blood.
- **Type 1 diabetes** is often diagnosed in childhood and is not associated with excess body weight.
  - It is treated with insulin injections or using an insulin pump.
  - It can't be controlled without taking insulin.
- **Type 2 diabetes** is usually diagnosed in people over 40 years of age and is often associated with excess body weight, high blood pressure and/or cholesterol levels at diagnosis.
  - It is treated initially with medication/tablets. It is sometimes possible to come off diabetes medication.
  - 90% of people with diabetes have Type 2 diabetes, which is best treated with a healthy diet and increased physical activity.

Allergies and Intolerances

- Coeliac disease is a condition where people have an adverse reaction to gluten, a protein found in wheat, barley, rye, and also oats, which contain a similar substance to gluten.
- Xanthan gum is added to gluten-free flour in order to make the product elastic and stretchy, which can be reduced by the absence of gluten.
- Coeliacs cannot absorb nutrients if they eat gluten. This causes severe pain and can lead to anaemia and malnutrition.
- Lactose intolerance is caused when the body is unable to digest lactose (a sugar found in milk and dairy products). Lactose intolerance causes stomach upset.
- An allergy to nuts can cause anaphylaxis, a reaction that can be fatal. People with severe allergies carry an epi-pen in case of an attack.
- Food products must be labelled if they contain nuts.
- People with a nut allergy have to check that food does not include nuts as an ingredient and that food has been produced in a nut-free environment.

GLUTEN FREE   DAIRY FREE   SOY FREE   EGG FREE   NUT FREE   PEANUT FREE   CORN FREE   NO TRANS FAT

NO SUGAR ADDED   NO SUGAR   VEGETARIAN   ORGANIC

Products displaying the Crossed Grain symbol have been licensed by Coeliac UK and are safe to eat for those following a gluten-free diet.

> ### Key Point
>
> If you can't tolerate certain foods, you have to change your diet.

> ### Key Words
>
> kosher
> halal
> vegetarian
> ovo-lacto vegetarian
> vegan
> lacto vegetarian
> ethical
> diabetes
> coeliac
> malnutrition
> lactose intolerance
> allergy
> anaphylaxis

> ### Quick Test
>
> 1. Which religions traditionally do not eat pork?
> 2. Which type of vegetarian would not eat honey?
> 3. Which foods can people with coeliac disease not include in their diet?

Review Questions

Protein and Fat

1 (Circle) **three** foods that contain High Biological Value (HBV) protein. [3]

bread   (chicken)   grapes   butter

(milk)   broccoli   (soya)   lentils

2 What is it called when Low Biological Value (LBV) protein foods are eaten together to provide a good supply of all the essential amino acids? [1]

Protein complementation

3 Over-consumption of saturated fat foods is likely to raise what level in the body? [1]

cholestrol

Carbohydrates

1 Unscramble the following starchy carbohydrate foods. [3]

astap *pasta*

ototpa *potato*

otsa *oats*

2 Anyone suffering from constipation needs to eat more foods high in dietary fibre/non starch polysaccharide (NSP). Underline **four** foods that are high in NSP. [4]

cornflakes   <u>lentils</u>   <u>cabbage</u>   cream crackers

eggs   <u>apples</u>   <u>shredded wheat</u>   milk

3 Which type of carbohydrate is linked to tooth decay? [1]

Sugars

Vitamins

1 (Circle) three foods that are a good source of Vitamin C (ascorbic acid). [3]

cheese   sardines   (Kiwi fruit)   peanut butter

(lemons)   margarine   (cabbage)

2 Explain why a pregnant woman needs an increased intake of folate (folic acid). [1]

For the development of the neural tube in the foetus

3 Give **two** reasons why raw vegetables contain more vitamins than cooked vegetables. [2]

I: _Water soluble vitamins like B1 and C get destroyed by heating_

II: _Vit C gets destroyed on exposure to oxygen after it has been cut_

4 What is the alternative name for Vitamin C? _Ascorbic acid_ [1]

Minerals and Water

1 Fill in the missing words. [3]

Iron supports the production of _haemoglobin_ in _red blood_

cells cells; this transports _oxygen_ around the body.

2 Why is iron deficiency anaemia common in teenage girls? [1]

Due to loss of blood during menstruation

3 Iodine is a component of thyroid hormones. What do these hormones regulate in the body? [1]

Basic metabolic rate

4 Give **two** reasons why someone may need to increase their water intake. [2]

I: _In hot weather perspiration increases water needs._

II: _Elderly — to prevent kidney problems._

Practice Questions

Making Informed Choices

1 Eating less salt and less fat are two of the current healthy eating guidelines. List **three** other healthy eating guidelines. [3]

I: _Drink 6-8 glasses of water a day._

II: _Base your diet on starchy carbohydrates._

III: _Eat at least 5 portions of fruits & vegetables daily._

2 What term is used to describe the gradual introduction of solid foods into a baby's diet? [1]

Weaning

3 What does the yellow group on the Eatwell Guide show? [1]

Carbohydrates

4 State the recommended number of glasses of water we should drink each day. [1]

_6 - 8_

5 As people become older their energy requirements change. Explain how the requirement changes and give a reason for this change. [2]

Older people need to have smaller portions

Reason: _Energy requirements are less because they are less active_

Diet, Nutrition and Health

1 What is the maximum daily recommended amount of salt? Tick (✓) **one** answer. [1]

a) 2 g ☐   **b)** 6 g ☑   **c)** 16 g ☐   **d)** 24 g ☐

2 Obesity is linked to many other health conditions. Name **two** of these conditions. [2]

I: _Coronary Heart Disease_   II: _High Blood Pressure_

3 People with Type 2 diabetes cannot produce enough of which hormone? [1]

Insulin

4 What are the health risks of a high-fat diet? [3]

high cholestrol
Fat blocks the blood vessels carrying oxygen to the heart
This leads to coronary heart disease. weight gain/obesity

5 Explain what is meant by basal metabolic rate (BMR). [2]

The amount of energy the body requires to power
our internal organs when at complete rest

6 Explain the meaning of the term 'energy density'. *calories (kcal) a kilojoules (kJ)* [2]

The amount of energy provided by a food
per gram . Eg: Fat = 9 kcal/g

Food Choices

1 Which of the following statements is **true**? Tick (✓) **one** answer. [1]

a) Vegetarians include gelatine in their diet. ☐

b) Kosher meat is eaten by Muslims. ☐

c) Lacto-vegetarians eat honey. ☑

d) Coeliac disease is caused by sensitivity to rice. ☐

2 Underline the correct answer. People with a severe allergy often carry their own medication in the form of… [1]

<u>an epi-pen.</u> insulin. a ball-point pen. Paracetamol.

3 State which nutrients may be missing from a vegan diet. [3]

Protein (HBV), vitamins D, Vitamin B12, Iron

Cooking of Food, Heat Transfer and Selecting Appropriate Cooking Methods

You must be able to:

- Know and understand the reasons why food is cooked and how heat is transferred to food
- Know the reasons for selecting different cooking methods.

Why is Food Cooked?

- Food is cooked in order to:
  - make it safe to eat (cooking destroys microorganisms)
  - change raw food to cooked food
  - make it palatable: develop flavours; improve mouthfeel; improve texture; reduce bulk; improve colour
  - help keep quality (extend shelf life)
  - make it easier to digest
  - give variety to diet.

How is Food Cooked?

- Cooking uses heat to change texture, flavour and colour of food.
- Cooking methods are **wet** (moist), **dry,** or **fat-based**:
  - Wet methods are boiling, steaming, stewing, poaching, casseroling and braising.
  - Dry methods are baking, roasting and grilling.
  - Fat-based methods are frying and stir-frying.
- Pre-cooking methods can improve tenderness and flavour, for example, a marinade for meat or fish.
- The selection of a cooking method depends on:
  - the type of food being cooked
  - the time available
  - the skill of the cook and the facilities available
  - the need to achieve desired characteristics, e.g. browning
  - the need to conserve vitamins, e.g. steam rather than boil to prevent loss of vitamins
  - the desire to improve palatability, which affects the appearance, colour, flavour, texture and smell.

> **Key Point**
>
> Cooking food makes it safe, allows it to keep for longer and makes it more palatable.

Microwave Cooking

- **Microwave** cooking uses a type of radiation called microwaves, which travel in straight lines and penetrate the food.
- The microwaves vibrate water molecules creating friction, which makes heat.
- **Hot spots** can occur, so food should be stirred and left to stand to allow the heat to be distributed evenly.
- Microwaves alone do not brown or crisp foods.

Summary of Cooking Methods

Method	Characteristics	Examples
Water-based		
Boiling	softens	vegetables, rice
Simmering	tenderises, evaporates	stews, sauces, curries
Poaching	tenderises	fish, chicken, eggs
Braising	tenderises, softens	meats, fish, vegetables
Steaming	tenderises	vegetables
Oven		
Moist or fat	tenderises	vegetables, joints of meat, potatoes
Dry		
Grilling	chars, browns, crisps	bacon, toast, cheese
Baking	browns, crisps	cakes, pastries
Dry frying	browns, crisps	bacon, lardons, chorizo, nuts
Roasting	browns, crisps	roast chicken, potatoes
Fat-based		
Deep frying	browns, crisps	battered fish
Shallow frying	sets, browns	eggs, onions
Stir fry	softens, reduces bulk	bean sprouts

Heat Transfer

- There are three ways in which heat is transferred through food:

Conduction	Convection	Radiation
Food molecules vibrate to transfer heat via conduction. Heat is transferred by contact of heat source to pan to food, e.g. frying.	Convection takes place in air (in ovens) or liquids. Currents occur as heated air or water rises and cooler air or water falls, e.g. boiling water.	Heat energy passing in direct lines to the food, e.g. grill to food. Energy from microwaves penetrate food to transfer energy.

Conduction

Convection

Radiation

Quick Test

1. Cooking food can make it more palatable. True or false?
2. What is the main heat transfer method when boiling food?
3. How can cooking methods be classified?
4. Name **three** types of heat transfer.

Key Words

palatability
radiation
conduction
convection

Proteins and Enzymic Browning

You must be able to:

- Understand protein denaturation and protein coagulation
- Know about the properties of protein in gluten formation
- Understand enzymic browning and oxidation in fruit and vegetables.

Protein Denaturation

- **Denaturation** occurs when the structure of amino acids found in protein is altered. They change shape or unfold because chemical bonds are broken.
- Protein in foods can be denatured (altered) by **heat, reduction of pH level** (more acid), **enzymes** and **mechanical actions**. (See the table below.)

Heat	• Cooking denatures proteins. • Denaturation occurs when the structure of amino acids found in protein changes shape after cooking – the protein molecule uncoils when cooked.	
pH	• pH is the level of acidity or alkalinity in a food. • pH is measured from 1, which is very acid, to 14, which is very alkaline. • Reducing the pH by using lemon juice or vinegar in a marinade denatures the protein in foods to make them tender, tasty and moist.	
Enzymes	• Meat tenderisers cause protein denaturation, making meat more tender. • Enzymic tenderisers are in the form of papain and bromelain. Papain can be found naturally in papaya and bromelain can be found in fresh pineapple. • Acidic pH from yoghurt, buttermilk, vinegar or citrus fruits helps to tenderise fish or meat (as marinades).	
Mechanical Actions	• Whisking egg white denatures the protein by uncoiling and unfolding, e.g. foam formation occurs (gas in liquid).	

Protein Coagulation

- Protein coagulation is a type of protein denaturation.
- Examples of coagulated foods are egg custards and quiches.
- It causes a change in texture, for example, runny eggs become coagulated (set).
- It usually starts at 60°C and is completed by 70°C.
- It is irreversible and causes loss of solubility.

Gluten Formation

- Gluten formation occurs when water is added to a wheat flour to form a dough. Wheat flour contains two proteins, glutenin and gliadin, which combine to form gluten.
- Strong wheat flour for bread making contains more gluten than plain flour.

Gluten in Bread

- Gluten makes dough stretchy and elastic.
- Salt and kneading help strengthen gluten.
- Gluten forms the structure of a baked loaf of bread.

Gluten in Pastry

- Rubbing fat into flour makes short gluten strands – the scientific term for this is **shortening.**
- Gluten forms the structure in baked pastry.

Gluten in Pasta Making

- Gluten in wheat flour helps pasta hold its shape, e.g. fusilli.
- Gluten also makes the pasta dough flexible and increases its ability to hold various shapes.

Proteins and Enzymic Browning

- Enzymic browing occurs on the surface of cut fruits, such as apples, and on the surface of cut vegetables, such as potatoes.
- It happens due to cell enzymes reacting with air (oxidation).
- Enzymic browning can be prevented (inhibited) by:
  - blanching cut fruits or vegetables in boiling water
  - blanching vegetables before freezing, which inhibits the enzymic action that can discolour food
  - dipping fruit or vegetables in acid, e.g. lemon juice
  - removal of air by submerging in water
  - cooking, e.g. stewing fruit, roasting parsnips.

Oxidation

- Oxidation causes discolouration, e.g, cut lettuce leaves turn pink-brown.
- Oxidation also causes vitamins to be lost, particularly vitamin C.
- Oxidation enables enzyme activity, e.g. browning, discolouration.
- Oxidation can be reduced during preparation and cooking by:
  - cooking vegetables in small amounts of water
  - using a quicker, shorter method of cooking, e.g. steaming, stir fry
  - serving vegetables immediately after cooking
  - keeping the lid on when boiling vegetables
  - using the cooking water in gravy.

> ### Key Point
>
> Wheat flour contains the protein gluten. Gluten forms the structure of pastries, breads and cakes.

> ### Key Point
>
> Enzymes can cause the browning of fruit and vegetables. Fruit and vegetables need careful handling during preparation to prevent enzymic browning.

> ### Key Words
>
> denaturation
> pH level
> marinade
> enzymic browning
> oxidation

Quick Test

1. What causes the browning of cut fruit or vegetables?
2. What is the term used to explain the way heat changes the texture of egg proteins?

Carbohydrates

You must be able to:

- Understand the functional and chemical properties of carbohydrates, which are gelatinisation, dextrinisation and caramelisation.

Gelatinisation

- **Gelatinisation** occurs when starches (wheatflour, cornflour or arrowroot) thicken liquids. The process needs heat and agitation (stirring), especially in sauce making. It occurs during the cooking of starchy food such as potatoes, rice or pasta.

Gelatinisation in Sauce Making

- When making a sauce gelatinisation occurs.
- Starch grains absorb liquid, swell, burst (at 80°C) and finally thicken a sauce. Starches complete thickening at just under 100°C, so it is important to cook to boiling point to avoid a sauce with a raw taste.
- Sauces need stirring (agitating) to prevent lumps forming, to stop the sauce from sticking to the bottom of the pan and burning, and to help the process of gelatinisation.
- Basic recipes use different methods and different thickening agents, as seen when using the roux method, the blending method and the all-in-one method.

Gelatinisation and Ratios

- A sauce is viscous, which means it can either be poured (e.g. parsley sauce) or used to coat an ingredient (e.g. cauliflower cheese) or to bind other dry ingredients together (e.g. rissoles).
- The change in viscosity is due to the ratio of thickening agent to liquid; more starch gives a thicker sauce. The ratio selected changes the consistency of the sauce from runny to thick.
- Retrogradation is the deterioration of a starch-based sauce on keeping – this results in shrinkage, drying and cracking.
- Synerisis is the loss of fluid from a foam or set mixture, e.g. lemon meringue pie, and in cheese making.

Modified Starches and Gelatinisation

- Modified starches are used to help gelatinisation occur in different ways. Quick-cook pasta or rice are modified by pre-gelatinisation.
- Milkshakes use starch modified to allow cold liquid thickening.
- Instant thickening gravy granules are modified starch that can be sprinkled into boiling liquids.

> ### Key Point
>
> Gelatinisation is the function of starches as thickening agents.

- Modified starches thicken cold desserts without the application of heat, and are used to thicken and stabilise salad dressings.

Dextrinisation

- Dextrinisation occurs when starch is toasted or cooked by dry heat, e.g. toasted or charred bread.
- It is a result of starch breakdown by dry heat to form dextrins.
- It changes the properties of starch as a result of heat application.
- Dextrinisation is known as non-enzymic browning.
- Dextrins taste sweeter than starch and add flavour to toasted, charred or baked goods.
- Dextrins are hygroscopic, absorbing moisture from the air, e.g. toasted or baked products soften slightly on keeping. Baked produce is best stored in an airtight tin or container with lid.
- Characteristics of dextrinisation are golden colours, browning, sweeter taste and crispness.

Caramelisation

- Caramelisation causes sugar to change colour and flavour due to dry or moist heat.
- It causes surface browning on baked goods containing sugar.
- It changes the properties of sugar; solutions become syrups.
- It is known as non-enzymic browning.
- Characteristics of caramelisation are a golden colour, browning, gloss, sweetness and stickiness.

Examples of Caramelisation (Browning) in Food Preparation

- Frying onions, or frying or roasting parsnips, potatoes or squash.
- Making a crème brulee or crème caramel.
- Spun sugar caramelisation is created through the application of **dry** heat to sugar.
- Fudge, toffee or halva are created through the application of **wet** heat to caramelise the sugar.
- Preparing glazed pork ribs or chicken wings.

Browning and Carbohydrates

- Dry methods of cooking gradually turn starches and sugars golden brown. This aids the palatability of the products by improving flavour, texture and colour.
- Browning is often used as an indicator of adequate cooking e.g. cook until golden brown.

> ### Quick Test
>
> 1. What term describes thickening a sauce using starch?
> 2. What sort of heat transfer commonly causes dextrinisation?
> 3. Dextrins attract and absorb moisture from the air. Is this true or false?

Fats and Oils

You must be able to:

- Understand the role of fats and oils in shortening, plasticity, aeration and emulsification
- Know the functional and chemical properties of fats and oils.

Types of Fat

- Fat from animal sources include butter and lard – these are saturated fats.
- Fat from vegetable sources include margarine and vegetable shortening – these are unsaturated fats and are suitable for vegetarians, vegans and certain religions.

Shortening

- Shortening is a process using fat that creates a characteristic short, crumbly texture.
- Shortening is seen in shortcrust pastry, shortbread biscuits, cookies and rich pastries.
- The process in food preparation most likely to bring about shortening is the rubbing-in method.

How Does a Fat Shorten a Pastry Mixture?

- Fats with plasticity are good shortening agents because they rub-in easily.
- Fat coats the flour grains, preventing gluten development.
- The cooked texture is short and crumbly.

What Happens During the Cooking of Pastry?

- The flour grains absorb the fat.
- Pastry changes from pliable to rigid (the gluten sets).
- Pastry turns golden brown.

Plasticity

- Plasticity means the ability of a fat to change properties over a range of temperatures. Temperature is an important factor in plasticity of fats.
- Cold fats are solid and firm.
- Fats at room temperature become spreadable and soft.
- Plastic fats such as butter or margarine can be used for spreading, rubbing-in, creaming, melting-method cooking or for muffins.
- Warmed fats melt and become runny.

> ### Key Point
>
> Fats make pastry short and crumbly. Fats give colour and flavour to pastry. The plasticity of fat allows it to be used for rubbing-in, spreading and creaming.

Aeration

- Aeration helps products have a light and open texture.
- Fats aerate mixtures during beating or creaming with sugar.
- Aeration increases the volume of a product by incorporating air.
- Beating, whipping, creaming and whisking are methods that help aeration.
- During preparation of a creamed mixture:
  - the fat and sugar are creamed together, trapping air (aeration)
  - the mixture becomes paler
  - an air-in-fat foam is formed.
- During baking:
  - trapped air expands
  - the cake rises.

 Key Point

Fats can help aeration in baking.

The creaming method aerates a cake mixture and helps it to rise.

Emulsions

- Emulsions are mixtures of liquids that do not normally mix (known as 'immiscible' liquids), e.g. oil and water.
- Emulsifiers have a hydrophilic end, which is water-loving and forms chemical bonds with water, and a hydrophobic end, which is water-hating and forms chemical bonds with oil.
- Fats and oils add texture, flavour and colour to emulsified sauces such as Hollandaise, which is a hot emulsion, and mayonnaise, which is a cold emulsion.
- Stabilisers keep emulsions mixed, preventing them separating.

Types of emulsions

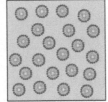
oil-in-water

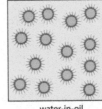
water-in-oil

Oil and balsamic vinegar

The Process of Emulsification

- Emulsification requires agitation by whisking, by mixer or food processor.
- It requires slow addition of oil to prevent the emulsion splitting.
- Emulsification is helped by a natural emulsifier called lecithin, which is present in egg yolks.
- A good example of emulsification is seen when making mayonnaise, a smooth, stable emulsion for salad dressing.
- Vinaigrette dressing (oil and vinegar) is not a stable emulsion – it will separate out on standing.

 Key Point

Emulsions are mixtures of liquids that do not normally mix, e.g. oil and water. Egg yolks contain lecithin, a natural emulsifier. Eggs help stabilise mayonnaise.

Key Words

shortening
plasticity
aeration
creaming
foam
emulsification

Quick Test

1. What term describes how fat makes a short texture product?
2. The ability of a fat to change properties is known as plasticity. Is this true or false?
3. Which basic cake-making process traps air into the cake?

Raising Agents

You must be able to:

- Understand the processes of raising or aerating using physical and mechanical methods
- Know and understand the working properties of chemical and biological raising agents.

Raising and Aerating

Physical Methods	Mechanical Methods
• Physical raising methods such as air, water vapour or steam help products to have a light, open texture. • Recipes that need to be light have ingredients that function as raising agents such as water, milk or egg whites.	• Food preparation methods such as sieving, whisking or beating can be used to trap air. • Combinations of physical and mechanical methods work well in food preparation to make mixtures light, e.g. batters for Yorkshire puddings.

Air, Steam and Foam as Raising Agents

- **Air** is a very effective raising agent because it expands when it is heated. Air pockets swell and volume increases.
- Food preparation techniques help prevent loss of air, e.g. folding in flour when making a whisked sponge cake.
- **Steam** is produced from water in a mixture; this is a physical change.
- Steam produces light, open and uneven textures and adds volume during cooking, e.g. profiteroles.
- Moist mixtures produce steam during cooking.
- **Foams** – whisking helps trap air, creating foam.
- Ingredients containing protein form foams, e.g. milk froth, egg whites.
- Egg whites stretch and unravel to trap air to form a gas-in-liquid foam.
- Sugar stabilises foam, e.g. cold-set soufflé.
- Egg white foams set mousses.
- Cooking stabilises foam, e.g. roulade, meringue.

Chemical Raising Agents

- Chemical raising agents produce carbon dioxide when heated with a liquid.
- They cause effervescent fizzing and bubbles of gas.
- Chemical raising agents must be carefully measured.

Bicarbonate of Soda

- Bicarbonate of soda is an alkaline powder.
- It can leave a soapy aftertaste but strong flavours (e.g. gingerbread) will mask the aftertaste.
- It works more effectively with an acid ingredient such as buttermilk or cream of tartar, e.g. soda bread.
- The acid neutralises the alkali and prevents soapy aftertaste.
- Cream of tartar is an acid raising agent, which is frequently used alongside bicarbonate of soda, e.g. in scones.

Bicarbonate of soda

Baking Powder

- Baking powder is a ready-to-use mixture of cream of tartar plus bicarbonate of soda and rice flour.

Self-raising Flour

- Self-raising flour is plain flour and baking powder added together to create rise. Plain flour alone does not contain a raising agent.
- Self-raising flour can be brown or white.
- Self-raising flour contains a pre-sieved precisely measured amount of baking powder for ease and speed of use.

Gingerbread

Biological Raising Agents

- Yeast is a biological raising agent. It ferments to give off carbon dioxide gas.
- Fermentation in yeast is a biological (also known as biotechnological) raising agent.
- The conditions for yeast fermentation are warm temperature (25°C–35°C); moisture; food; time.
- Temperatures above 60°C during baking will inactivate and finally destroy yeast cells.
- Boiling liquids will inactivate yeast, preventing fermentation from taking place.
- Yeast is the raising agent in bread, bread rolls, buns and rich pastries (Danish pastries).
- Leavened bread contains raising agent in the form of yeast or bicarbonate of soda.
- Unleavened bread contains no raising agent and is flat in structure.

Quick Test

1. What is the raising agent in a whisked sponge cake?
2. What happens when air is heated?
3. How does egg white trap air?
4. How can water help make a mixture light during cooking?

Key Words

physical raising methods
chemical raising agents
yeast

Review Questions

Making Informed Choices

1 Which of the following foods would you serve to someone who needed to increase their intake of iron? Circle **three** foods. [3]

oranges   chocolate   digestive biscuits

beef   apricots   salad

2 What is the Eatwell Guide? Tick (✓) **one** answer. [1]

a) A chart that shows you how long foods can be kept for. ☐

b) A guide that informs you of where to shop for the healthiest food. ☐

c) A guide that shows the proportions of food groups that should be eaten daily for a well-balanced diet. ☐

d) A guide that tells you for how long foods have to be reheated. ☐

3 Fill in the missing words. [2]

Babies are born with a supply of i_____ stored in the l_____.

Diet, Nutrition and Health

1 What is obesity? Tick (✓) **one** answer. [1]

a) Abnormal accumulation of body fat ☐

b) Lack of thyroid hormone ☐

c) Weakened teeth and gums ☐

d) Narrowing of the arteries ☐

2 Which of the following foods would you serve to an elderly person to keep their bones as healthy as possible? Circle **three** foods. [3]

oranges   milky drinks   digestive biscuits

sausages   cheese   yoghurts   salad

3 How does someone with type 2 diabetes manage the condition? [2]

....

....

....

4 What is a healthy BMI for adults? Tick (✓) **one** answer. [1]

a) 7.5–12 ☐   **b)** 13.5–18 ☐   **c)** 18.5–25 ☐   **d)** 32–38.5 ☐

5 What is osteoporosis? [1]

....

....

....

Food Choices

1 Which religious dietary law forbids shellfish? Tick (✓) **one** answer. [1]

a) Islam ☐   **b)** Hinduism ☐   **c)** Sikhism ☐   **d)** Judaism ☐

2 What condition can be caused if a person has a serious allergy? [1]

....

3 What is lactose? [1]

....

4 **a)** Who is most likely to develop Type 2 diabetes? [2]

....

....

b) Explain **two** main recommendations for a diabetic person's diet. [2]

I: ....

II: ....

Practice Questions

Cooking of Food, Heat Transfer and Selecting Appropriate Cooking Methods

1 Show you understand the key reasons for cooking food. Complete the following statements using the words in the boxes below.

| shelf life | digest | variety | microorganisms | keep quality |

Food is cooked to:

a) make it safe to eat by destroying .... [1]

b) help extend .... and .... [2]

c) improve .... in the diet. [1]

d) make it easier to .... [1]

2 Name **three** methods of heat transfer. [3]

I: .... II: .... III: ....

3 Listed below are the three classifications of cooking methods. Name **two** examples of each classification. [6]

	Water-based Methods	Dry Cooking Methods	Fat-based Methods
Example 1			
Example 2			

Proteins and Enzymic Browning

1 Protein foods can be denatured in four ways. What are the **four** ways? [4]

I: .... II: ....

III: .... IV: ....

2 During the cooking of a quiche the egg filling changes texture.

   a) In what way does the texture of the quiche filling change during baking? [1]

   _____

   b) Why does the texture of the quiche filling change during baking? [2]

   _____

   _____

3 a) What is the name of the protein in wheat flour? [1]

   _____

   b) In what way is the protein content of strong flour different to plain cake flour? [1]

   _____

4 a) State **two** actions that are required for wheat flour to form gluten. [2]

   I:_____

   II:_____

   b) Gluten is formed from two proteins in wheat: glutenin is one; what is the other protein? [1]

   _____

5 a) What is the term used to explain browning in foods **not** as a result of either
      dextrinisation or caramelisation? [1]

   _____

   b) Explain **one** way to prevent browning of cut apples. [1]

   _____

   _____

Practice Questions

Carbohydrates

1 Circle the correct words in the following passage. [5]

The function of starch in thickening a **solid / liquid** is known as **gelatinisation / caramelisation**. For a sauce to thicken it needs to be **chilled / heated** and also **stirred / sieved** to ensure a smooth sauce. A sauce should be heated to **setting point / boiling point** to prevent it tasting raw.

2 a) As bread is toasted dextrins are formed. How does dextrin affect the colour, flavour and texture of toast slices? [3]

Colour: ....

Flavour: ....

Texture: ....

b) What is the scientific term for the effect of dry heat on starch? [1]

....

c) Dextrins attract moisture from the air. What is the scientific term for this? [1]

....

d) How does this process affect the quality of the toast? [1]

....

Fats and Oils

1 Which of these statements is **not** true? Tick (✓) **one** answer. [1]

a) Shortening is a process that creates a hard texture in products. ☐

b) Shortening is seen in shortcrust pastry, shortbread biscuits, cookies and rich pastries. ☐

c) The process in food preparation most likely to bring about shortening is the rubbing in method. ☐

2 Fats are used in food preparation to promote characteristic textures, flavours and colours. Identify the functional properties of fat in the preparation processes on the following page. [6]

Process	Function of Process	End Product Characteristic
a) Margarine and sugar beaten (creamed) together in a mixture	Explain **two** functions	Give **two** characteristics ....
b) Margarine or butter rubbed into a flour mixture	**One** function	**One** characteristic ....

Raising Agents

1 Describe **three** functions of raising agents in food preparation. [3]

I: .... II: .... III: ....

2 A baker wants her shop assistants to understand raising agents. She uses examples from her shop.

Example 1 is a whisked sponge flan.

a) What is the raising agent in the flan sponge? [1]

....

b) Describe how the raising agent is incorporated into the sponge. [1]

....

....

Example 2 is a cheese scone.

c) Which raising agent is used in scones? [1]

....

d) What gas would the raising agent produce? [1]

....

e) Explain how the raising agent works during baking. [2]

....

....

Microorganisms, Enzymes and Food Spoilage

You must be able to:

- Know the growth conditions for microorganisms and enzymes and the control of food spoilage
- Know and understand that bacteria, yeasts and moulds are microorganisms
- Explain that enzymes are biological catalysts usually made from protein.

Bacteria

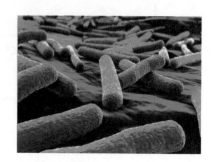

- **Bacteria** are single-celled organisms that are able to reproduce rapidly. They are also called **microorganisms.**
- Bacteria are sometimes useful and are used in cheese-making and in yoghurt.
- They are sometimes harmful (pathogenic) and can cause food poisoning.

Conditions for Growth

Temperature	• Bacteria generally multiply between 5 °C and 63 °C – this is known as the 'danger zone'. • The average ideal temperature for rapid bacterial multiplication is 37 °C, which is body temperature.
Moisture	• Bacteria need moisture to live and multiply.

Time	• Under optimum conditions, bacteria will multiply every 10–20 minutes, so within seven hours one bacterium can become one million.
	• To control bacteria multiplying:
	  – eat food as soon as possible after making/cooking
	  – if food is not being eaten straight away, cool down as quickly as possible (within 90 minutes is recommended) and store in the fridge or freezer. A blast chiller will cool food more quickly than the recommended 90 minutes.

Nutrients	• Bacteria can multiply to large numbers on high-risk foods such as meat, poultry, fish, eggs and milk. These are all high-risk foods.
pH level	• Bacteria grow best at a neutral pH level, between 6.6 and 7.5. • Bacteria are unable to survive below pH 4.5. • Vinegar (acetic acid) has a pH of 3.5.

Yeast

- Yeast are single-celled plants found in the air and on skins of fruit.
- Yeast spoils the taste of food but is not harmful.
- It grows only on sugary foods, but not in sugar concentrations above 50% (jams should be made with 60% sugar).
- It can survive without air.
- It can't grow at low temperatures or survive in vinegar.
- It is destroyed at temperatures above 70 °C.

> ### Key Point
>
> Bacteria are found everywhere and need the right temperature, warmth, time, nutrients, pH level and oxygen to grow and multiply.

- Yeast is a very helpful organism. It is used in baking bread, where carbon dioxide is used as a raising agent, and in wine making and brewing.

Moulds

- Moulds are a type of fungus, which settle on food and grow into a visible plant.
- Moulds grow on many foods, such as bread, cheese and meat.
- They like slightly acid conditions.
- They need moisture and warmth (20 °C–40 °C), but are destroyed by heat <70 °C.
- Moulds can survive in the fridge but not in the freezer.
- Mould on food is a sign that it is not very fresh or has been stored incorrectly. Some mould can result in allergic reaction and respiratory difficulties.

Enzymes

- Enzymes in food can be a problem for food storage.
- The cells break open, the enzymes escape and react with other parts of the food. Soft spots appear on fruit and vegetables and make meat smell and taste bad.
- Denaturing the enzymes can help to preserve the food, e.g. through heat, use of acids, strong alkalis or salt.
- Enzymes are chemical catalysts that are found in all cells.
- Enzymes break down plant and animal tissues, causing fruit to ripen, meat to tenderise and enzymic browning (also known as oxidation) to speed up.

Ways to Prevent Oxidation (Enzymic Browning)

- Adding lemon juice (an acid) to a fruit salad prevents browning.
- Blanching vegetables before freezing prevents discolouration.
- Removing air by immersing potatoes in water will prevent browning.
- Refrigeration or freezing will slow down browning.
- The removal of moisture (dehydration) will prevent browning, however it is a slow process and the browning reaction is quick.

Quick Test

1. What are microorganisms?
2. What is the ideal temperature for bacterial growth?
3. How can we control bacterial growth?
4. Name **two** food products that use yeast.

Key Words

bacteria
microorganisms
moulds
enzymes

Microorganisms in Food Production

You must be able to:

- Demonstrate knowledge and understanding of the use of microorganisms in food production, including moulds in the production of blue cheese, yeasts as a raising agent in bread and the use of bacteria in yoghurt production.

The Dairy Industry

- It would be impossible to make cheese without a starter culture.
- As the culture grows in the milk, it converts the sugar lactose into lactic acid, which ensures the correct level of acidity and gives the cheese its moisture.
- As the cheese ripens, the culture gives it a balanced aroma, taste and texture.
- Choosing the right mixture of culture is essential for a high-quality cheese.

Cheese Production and Moulds

- Cheeses that rely on moulds for their characteristic properties include:
  - blue cheese
  - soft ripened cheese (such as camembert and brie)
  - rind-washed cheese (such as époisses and taleggio).

Blue Cheese

- To make blue cheese:
  - the cheese is treated with a mould
  - as the cheese matures, the mould grows
  - this creates blue veins within the cheese, giving the cheese its characteristic flavour, e.g. stilton and roquefort.

Blue cheese

Soft Ripened Cheese

- To make soft ripened cheese:
  - P. camemberti is allowed to grow on the outside of the cheese, causing the cheese to age from the outside in, forming a soft white crust and runny inside, e.g. brie and camembert.

Soft ripened cheese

Rind-washed Cheese

- To make rind-washed cheeses:
  - rind-washed cheeses also ripen inwards but they are washed with brine and other ingredients, e.g. beer and wine, which contain mould
  - this makes them attractive to bacteria, which adds to the flavour, e.g. limburger.

Rind-washed cheese

Yoghurt

- In yoghurt, the culture is responsible for the taste and texture of the final product.
- In recent years probiotic cultures have become popular in dairy products because of their health benefits.
- Probiotic cultures are carefully selected strains, and there is good evidence that they help improve digestion, safeguard the immune system, and keep the body's intestinal flora in balance.
- Probiotic cultures are classified as a functional food.

The Meat Industry

- Meat starter cultures are used to make dried, fermented products such as salami, pepperoni, chorizo and dried ham.
- Lactic bacteria develop the flavour and colour of the products.
- A wide variety of moulds are used to ripen the surface of sausages, preserving the natural quality of the product and controlling the development of flavour.

> **Key Point**
>
> Microorganisms (bacteria) are used to make a wide range of food products. Bacteria are used to make cheese, yoghurt, and bread. The most important bacteria in food manufacturing are the Lactobacillus species.

Yeast

- Yeast is used in bread-making as well as in making beer and wine.
- Yeast is a microorganism.
- Yeast requires sugar to grow.
- In bread making, yeast will:
  - leaven the dough by producing CO_2
  - through fermentation and its enzymic action on other ingredients, create a stretchy dough
  - contribute to the flavour of the bread.
- Yeast and sugar that has fermented can also be used to make fizzy drinks.
- Yeast and sugar are combined to produce a 'starter'.
- This will lead to lactic acid bacteria developing, which then produce carbon dioxide that makes the drinks fizzy.

 Quick Test

1. What is the most important bacteria used in food manufacturing?
2. What is blue cheese treated with to give it its taste and texture?
3. In what ways are probiotic cultures considered to have health benefits?

 Key Words

starter culture
probiotic

Bacterial Contamination

You must be able to:

- Know and understand the different sources of bacterial contamination
- Know and understand the main types of bacteria that cause food poisoning
- Demonstrate knowledge and understanding of the main sources and methods of control of different food poisoning bacteria types
- Recognise the general symptoms of food poisoning.

Bacteria

- Bacteria can be found everywhere, including raw food, people, air and dust, equipment and utensils, soil, pests, water and food waste.

The Dangers of Bacteria

- It is essential to control the conditions that allow bacteria to multiply and cause illness, e.g. stick to strict time and temperature controls.
- You can become ill if you eat food that is contaminated by certain bacteria (pathogens) and viruses.
- Kitchens provide the ideal conditions for bacteria growth.
- Bacteria are microscopic. You cannot tell if a food is contaminated by just looking at it.

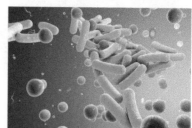

Food Poisoning Bacteria

- Food poisoning is caused by bacteria multiplying in or on food.

Pathogenic Bacteria	Foods Affected	Symptoms	Onset	Special Note
Salmonella	Raw meat; Eggs; Seafood; Dairy products	Diarrhoea; Vomiting; Fever	12–36 hours	May be fatal to the elderly and babies; Found in human and animal excreta
Staphylococcus Aureus	Cooked sliced meat; Dairy products; Anything touched by hand	Vomiting; Diarrhoea; Abdominal pain	1–6 hours	Present in nasal passages, throat and skin; Associated with dirty food handlers; Good personal hygiene is crucial
Clostridium perfingens	Raw and cooked meat and meat products	Nausea; Diarrhoea; Abdominal pain	8–22 hours	
Clostridium Botulinum	Incorrectly canned meat, fish or vegetables	Paralysis; Difficulty breathing; Double vision; Nausea; Vomiting	12–48 hours	Rare
Bacillus cereus	Cooked rice, pasta and cereal foods	Nausea; Vomiting; Diarrhoea	1–6 hours	

Food-borne Disease

- Food-borne diseases are caused by pathogenic microbes (bacteria and viruses) carried on food. These microbes do not multiply in the food but in the person who has eaten the food.

Pathogenic Microbes	Foods Affected	Symptoms	Onset	Special Note
Escherichia-Coli (E-Coli)	Raw meat; Untreated milk and water	Vomiting; Blood in diarrhoea; Kidney damage or failure	12–24 hours	Causes gastroenteritis in humans
Listeria Monocytogenes	Soft cheeses; Pâté; Unpasteurized milk; Undercooked meat; Incorrectly heated cook-chill meals	A range of symptoms from mild flu-like symptoms to septicemia, meningitis and pneumonia	No specific time	Can cause miscarriage, premature labour and birth
Campylobacter	Meat; Shellfish; Untreated water; Washing raw poultry	Diarrhoea; Headache; Fever; Abdominal pain	1–11 days	Easily transmitted between humans. Raw meat and poultry **MUST NOT** be washed as this spreads the bacteria
Norovirus	Shellfish; Raw vegetables; Salads	Nausea; Vomiting; Diarrhoea; Abdominal pain; Fever	1–2 days	Projectile vomiting The virus can survive for several days if not cleaned up properly

Preventing Contamination

- Preventing contamination is the key to food safety.
- Keep the kitchen clean and tidy. Clean and disinfect all areas, equipment and utensils used to prepare food.
- Keep food covered. Handle the food as little as possible.
- Store food correctly. Cook food thoroughly.
- Remove food waste and rubbish.

Food Poisoning

- Food poisoning is caused by harmful bacteria multiplying in or on food.
- Symptoms usually pass in a few days and the sufferer will make a full recovery.
- Food poisoning can affect anyone, but some people may suffer more than others, such as very young children and babies; elderly people; those who have had a serious illness or are recovering from a serious illness; pregnant women and nursing mothers; people who have allergies.

> ## Key Point
>
> Bacterial contamination is the presence of harmful bacteria in our food, which can lead to food poisoning and illness. As a food handler, you must do everything possible to prevent this contamination.

Quick Test

1. What are the main symptoms of food poisoning?
2. Name **three** bacteria responsible for food poisoning.
3. What are the typical sources of food poisoning?
4. Which groups of people are more at risk of food poisoning?

> ## Key Words
>
> pathogens
> contamination

Buying and Storing Food

You must be able to:

- Know and understand the food safety principles when buying and storing food
- Know and understand temperature control and ambient storage
- Understand danger zone temperatures and be able to describe the correct uses of domestic fridges and freezers
- Understand date marks.

Buying Safe Food

- Make sure the food is safe for consumption.
- Check for signs of damage to tins, packets and packaging.
- Check the date marks – the use-by date and best-before date.
- Stock rotation makes sure that food is used within date (when it is safe) and prevents unnecessary waste.

Use-by Dates

- A use-by date is a safety date found on foods and their packaging.
- Use-by dates are found on highly perishable, packaged food such as meat, fish and dairy products that require chilling and have a short shelf life.
- It is an offence for businesses to sell or use food that has passed its use-by date.

Best-before Dates

- Best-before dates usually appear on less perishable foods that have a long shelf life, such as canned, dried and frozen food products.

Storing Food

- It is important to store food properly.
- Food should be wrapped, covered or kept in a suitable clean container.
- Raw meat, poultry, fish and eggs should always be stored away from ready-to-eat foods. Raw vegetables, including salad leaves, may contain pathogens from the soil and should be kept away from ready-to-eat/high-risk foods.
- The refrigerator should be cleaned regularly.
- Dry and canned foods, e.g. dried pasta, tinned tomatoes, herbs and spices should be stored in cupboards that are clean and dry.
- Frozen food still could have bacteria present but they are dormant. Enzymes that cause food spoilage are slowed but not stopped unless inactivated – this is the reason for blanching vegetables before freezing.

- Food ingredients and finished products must be:
  - at the correct temperature
  - protected from contamination
- Food ingredients should be used according to the date marks on the food or its packaging.
- Using food within the date marks avoids waste and reduces the risk of cross contamination.

Chilled Food Storage

- Fridges should be set to operate at a temperature between 1 °C and 4 °C to make sure that chilled food is held below 5 °C.
- Door handles should be cleaned and disinfected.
- Raw ready-to-eat food and high-risk foods should be kept above raw food (for cooking) in the fridge.
- Food must be kept covered, and food-safe containers and food labels used.
- Never put warm food in a fridge, it will cause the temperature in the fridge to rise into the danger zone (5 °C–63 °C).

Frozen Food Storage

- Bacteria are dormant in the freezer.
- Frozen food should be stored at −18 °C or below.
- Food should be well wrapped to prevent freezer burn through loss of moisture.
- Food bought as frozen should be stored in the freezer as soon as possible.

Defrosting

- If frozen foods are not defrosted thoroughly, ice crystals remain at the centre. Cooking will melt the ice but the correct core temperature may not be achieved and bacteria may survive.
- Protect defrosting food from being contaminated.
- If high-risk food is defrosted at room temperature, bacteria will start to multiply on the surface of the food.
- Defrosted food must be treated like chilled food.

> ### Key Point
>
> When handling food at any stage, from buying the food through to correct storage, steps must be taken to prevent contamination. Everything possible must be done to control the conditions that allow bacteria to multiply, causing food poisoning.

> ### Quick Test
>
> 1. What are the **two** date marks you need to check when buying food?
> 2. What is the recommended temperature for chilled food?
> 3. It is acceptable to put warm food in the fridge. True or false?
> 4. What is the recommended temperature for a freezer?
> 5. What happens to food that is not defrosted thoroughly?

> ### Key Words
>
> use-by date
> best-before date
> chilled food

Preparing and Cooking Food

You must be able to:

- Know and understand the food safety principles when preparing and cooking food, including the importance of personal hygiene and clean work surfaces
- Understand about cross contamination and temperature controls
- Know the factors surrounding high-risk food
- Demonstrate knowledge of the correct use of temperature probes.

Personal Hygiene

- Food handlers are a common source of pathogenic bacteria.
- When preparing food, you must maintain the highest possible standards of personal hygiene in order to avoid contaminating food and causing illness.
- A clean apron should always be worn to protect the food from contamination from your clothes.
- All jewellery should be removed when cooking, food handlers must tie back long hair or wear a hairnet/hat, and fingernails should be kept short and clean with no nail varnish.
- Licking your fingers or utensils when cooking must be avoided.
- Wash your hands:
  - before preparing food
  - between handling raw and high-risk foods or ready-to-eat foods
  - after you have been to the toilet
  - after sneezing/coughing
  - after changing a waterproof plaster
  - after cleaning
  - after handling food waste or rubbish and known allergens.

Preparing Food

- Food needs to be protected from contamination during preparation, as the food is usually uncovered while being handled.
- Food should be handled as little as possible.
- Food must be kept out of the danger zone (5 °C–63 °C) as bacteria will multiply.
- To prevent cross contamination, raw food and cooked food must be prepared separately using separate utensils (different chopping boards and knives). Red chopping boards and knives are used for raw meat and should only be used for this purpose.

Preparing High-risk Foods

- When preparing food, some foods are more of a risk than others: these are high-risk foods (See alongside).
- Protein-based foods, moist foods and ready-to-eat foods that require no further cooking are high-risk foods.
- High-risk foods require strict time and temperature controls.

Key Points

When preparing and cooking food it is important to have high personal and food hygiene standards.

High-risk foods include:
- cold cooked meat
- poultry
- fish and seafood
- ready meals containing gravy or sauce
- egg products, such as quiche and homemade mayonnaise
- although not high in protein, cooked rice, pasta and cereals are classed as high-risk as they can provide a moist environment where certain bacteria can multiply
- dairy-based products, e.g. cream cakes and desserts.

Cooking and Reheating

- Pathogenic bacteria can be destroyed and food made safe by thorough cooking. If food is not cooked correctly, pathogenic bacteria may survive and cause food poisoning.
- To make sure bacteria are killed, the thickest part of the food (the core) should reach 70 °C for two minutes.
- Liquids should be stirred to avoid cold spots.
- Large items should be turned to ensure even cooking.
- Poultry, pork and minced meat products must be thoroughly cooked to kill the bacteria.
- If a microwave oven is to be used, always follow the manufacturer's guidelines.
- Hot holding is the process of storing food warm for service. Food must be kept at a temperature of no lower than 63 °C for a maximum of 90 minutes before being discarded.
- Food must not be reheated more than once.
- Bacteria will multiply during repeated cooling and reheating.
- Reheated food should reach a core temperature of 75 °C.

Cleaning

- All food contact surfaces and hand contact surfaces must be cleaned and disinfected after use. Best practice is to 'clean as you go'.
- Food preparation areas must be kept clean to protect food from bacterial contamination, physical contamination and chemical contamination.
- Food preparation areas must be kept clean to prevent slips and trips.

Types of Food Poisoning

- Food poisoning can occur through:
  - Microbiological contamination – this is the germ itself contaminating the food.
  - Physical contamination – this is when items physically drop into food, i.e. rings, nails, hair.
  - Chemical contamination – this is when chemicals get into food, i.e. cleaning chemicals.

Temperature Probes

- Temperature probes are used to take the core temperature of food.
- Care must be taken to ensure the probe does not cause cross contamination: it must be cleaned and disinfected after every use.

> **Key Point**
>
> Food must be cooked thoroughly to make it safe to eat.

> **Key Point**
>
> Bacterial contamination can be direct and indirect:
>
> – **Direct contamination** is when a high-risk food such as raw meat is touching cooked meat.
>
> – **Indirect contamination** occurs when bacteria are transferred to the high-risk foods by a vehicle such as hands or a knife.

> **Key Words**
>
> hygiene
> high-risk foods
> danger zone
> reheating
> core temperature

> **Quick Test**
>
> 1. List **four** occasions during food preparation when you must wash your hands.
> 2. What temperature control and time during cooking kills most bacteria?

Food Preservation

You must be able to:

- Know and understand how processing affects the sensory and nutritional properties of ingredients.

Preservation

- There are four main types of food preservation: high temperature; low temperature; drying; chemical.

High Temperature

Method	Details	Further Information
Canning	• Foods are placed in liquids in cans, sealed and heated to 121 °C • Long shelf life	• Loss of water-soluble vitamins C and B • Change in taste of the food
Irradiation	• Strictly controlled X-rays are passed through the food to delay ripening	• Vitamins A, C, E, and K may be lost • Food looks fresh and tastes the same
Pasteurisation	• Used mainly for milk, heating it to 71 °C for 15 seconds, then rapidly cooling it to 10 °C • Limited shelf life	• Little or no change to taste • Loss of vitamin B2 • Often fortified with vitamin D
Sterilisation	• Heated to 104 °C for 40 minutes or 115 °C for 15 minutes • Used mainly for milk and juices to prolong storage	• The process causes a slight caramelisation of the milk sugar content, resulting in a creamy flavour
Ultra-Heat Treatment (UHT)	• Heated to 140 °C for up to 5 seconds then put in an airtight container • Allows milk to be stored for up to six months	• There is a slight change in taste, colour remains similar and little change in nutrients

- Milk can also be preserved in cans – evaporated milk has water evaporated and is sterilised so it is much thicker and sweeter.
- Condensed milk is not sterilised and has added sugar so it is very sweet and thick.

Low Temperature

Method	Details	Further Information
Freezing	• Food is preserved for up to one year in temperatures between -18 °C and -29 °C	
Chilling	• This just extends shelf life	• Generally, no changes to food or nutrient content
Cold storage (CA)	• This just extends shelf life in an atmosphere of carbon dioxide	

Drying

Method	Details	Further Information
Sunlight	• An old method, which allows moisture to evaporate from the food in the Sun, e.g. fish, meats	• Dehydrating foods can affect colour, e.g. purple plums turn dark brown • They may develop a wrinkly surface/skin • The texture may change as well as the concentration of the flavour • Vitamins C and B6 (and others) may be lost
Oven drying	• Warm ovens are used to dry foods slowly	
Roller drying	• Used for foods that are reconstituted as 'instant' foods, e.g. baby foods	• Loss of vitamins A and C
Spray drying	• This method is used for some foods that are damaged by high heats	
Accelerated Freeze Drying (AFD)	• Food is frozen and the temperature is then increased to make the ice vaporise	• There is no change to the nutrient content of the food and flavour, colour and texture is mostly unaffected

Chemical

Method	Details	Further Information
Vinegar (pickling)	• The strong acid solution preserves the food, e.g. chutney, onions	• Changes to taste, flavour and texture • Shelf life is increased
Sugar	• Fruit is preserved, e.g. jam making	
Salt	• Meat and fish can be salted • Brine solutions can be used to preserve vegetables and canned fish	
Smoking	• Food is 'cooked' by exposing it to heat from wood fires	• Distinctive smoky taste
Alcohol	• Fruits are prepared and stored in brandy	• Changes to taste
Vacuum packaging	• Oxygen is removed from a sealed package, e.g. fish, cheese	• Long shelf life with fresh appearance and taste
Modified Atmospheric Packaging (MAP)	• Sealed packages have oxygen removed and the gas content inside changed, e.g. ready-prepared salads	

Quick Test

1. Which vitamins may be lost during irradiation?
2. What shelf life does UHT milk have?
3. How does vacuum packaging differ from MAP?

Key Words

preservation
temperature
drying
chemical preservation

Review Questions

Cooking of Food, Heat Transfer and Selecting Appropriate Cooking Methods

1 Improving palatability is one of the main functions of food preparation and cooking. Fill in the blanks to complete the following text. [5]

Palatability means how acceptable the sensory characteristics of a food are, e.g. how

appetising it is. Making food palatable develops ....

improves .... and .... , reduces

.... and changes ....

2 Many methods of cooking use a combination of heat transfer. Explain how methods of heat transfer can combine when boiling potatoes. [6]

....

....

....

....

....

....

Proteins and Enzymic Browning

1 What does protein denaturation mean? Give **one** example, and explain this example.

Meaning [2]

....

....

Example [2]

....

....

2 Choose the correct words from the boxes below to complete the sentences. [5]

| elastic | kneading | short | gluten | structure |

Wheat flour contains the protein .... which makes a dough

stretchy and .... Different cooking techniques can affect gluten

formation, e.g. .... helps increase gluten formation in breadmaking,

whereas rubbing fat into flour makes .... gluten strands to aid the

texture. Gluten forms the .... of pastries, breads and cakes.

Carbohydrates

1 What are **two** changes that can be noticed when a solution of sugar and water is heated? [2]

I: ....

II: ....

2 A chef is planning to use a roux sauce to coat steamed cauliflower. Which recipe would be his best choice and why?

Recipe A	Recipe B
500 ml milk	500 ml milk
10 g flour	25 g flour
10 g butter	25 g butter

a) Choice .... [1]

b) Explain your answer. [4]

....

....

Fats and Oils

1 A student decides to make shortcrust pastry by hand.

What is the name of the method he would use? .... [1]

2 A student is using the creaming method to make some small cakes.

a) Which **two** ingredients would be creamed together first? [2]

I: .... II: ....

b) During the preparation of the cakes he needs to check the mixture. State **one** characteristic of the creamed mixture he might look for. [1]

....

c) Explain why the mixture would show this characteristic. [2]

....

....

d) How would this help the cakes during baking? [2]

....

....

Raising Agents

1 Explain **four** conditions needed for yeast fermentation.

I: .... [2]

II: .... [2]

III: .... [2]

IV: .... [2]

2 A student has been asked to investigate raising agents to make products with light and airy textures.

What are raising agents? [3]

....

....

....

Practice Questions

Microorganisms, Enzymes and Food Spoilage

1. What is an enzyme? [1]

_____

2. Some fruits and vegetables go brown when they are cut and exposed to oxygen. What is the scientific term for when fruits and vegetables go brown? [1]

_____

3. Name **one** fruit that could turn brown. [1]

_____

4. Suggest **one** method that can be used to slow down the browning process. [1]

_____

_____

Microorganisms in Food Production

1. Tick (✓) the correct option. Microorganisms are used in the production of: [1]

   a) milk, butter and cheese. ☐

   b) bread, cheese and yoghurt. ☐

   c) salami, sausages and burgers. ☐

   d) bread, butter and oil. ☐

2. Which microorganism is used to make salami, pepperoni and chorizo? [1]

_____

3. Yeast is most active at cold and high temperatures. Is this true or false? Tick (✓) **one** answer. [1]

   True ☐   False ☐

Practice Questions

Bacterial Contamination

1 Bacterial contamination causes food poisoning. Is this true or false? Tick (✓) **one** answer. [1]

True ☐ False ☐

2 Which of the following is important in helping prevent bacterial contamination?
Tick (✓) **one** answer. [1]

a) Clean as you go. ☐

b) Make sure all the kitchen lights are working. ☐

c) Check all equipment is working. ☐

d) Store heavy equipment at a lower level. ☐

3 Explain what the 'use by' date means on a food product. [1]

_____

_____

Buying and Storing Food

1 Refrigeration is used for food storage to slow down spoilage. Is this true or false?
Tick (✓) **one** answer. [1]

True ☐ False ☐

2 Complete the following sentences using the words in the boxes (continued on the next page).

perishable	1 °C and 4 °C, below 5 °C
cooked	−18 °C and below

a) When preparing food, keep raw and _____ foods separate. [1]

b) Chilling high risk/_____ foods will slow down the growth of
bacteria. [1]

c) Check the internal temperature of a refrigerator to make sure it is between

_____. [1]

d) The temperature of your freezer should be _____. [1]

Preparing and Cooking Food

1 Which of the following is most likely to cause cross contamination? Tick (✓) **one** answer. [1]

a) Using ready to eat foods within their use-by-date. ☐

b) Placing ready-to-eat foods above raw foods in a fridge. ☐

c) Using the same knife to cut raw chicken and cooked ham. ☐

d) Storing raw chicken in a covered container at the bottom of the fridge. ☐

2 Why should leftover food only be reheated once? [1]

_____

_____

_____

3 Circle the foods that are considered to be high risk. [2]

cooked rice   potatoes   chocolate

tomatoes   cooked chicken   bananas

apples   biscuits

Food Preservation

1 Name **three** methods of preserving foods using high temperatures. [3]

I: _____

II: _____

III: _____

Food Provenance and Production Methods

You must be able to:

- Demonstrate knowledge and understanding of where ingredients are grown, reared and caught
- Have a clear understanding of different farming methods and their effect on the environment.

Traceability

- Traceability means the ability to track any food, feed, food-producing animal or substance that will be used for consumption, through all stages of production, processing and distribution.
- This is so that when a risk is identified it can be traced back to its source in order to swiftly isolate the problem and prevent contaminated products from reaching consumers.

Modern Intensive Farming

- After the Second World War, farmers were offered subsidies to farm intensively to produce large scale, low cost products.
- This policy has resulted in:
  - fewer small farm communities
  - a greater number of larger business farms
  - large numbers of animals and poultry being kept in massive buildings and fed on high nutrient feeds in a short period of time, which is designed to maximise growth
  - the widespread use of antibiotics, growth enhancers, fertilisers and pesticides
  - small farm fields being opened up – woodland destroyed to make room for large machinery access.
- These methods are also employed all over the world, resulting in large surpluses of food being produced.

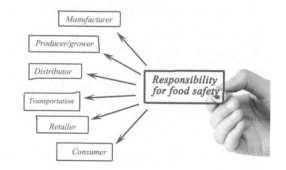

Farming Methods

Barn-reared Animals

- Barn-reared animals live in an environment similar to intensively-reared animals.
- They have access to natural light from windows.
- They live in a lower density of animals per square metre.
- They have access to environment enrichment such as fresh straw.

Organic Foods

- Organic foods are grown naturally without help from any chemical or synthetic treatments.
- They rely on natural compost and manure as fertilisers.
- Organic foods are not Genetically Modified – they are GM-free.

- There is no proof that organic food is more nutritious – buying organic food is a lifestyle choice.

Free-range Farming

- Free-range farming allows animals or poultry access to outdoor areas for part of their lives.
- Hens that are free-range produce eggs that are more nutritious and tasty. Animals reared this way also have better meat quality.
- Organic and free-range farming are more ethical and have a lower negative environmental impact.

Hydroponic Farming

- Hydroponic farming is the production of food using specially developed nutrient-rich liquids rather than soil.
- Hydroponic farming takes place in vast polytunnels or greenhouses in carefully controlled conditions.
- It is an expensive method, so is only used for high-value crops.

Fish Farming

- Increasing demand for fish has seen stocks diminishing in the wild through overfishing.
- The reduction of fish stocks may be due to lack of controls or the use of factory ships that strip the sea of every type of creature.
- Hatcheries release young fish into the wild.
- Some fish farms are on land, with the fish never exposed to natural resources.
- Fish farm tanks may be giant nets in fresh or seawater, where the fish are controlled, but still in a semi-natural environment.

Genetically Modified (GM) Foods

- This form of intensive farming is widely used in agriculture and the food processing industry. It is carefully controlled and regulated.
- GM foods are produced to be more resistant to plant disease, insect pesticides and viruses.
- The DNA in the product can be changed in order for the product to display particular characteristics, e.g. cattle with a higher milk yield, or sheep with a higher meat yield.
- As a result of higher yield, food products are cheaper and harvested in a shorter period of time.
- There are concerns about the use of GM food production:
  - it is altering and playing with nature
  - possibilities for new strains of microorganisms to develop
  - there are potential risks to long term human (and animal) health and allergic reactions
  - pollen from GM and non-GM crops may potentially be mixed.

> **Key Point**
>
> Best quality protein foods are ones where the welfare of the animals has been considered.

> **Key Words**
>
> traceability
> field to fork
> barn-reared animals
> organic
> Genetically Modified (GM)
> free range farming
> hydroponics
> hatcheries
> fish farms
> intensive farming

> **Quick Test**
>
> 1. Why is it important that the origins of food can be traced?
> 2. What are the benefits of free-range farming?
> 3. Why is hydroponics an expensive farming method?

Food Provenance: Food and the Environment

You must be able to:

- Demonstrate knowledge and understanding of the environmental issues associated with food and its production.

Food Origins

- Seasonal foods are home-grown products that are traditionally grown or produced during particular seasons of the year, e.g. in the UK strawberries are harvested between June and September.
- Transportation development around the world has meant that when seasonal products are not available they can be imported from hotter climates where they are grown all year round.

Food Miles

- Food miles are the distance food travels from its point of origin to your table.
- The planes, boats and lorries used to transport food around the world all create carbon dioxide gas (CO_2), which is a contributory factor to global warming and climate change (carbon footprint). — *Amount of CO_2 released into the atmosphere by an individual or community's actions*
- Food miles can be reduced by:
  - supporting British farmers and the economy – use farmers' markets, which showcase local and regional producers
  - eating seasonal products – our bodies get the right delivery of nutrients, minerals and trace elements that we need at the right time of year
  - being a wise shopper – purchase foods that have been produced nearer to Britain.

> **Key Point**
>
> Food and packaging waste contributes to greenhouse gases (GHGs).

Reducing Carbon Emissions

- Recycling and producing less waste also helps to reduce carbon emissions.
- Reducing the amount of packaging or using biodegradable packaging, which rots naturally, could help our environment.
- Recycling (re-using) using local collection facilities or bottle banks is 'green', however some of the chemicals used to clean recycled waste can cause pollution. Recycling may also use more energy than making packaging from new resources.

Food Waste and Landfill

- Nearly a third of all food produced ends up in landfill sites where it gives off methane gas as it decomposes. This gas adds to GHG emissions.

- Food waste can be reduced by:
    - using FIFO (First In First Out) storage
    - wise shopping and planning ahead
    - only preparing the food you need
    - using food before it goes out of date
    - using left-over food to make other dishes, e.g. mashed potato can be used to make croquettes for another day.
- Home composting is efficient, easy and clean. It benefits the garden and plant life by returning goodness to the soil – just food waste and the earthworms in the ground are needed.

Sustainable Food

- Sustainable food means food that will continue to be available for many years to come.
- Intensive farming can diminish the quality of food stocks for future generations.

Fruit and Vegetables

- Follow healthy eating guidelines and eat more fruit, vegetables, grains and pulses, and less animal protein.
- Home-grown garden or allotment fruit and vegetables provide a cost-effective variety of vegetables.

Fish

- Fish can be made more sustainable by:
    - restricting catch sizes
    - imposing minimum sizes of fish for sale
    - widening the selection of fish being eaten to more species
    - putting back young fish so that they can go on to breed and reproduce.
- Dolphin-friendly tuna makes the consumer aware that no dolphins have been accidently trapped in nets during fishing.
- Fishermen have allocated strips of ocean in order to fish sustainably in different areas of the world. There are set fishing regulations and quotas for their area.

Marine Stewardship Council – Seafood can be traced back to a certified sustainable fishery.

> **Quick Test**
>
> 1. Explain what food miles are.
> 2. How can recycling sometimes produce more pollution than making something from new?
> 3. Give **two** ways that fish stocks can be made more sustainable than intensive fishing.

> **Key Words**
>
> transportation
> food miles
> climate change
> carbon footprint
> recycling
> packaging
> food waste
> composting
> sustainable food

Food Provenance: Sustainability of Food

You must be able to:

- Demonstrate knowledge and understanding of the impact that food has on local and global markets.

Carbon Emissions

- As our greenhouse gas (GHG) emissions increase, the planet traps more energy from the Sun.
  - This damages the Earth's ozone layer.
  - This in turn causes changes to climate, and ultimately food and water supplies throughout the world.
- Livestock, especially cows, produce methane gas, which is 20 times more harmful than CO_2.

Key Point

Carbon emissions and global climate change affect food and water supplies.

Global Climate Change Issues

- There are several issues arising from global climate change:
  - Air temperature and rainfall levels rising and falling have an effect on soil. Crops can easily fail as a result.
  - Flooding of areas of land, both coastal and inland.
  - CFCs have depleted the atmosphere's ozone layer and this can have a reduction in yield in some crops with ultraviolet radiation affecting them.
  - Photosynthesis of plants relies on carbon dioxide; increased cloud cover as a result of global warming restricts this from being as efficient.
  - Changes in climate can affect the pests that attack crops, and can change the foods that some helpful bugs use, e.g. bees dying and so not pollinating plants.

Tackling Sustainability of Food Sources

- There are ways that the sustainability of food sources can be addressed:
  - Prevent soil erosion from winds, high rainfall and flooding.
  - Look to improve crop varieties to match climate change, e.g. in drier climates grow crops that require less moisture.
  - Look at crop rotation to reduce soil erosion, and the general health of crops.
  - Put in irrigation systems in drier areas.
  - Increase crop diversity.
  - Improve soil organics by using animal waste.
  - Develop wind breaks.
  - Change the dependence on fossil fuels for transporting foods.

- Tackle deforestation issues – trees remove CO_2 from the atmosphere. Large areas of forest are being cut down in order to graze animals or grow crops. As a result, CO_2 builds up, contributing to global warming, e.g. palm oil producers in Asia have cut down rainforest, which has also affected the habitat of many animals now in danger of extinction.

Sustainable Food

- Sustainable food is food that should be produced, processed, distributed and disposed of in ways that:
  - contribute to thriving local economies and sustainable livelihoods – both in the UK and, in the case of imported products, in producer countries
  - protect the diversity of both plants and animals and the welfare of farmed and wild species
  - avoid damaging or wasting natural resources or contributing to climate change.

Fairtrade

- Fairtrade is a foundation that pays a realistic income to farmers in developing countries.
- It ensures a fair price for the goods, giving a steady income, and covers the cost of sustainable production.
- It invests in the locality and in better working conditions.
- Many products now display the Fairtrade mark, e.g. bananas, tea, chocolate and coffee.

Food Assurance Schemes

- Food assurance schemes give guaranteed standards of animal welfare or food safety that the consumer can rely upon.

Red Tractor

- Red Tractor is a logo that tells the consumer that the food has been produced, processed and packed to Red Tractor standards.
- The flag on the logo shows the country of origin of the food.
- Red Tractor assures...
  - standards of food hygiene and safety
  - standards of equipment used in production
  - animal health and welfare
  - environmental issues and responsible use of pesticides.
- Red Tractor is controlled and monitored by Assured Food Standards (AFS).
- Any product with this logo can be traced from farm to fork.

> ### Quick Test
>
> 1. What does the flag on the Red Tractor logo mean?
> 2. How does Fairtrade support farmers in developing countries?
> 3. Why are large areas of the world being deforested?
> 4. Which **two** gases contribute to global warming?

British and International Cuisines

You must be able to:

- Understand the meaning of 'cuisine' in terms of the foods related to the traditional eating habits of certain countries
- Learn about the cuisine of two other countries as well as British traditional cuisine.

Traditional British Food

- British food makes use of ingredients produced in the local area.
- British cheeses originate from different parts of the country, e.g. Cheddar (Somerset), Wensleydale (Yorkshire), Red Leicester, Double Gloucester.
- Each cheese has its own distinctive colour, flavour and texture and is made using ingredients from its region of origin.
- There are lots of regional dishes, including Cornish pasties, Lancashire hot pots, Melton Mowbray pies, Eccles cakes, fish and chips and suet-based puddings such as Sussex Pond Pudding.
- Regional dishes normally have historic links. For example, Cornish pasties were eaten by tin miners working underground. The crimped edge was the handle for dirty hands so that the rest of the pastry could be eaten quickly and without mess.

Traditional British meal

British blue cheese (Stilton)

Modern British Food

- We now live in a country that is multicultural and people travel to holiday destinations worldwide and are exposed to the cuisines of many other countries. Cheaper air travel prices mean that these countries are more easily accessible to a greater number of people than ever before.
- Supermarkets and specialist shops provide a vast range of ingredients, such as herbs, spices, fruit and vegetables from global cuisines.
- Because of influences from other countries, meals in the UK now contain a wide variety of foods.
- Recipes have been adapted to meet our tastes, e.g. Chicken Tikka Massala (a rich, flavoursome chicken dish without chilli) was invented in the UK but is probably based on Bangladeshi cuisine.

Cornish pasty

Other Cuisines

Spain: Tapas and Paella

- Tapas consist of a wide variety of appetisers or snacks served on small plates and chosen from a menu list.

- Tapas may be cold, e.g. mixed olives or tortilla (a potato omelette) or hot, e.g. chopitos (battered and fried baby squid), garlic prawns (gambas pil pil) and patatas bravas (cubes of potato in a spicy tomato sauce).
- Paella is widely served in restaurants and is traditionally eaten by large groups of people in the street during fiesta times.
- Paella is based on rice from Valencia (a region of Spain) and cooked in a wide flat pan with a mixture of locally sourced foods such as seafood, meat, vegetables and spices, e.g. saffron.

Japan: Fish, Noodles and Rice

- Fish is common in traditional Japanese cuisine as most of the population live near a coastline.
- Other seafoods such as seaweed are also important in the Japanese diet as it is rich in protein and has a flavour that many people love.
- As well as rice, udon noodles are an important ingredient.
- A typical Japanese meal consists of a bowl of rice (**gohan**), a bowl of miso soup (**miso shiru**), pickled vegetables (**tsukemono**) and fish or meat.
- Sashimi consists of thin slices of raw fish pH cooked or other seafood served with spicy Japanese horseradish (**wasabi**) and soy sauce (shoyu).
- Sushi consists of seafood, vegetables and egg served on vinegared rice.

> **Key Point**
>
> 'Cuisine' relates to the established range of dishes and foods of a particular country or region.

> **Key Point**
>
> 'Cuisine' is also concerned with the use of distinctive ingredients and specific cooking and serving techniques.

> **Quick Test**
>
> 1. Name **two** British cheeses that are not mentioned on this spread.
> 2. How well does the traditional British meal match the Eatwell Guide?
> 3. Why does a Cornish pasty have a crimped edge?

> **Key Words**
>
> multicultural
> cuisine

Food Manufacturing

You must be able to:

- Demonstrate a knowledge and understanding of the primary and secondary stages of food processing
- Understand the positive and negative effects of the use of additives during food manufacturing.

Primary Processing

- Primary foods cannot be eaten in their original condition. They have to be prepared or go through some form of change before they can be eaten.
- Examples of primary foods include untreated milk, sugar beet and raw potatoes.
- Primary processing is the initial process that a primary food goes through in order for it to be usable.
- Sometimes primary processing can be very basic, e.g. peeling and slicing raw carrots, washing salad leaves. Sometimes it can involve more stages, such as heating and cooling, as in processing milk to produce different types.
- A grain of wheat is a primary food. When wheat is primary processed, it is made into flour. The process is called milling:
  - The grains are blended with other varieties and washed to remove grit and dirt.
  - Huge rotating rollers crush the grains at varying speeds.
  - If white flour is wanted, the bran is removed by further rolling.

Fresh red lettuce, washed ready to sell

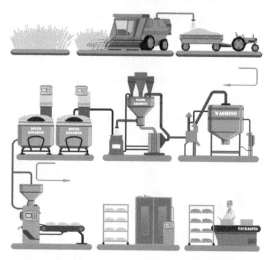

Bread production process from wheat harvest to freshly baked bread

Secondary Processing

- Secondary processing is a further process that can take place using the primary processed product to make a new food product.
- An example of secondary processing would be the processing of milk into other dairy products, for example:
  - Cream – the fat removed from milk is used. Types of cream are single, whipping, double and extra thick. Cream can be further processed to make soured cream, clotted cream and crème fraiche.
  - Butter – cream is churned to make butter. It can then be salted and made into regional varieties, e.g. ghee, continental.
  - Cheese – this is milk in its solid form. It can be processed into many different types, e.g. hard pressed cheese such as cheddar, soft cheese such as goat's cheese and blue veined such as stilton.

Butter made from milk

Dairy products made from milk

– Yoghurt – milk has a bacteria culture added to it to make yoghurt. Probiotic products contain live bacteria that are beneficial to the digestive system.

The Use of Additives During Food Manufacturing

- Many food manufacturers will use additives during food processing.
- Additives can be put into groups:
  - natural, e.g. beetroot juice used to provide colour
  - nature identical (synthetic) – made using chemicals to be the same as a natural product
  - artificial – made entirely from chemicals.
- There are different types of additives used for many different reasons:
  - **Colourings** – these are used to replace colour lost during food processing or to make a food look more appealing.
  - **Flavour intensifiers** – these are used to replace flavours lost during food processing or to enhance the flavour of a food.
  - **Preservatives** – these are used to stop foods from spoiling, to provide a food with a longer shelf life.
  - **Stabilisers and** emulsifiers – these help mix ingredients together and prevent them from separating, e.g. oil and water. They are used to give a creamy, smooth texture to foods.
- The advantages and disadvantages of the use of additives are shown in the table:

Advantages of Using Additives	Disadvantages of Using Additives
Consumers can have an extended range of foods.	Additives can be used to conceal the use of lower quality ingredients.
Foods can be kept for longer and be safe to eat.	They can cause allergies such as skin rashes or breathing difficulties.
To allow manufacturers to produce a product range, e.g. different flavoured snacks.	The use of some artificial colours can make children hyperactive.
To put back any colours that have been lost so the food looks as expected.	

Popped wheat (breakfast cereal) with colorings and flavorings added

> **Quick Test**
>
> 1. Describe what a primary food is.
> 2. Name two different types of cream.
> 3. Name one of the groups of additives.
> 4. Why are colourings added to foods?

> **Key Words**
>
> primary processing
> milling
> secondary processing
> additives
> emulsifiers

Review Questions

Microorganisms, Enzymes and Food Spoilage

1 Bacteria are microorganisms that cause food spoilage. Name **two** other microorganisms that cause food spoilage. [2]

I: .... II: ....

2 State and explain **three** conditions needed for microorganisms to grow. [3]

I: ....

II: ....

III: ....

3 Name **three** foods that spoil easily. [3]

I: .... II: .... III: ....

4 Enzymes cause fruit and vegetables to ripen. How does ripening affect fruit? Tick (✓) **one** answer. [1]

a) They gradually lose their colour.   ☐

b) They start to go brown.   ☐

c) They may go green.   ☐

d) They start to dry out.   ☐

Microorganisms in Food Production

1 Microorganisms are used in the manufacturing of certain foods. Explain how they are used in the production of bread. [3]

....

....

....

....

....

2 What is used in yoghurt production to develop the taste and texture? [1]

3 Why have probiotic cultures become popular in dairy products? [3]

4 Explain why microorganisms are important in the production of blue-veined cheese. [2]

Bacterial Contamination

1 Bacteria in food can cause food poisoning. Name **two** high-risk foods. [2]

I: .... II: ....

2 Describe the main causes of food poisoning. [8]

Review Questions

Buying and Storing Food

1 Complete the following sentences about temperature controls. [4]

a) Water boils at .... °C.

b) The temperature of a freezer should be below .... °C.

c) Bacteria multiply rapidly between .... °C and .... °C.

d) When heating food, the internal temperature should reach .... °C.

2 Tick (✓) the correct box next to each statement to show if it is true or false. [3]

	True	False
a) Lettuce should be stored at the top of the refrigerator.		
b) Hot food should be placed in a refrigerator.		
c) Raw meat should be stored at the bottom of a refrigerator.		

3 Describe **four** ways of reducing the risk of food poisoning when storing food. [4]

I: ....

....

II: ....

....

III: ....

....

IV: ....

....

Preparing and Cooking Food

1 Complete the following sentences using the correct temperature. [4]

| 5 °C | 63 °C | 75 °C | 18 °C |

a) Food should be stored in the refrigerator below ....

b) The core temperature of cooked food should reach ....

2 What are the recommended temperatures for the following?

Reheating cooked foods: .... [1]

Storing chilled foods: .... [1]

3 Name an item of equipment used to check the temperature of foods when reheating. [1]

....

4 Describe the correct procedures to follow when using the equipment named in question 3. [6]

....

....

....

....

....

....

....

....

Food Preservation

1 Name **two** vitamins that may be lost during the natural sunlight drying process. [2]

I: ....   II: ....

2 Suggest **one** benefit of low temperature storage. [1]

....

Practice Questions

Food Provenance and Production Methods

1 Which of these will help to make the food resource more sustainable? Tick (✓) **one** answer. [1]

    a) Eat more animal proteins. ☐   **b)** Buy fish that are smaller. ☐

    c) Eat a larger variety of fish species. ☐   **d)** Eat less fruit and vegetables. ☐

2 How would eating less beef and lamb help the environment? [2]

....

....

3 Circle the correct answer. [1]

Intensive farming produces food products that are **high cost / low cost**.

4 Name **three** things that are needed by organic farmers so that they can call their products 'organic'. [3]

....

....

Food Provenance: Food and the Environment

1 Circle the correct options in the following sentences.

    a) Planes, boats and lorries all create **carbon dioxide / carbon monoxide** emissions. [1]

    b) Food miles are the distance food has travelled from its point of origin to **your supermarket / your table**. [1]

    c) Heavily fertilised crops grown in the UK in heated greenhouses may be responsible for creating **less / more** carbon emissions than imported foods. [1]

    d) FIFO places existing food stock to the **front / back / floor** of food storage areas. [1]

2 What is biodegradable packaging? [2]

....

....

3 Give **two** benefits of eating seasonal products.   [2]

I: ....

II: ....

Food Provenance: Sustainability of Food

1 What does GHG stand for? Tick (✓) **one** answer.   [1]

a) Good Healthy Goods ☐   b) Global Heating Gas ☐

c) Greenhouse Gas ☐   d) Genetically Healthier Groups ☐

2 Explain what a Fairtrade product is.   [4]

....

....

....

British and International Cuisines

1 Which of these Indian curry dishes was invented in the UK? Tick (✓) **one** answer.   [1]

a) Prawn Rogan Josh ☐   b) Chicken Tikka Massala ☐

c) Lamb Khadery ☐   d) Chicken Dopiaza ☐

2 What four things make a British cheese distinctive?   [4]

I: ....   II: ....

III: ....   IV: ....

Food Manufacturing

1 Give **two** examples of different actions that have to be carried out in order to make a primary food usable.   [2]

I: ....

II: ....

Factors Affecting Food Choice: Sensory Evaluation

You must be able to:

- Understand how to taste food products, using your senses, accurately
- Know about a range of sensory testing methods.

Tasting Food and Drink

- There are five senses that are used to taste food and drink. A combination of these senses helps you decide if you like a food.
- **Taste**: the tongue can detect five basic tastes: bitter, sweet, salt, umami (a savoury taste), acid/sour
- **Sight**: food's appearance influences how much we want to eat it.
- **Smell**: the aroma of food reaches the nose before it reaches the mouth and is tasted.
- **Touch**: what food feels like in the mouth (texture).
- **Hearing**: what food sounds like, e.g. sizzling.
- The senses help to develop personal food preferences (likes/ dislikes) and evaluate foods, either through preference or discrimination tests.
- A range of accurate sensory words should be used when describing food. These usually come under the headings of: appearance, flavour, texture and aroma.

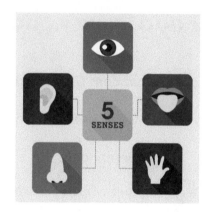

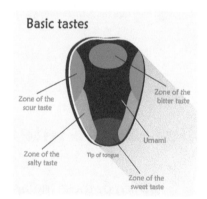

Basic tastes

Zone of the sour taste

Zone of the bitter taste

Zone of the salty taste

Tip of tongue

Umami

Zone of the sweet taste

Controlled Sensory Analysis

- Here are the stages in carrying out a controlled sensory analysis:
  - Invite people to be your testers in the sensory analysis.
  - Find a quiet area to work.
  - Give each tester a cup of water to cleanse their palate between each sample.
  - Provide small samples of food with clean spoons or forks for each sample. Provide a sheet to record results for each tester.
  - Foods should be identified using codes or symbols so that tasters are not influenced by brand names.
  - Food products should be tested carefully and results recorded accurately.

> **Key Point**
>
> The human **olfactory** system (smell) and taste sensors are important when tasting food.

Paired Preference Tests

- Testers are asked to taste two similar products.
- They are then asked which product they prefer.

Triangle Testing

- Three samples are tested but two are the same.
- The aim is to find out if the tester can pick out which sample is different, e.g. a sauce made with 15% fat or 5% fat.

Triangle Testing

Which one is the odd one out?

This test helps to work out whether a 'healthier' product can be developed without losing taste.

Ranking Tests

- People are asked to taste several products and award scores to decide on the order of preference (best to worst).
- All the samples should be coded.

Rating Tests

- People are asked to say how much they like or dislike a sensory characteristic of a product. This is called a rating.
- They use a hedonic scale to award a number (using a list provided), or they can indicate which symbol they think is best (most useful for young children).
- Sensory characteristics include sweetness, flavour, colour, texture.

Sensory Characteristic	Testers				Total
	1	2	3	4	
Evenly spread toppings					
Golden brown cheese					
Cheese aroma					
Tomato flavour					
Pizza base texture					
Overall flavour					

KEY
1 = dislike a lot
2 = dislike a little
3 = neither like nor dislike
4 = like a little
5 = like a lot

Sensory Profiles

- The results of sensory tests are often displayed visually using charts and sensory profiles, such as the star profile/radar diagram below.

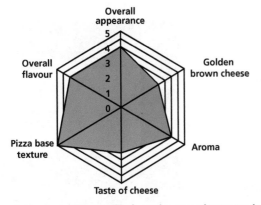

Example: sensory profile for a cheese and tomato pizza.

Quick Test

1. What is another name for the feeling of food in mouth?
2. Where are the taste sensors in your body?
3. Why is it important to use codes/symbols when tasting foods?

Key Words

senses   palate
texture   sensory
olfactory   characteristic
sensory   rating
 analysis

Factors Affecting Food Choice

You must be able to:

- Show that you understand that people choose what to eat for a complex variety of reasons
- Provide some reasoned suggestions for food choice based upon occasion, health, lifestyle and income.

Physical Activity Level (PAL)

- There are UK Government guidelines for 5–18 year olds regarding physical activity.
- These guidelines promote the benefits of being active for young people.
- The guidelines suggest at least 60 minutes of physical activity each day.
- Physical activity improves cardiovascular and bone health.
- Physical activity helps to maintain a healthy weight.

Healthy Eating

- The Eatwell Guide is a government guide that advises the public what and how much to eat.
- It makes healthy eating easier to understand by showing a visual image of the types and proportions of foods needed for a well-balanced diet (see page 44).

> **Key Point**
>
> Many factors affect the food choices that people make.

Income and Cost of Food

- The income a household has influences food choices.
- Low-income households have to make difficult choices regarding healthy foods, cost and quality, e.g. protein foods and fresh fruit and vegetables are generally more expensive than starchy foods.
- Where people shop and what they buy is affected by cost.
- Some food retailers market their foods based on high quality and others aim for low cost.
- Food banks are used by people on very low incomes.

Availability of Food

- There is a vast array of foods to choose from including organic, multicultural and gluten-free.
- The best strategy for a healthy and varied diet is to plan a meal diary for the week, create a shopping list, then look for 'best buys'.

Seasonality

- Seasonal foods are foods that are harvested and consumed in the season they are naturally harvested in.
- In-season foods that are grown and sold locally should have more flavour and nutritional value than imported foods, e.g. English strawberries in June and July.

Enjoyment of Food

- Our enjoyment of food is affected by what the food looks, smells, tastes and feels like.
- We get maximum enjoyment from eating a variety of textures, flavours and colours.

Lifestyle

- Factors affecting household eating patterns include:
  - work (type of work done/hours worked)
  - travelling time
  - pastimes of individuals
  - who plans, prepares and cooks the meals.
- The amount of time available to prepare and cook food influences:
  - whether to use a microwave oven, a slow-cooker or a conventional oven.
  - the decision to use pre-prepared vegetables or from a greengrocer.
  - the type of food cooked, e.g. a casserole or a steak to fry.

Celebrations/Occasions

- Many religious festivals have strong eating traditions, e.g. hot cross buns at Easter, unleavened bread at Jewish Passover.
- Birthday parties or weddings generally include a selection of more expensive and extravagant foods as they are a special time for families.

Quick Test

1. What does PAL mean?
2. What is the name of the government guide that advises the general public on how much to eat and what to eat?
3. To enjoy eating food, what should our meals contain a variety of?

Key Words

cardiovascular
Eatwell Guide
proportions

Food Labelling

You must be able to:

- Know which information is legally required for a food label
- Explain how this information will help the consumer
- Understand the ways in which nutritional labelling can be presented.

Food Labels

- The information on a food label is controlled by EU regulations.
- Pre-packaged foods have information labels to inform consumers.
- The following information on food labels is required by law:
  - the name of the food
  - weight or volume (indicated by 'e', which stands for 'estimated weight', is normally placed after the total weight of the product in grams – this explains that the weight is estimated and allows for differences)
  - ingredients list (from largest to smallest)
  - allergen information
  - GM (genetically modified) ingredients
  - date mark and storage
  - cooking instructions – to ensure food is safe to eat
  - place of origin
  - name and address of manufacturer (in case of complaint)
  - lot or batch mark (for traceability)
  - E numbers – chemical additives that have been approved for use in the European Union
  - nutritional information (from 2016).

Recent Changes to Food Labels

- From December 2016 the rules for nutrition labelling in the EU and the FSA in the UK have had to be followed on pre-packed foods.
- The nutrition declaration must include the:
  - energy value in both kilojoules (kJ) and kilocalories
  - amounts in grams (g) of fat, saturates, sugars, protein and salt.
- You must have nutrition labelling if:
  - you make a nutrition or health claim
  - vitamins or minerals are added to the food.

Date Marks and Storage

- **Use by/best before** dates indicate the date when the food is safe to eat before the quality begins to deteriorate and bacterial numbers rise.
- **Display by** dates indicate shelf-life in the retail store.
- **Sell by** dates show when the product should be removed from sale to the customer.
- **Storage** instructions indicate how the food should be stored in order to maintain freshness and quality.

Key Point

Make sure that you have a good working knowledge of all the information that must be present on a food product label to inform a consumer.

Key Point

EU = European Union

FSA = Food Standards Agency

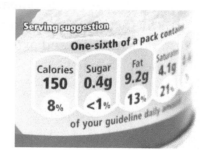

Key Point

You should know the accepted methods of displaying nutritional information on food labels.

The **name** identifies the food. Processed foods must also be identified by the cooking method, e.g. smoked, roast.

Contains GM soya or maize allows consumers to make an ethical choice.

Weight / volume: 'e' indicates approximate weight – allows for tolerances.

Ingredients are listed in **descending order of weight**. The largest amount is first and the smallest amount is the last.

Contains nuts or **may contain traces of nuts** indicates whether the product may have been in contact with nuts during manufacture.

Manufacturer's name or address allows consumers to contact the manufacturer. **Country of origin.**

Shelf life details: the best before date indicates that food is safe to eat but the quality will begin to deteriorate. After the use by date there is a risk of food poisoning. The display by / sell by date tells the retailer what to do with the product.

Instructions for use / heating instructions ensure that the product is cooked at the right temperature and that it's safe to eat.

Storage instructions are shown in words, symbols or temperatures.

The allergens that must be shown on the label are:
- celery
- cereals containing gluten
- crustaceans
- eggs
- fish
- lupin
- cow's milk
- molluscs
- mustard
- nuts
- peanuts
- sesame seeds
- soybeans
- sulphur dioxide (sulphites).

Allergen Information

- There are 14 allergen foods that must be indicated on the label if they are present in the food (see alongside).

Nutrition Labelling Methods

- A front of package label should contain:
  - Information on the energy value in kilojoules (kJ) and kilocalories (kcal) per 100g/ml and in a specified portion of the product.
  - Portion size information expressed in a way that is easily recognisable by, and meaningful to, the consumer.
  - % RI (Reference Intake) information based on the amount of each nutrient and energy value in a portion of the food.
  - Colour coding of the nutrient content of the food. Companies may additionally include the descriptors 'High', 'Medium' or 'Low' (HML) together with the colours red, amber or green respectively to reinforce their meaning.
- Back of pack labelling (compulsory in the EU from 2016).
  - The current rules specify the nutrients that can be included.
  - The information has to be presented per 100 g/ml but could also be provided per portion.

Each 1/2 pack serving contains

MED	LOW	MED	HIGH	MED
Calories	Sugar	Fat	Sat Fat	Salt
353	0.9g	20.3g	10.8g	1.1g
18%	1%	29%	54%	18%

of your guideline daily amount

Source: Food Standards Agency

Quick Test

1. When reading a food label, what weight of the food is used?
2. What does EU stand for?
3. What must be included in the nutrition declaration as well as fat, saturates and salt?

Knife Skills

You must be able to:

- Understand two different methods of using knives to prepare food safely
- Explain the techniques used when preparing different foods that require knife skills.

Knife Holds

Claw Grip

- To use the claw grip, shape your hand into a claw shape, tucking the thumb inside the fingers – the knuckle to fingertips part of the hand acts as a barrier against the knife blade when being held in the claw grip shape. It is safer to use a large knife with a flat-sided blade than a smaller one for this reason.
- Place the item you want to cut flat side down on a chopping board and rest the claw on the item to be sliced.
- Hold the knife in the other hand. Use the knife point as a pivot (it should not leave the board). As you slice, the food moves towards the knife; this reduces the health and safety risk.

Claw grip

Bridge Hold

- To use the bridge hold, first place the flat surface of the item on a chopping board.
- Now form a bridge with the thumb and index finger of one hand and hold the item on the chopping board.
- Hold a knife in the other hand and position the blade under the bridge formed with your hand. Firmly cut downwards.

Bridge hold

Knife Safety Rules

- The correct knife should be used for the appropriate job.
- Knives must be kept sharp and clean; a blunt knife is more likely to cause a cut because more pressure needs to be applied to use it to cut.
- Knife handles must be grease-free.
- The point must always be downwards when carrying a knife.
- Knives should not be put in the washing-up bowl.
- A knife must not be left on the edge of a table or chopping board.

Knife Skills for Vegetable Preparation

- The classic cuts for vegetables are shown in the table.

 Key Point

Knives are dangerous if not handled correctly and care should be taken at all times.

A flat and stable cutting surface is essential to avoid injury when cutting food.

 Key Point

Specific types of knives are designed for different cutting and shaping tasks.

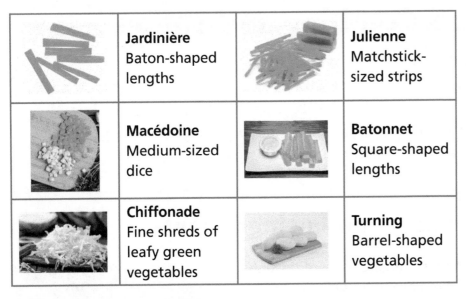	**Jardinière** Baton-shaped lengths		**Julienne** Matchstick-sized strips
	Macédoine Medium-sized dice		**Batonnet** Square-shaped lengths
	Chiffonade Fine shreds of leafy green vegetables		**Turning** Barrel-shaped vegetables

> **Key Point**
>
> There are specific terms used for vegetable cuts relating to the size and shape of the outcome.

Specific Types of Knives

Knife	Description	Uses
Cook's knife	Comes in different sizes. Strong, ridged blade is suitable for a range of tasks.	Dicing, chopping and trimming vegetables, meat, poultry, and fresh herbs.
Paring **knife**	A small knife with a thin and slightly flexible blade.	Fruit and vegetable preparation.
Boning knife	A very strong blade that will not bend or break easily. May have a straight or curved blade.	Removing bones from meat joints and poultry.
Filleting **knife**	Thin-bladed, flexible, very sharp knife.	Filleting fish.
Carving knife	Long blade with a serrated or plain edge. Can be rounded or pointed.	Carving meat joints or cooked hams.
Bread knife	Long serrated edge.	Slicing loaves and other bread products.
Palette knife	Flexible blade, which is rounded at the top.	Icing cakes; turning food during cooking; moulding and smoothing food.

> **Quick Test**
>
> 1. How would you carry a knife?
> 2. Is a blunt knife safer to use than a sharp knife?
> 3. Why is a flat surface needed to prepare food?
> 4. Name the two methods of holding food when cutting it.

> **Key Words**
>
> claw grip   chopping
> bridge   paring
> hold   filleting
> dicing   serrated

Prepare, Combine and Shape

You must be able to:

- Understand that a recipe consists of specific quantities of ingredients that are prepared, using a variety of skills, to produce the required outcome
- Know that ingredients can be combined and shaped to make the finished dish more attractive and appetising to the consumer.

Methods for Cutting and Preparing Ingredients

- **Slicing:** slicing even-sized cuts to suit the requirements of the dish.
- **Peeling:** using a peeler or knife to remove skin from fruit or vegetables, although it can be beneficial to leave skin on as it contains Non-Starch Polysaccharides (NSP) or fibre.
- **Chopping:** cutting ingredients into small pieces, precise sizes or roughly chopped.
- **Dicing:** cutting into cubes.
- **Grating:** passing food over a blade to reduce food in order to achieve the required size or thickness.
- **Coring:** removing the centre core of vegetables and fruit.
- **Mashing/crushing:** pressing into a puree or crushing into small pieces perhaps with the skin left on for added fibre.
- **Shredding:** grating or slicing into thin, long, flexible strips.
- **Scissor snipping:** using scissors to cut to the required shape, size or length.
- **Scooping:** using a spoon, scoop or melon baller to remove small circular pieces from the ingredient.
- **Segmenting:** cutting even-sized pieces from the ingredient, removing pith, zest and membrane.
- **Skinning:** peeling, grating, zesting or slicing off the outer skin from the ingredient.
- **Blanching:** placing the ingredient into boiling water for a few minutes to quickly cook, soften and inhibit the enzymic activity.
- **Blending:** using an electric food processor or blender to process different food ingredients together to form one product or sauce.
- **Juicing:** squeezing an ingredient to remove the liquid from it.
- **Preparing garnishes** – for example, zesting, carving, making ribbons, crisps, twists, roses, and using edible flowers.

Peeling food

Grating food

Combining and Shaping Ingredients

- Ingredients can be combined or mixed in a number of ways:
  - Whisking – combining ingredients to incorporate air into a mixture, e.g. meringues.
  - Stirring – gently mixing ingredients with a spoon.
  - Folding – gently incorporating mixtures together, such as flour into a cake mixture.

Key Point

Enzymic activity occurs when cut fruit and vegetables react with oxygen to turn them brown.

Stirring food (Stir-fry)

- Creaming – mixing two ingredients together, such as sugar and butter in cake making.
- Rubbing-in – incorporating fat into flour when making pastry.
- Ingredients can be shaped in a number of ways:
  - By hand – to achieve an even shape, for example, when making fishcakes, meatballs and koftas.
  - In a mould – e.g. to form the shape of bread loaves, mousses.
  - Using cutters – dough can be cut precisely to keep consistency.
  - With a rolling pin – used to achieve a desired thickness.
  - Using a piping bag – shaped nozzles create patterns, e.g. duchess potato.

Binding, Coating and Glazing

Binding

- Binding means holding ingredients together.
- Egg acts as a binding agent to hold ingredients together in burgers.
- Water binds flour and fat in pastry to help form a dough; some enriched shortcrust pastries use egg yolk to bind.
- Potato and/or flour are used as a binding material in fish cakes.
- Breadcrumbs are used as a binder in sausage mixtures.

Coating

- Coating means adding an outer layer to a food.
- Breadcrumbs are used for coating fish cakes and chicken goujons.
- Batters are used to enrobe, coat and protect fish and fritters that are deep-fried.
- Chocolate can be used as a coating to hold food together.

Glazing

- Egg wash **glaze** has a golden, shiny finish and is good for pastry and dough.
- Egg white has a crisp, golden texture and is good for sweet pastry dishes.
- Egg yolk gives a golden brown colour and works well on potato dishes.
- Milk gives a golden brown glaze to scones, pastry and biscuits.
- Sugar and water form a sweet sticky covering used on enriched dough.
- Jam gives a shiny finish and is brushed over fruit flans.
- Arrowroot is a clear shiny gel that is used to finish fruit flans.

> **Key Point**
>
> Various foods can be coated with ingredients to create a new layer to protect, add texture and flavour – this is called coating or enrobing.

> **Quick Test**
>
> 1. How would you shape meatballs?
> 2. What would you use to shape a burger?
> 3. What glaze would you use on enriched dough?

> **Key Words**
>
> combined
> rubbing-in
> binding
> coating
> goujons
> enriched dough

Dough

You must be able to:

- Know that making and shaping dough is a precursor to making a variety of flour-based mixtures
- Understand the function of ingredients in dough.

Bread Dough

- Bread dough is made with a strong plain flour, which contains a high level (17%) of the proteins gliadin and glutenin.
- Gluten is produced when water is added to the flour, enabling strong elastic dough to be formed.
- The elasticity of the dough helps to trap carbon dioxide gas (CO_2), which is produced by the yeast to raise the dough.

The Function of Ingredients in Bread

- Each ingredient in bread has a specific function:
    - A **strong flour** is used as it has a high gluten content.
    - **Yeast** is the raising agent, producing carbon dioxide.
    - **Warm liquid** is needed to form the dough and encourage the yeast to grow.
    - **Salt** adds flavour, and aids gluten development.
    - **Fat** extends the shelf-life and adds colour and flavour.

> **Key Point**
>
> Dough is made by mixing flour with liquid, and sometimes includes leavening (raising) agents as well as other ingredients and flavourings.

Enriched Dough

- **Enriched dough** is a basic bread dough with the addition of sugar, butter and sometimes egg.
- Additional flavourings such as mixed spices, dried fruit and nuts can be added.
- Examples of enriched dough include teacakes and stollen.

Pastries

- Different types of pastry are used for sweet or savoury dishes. They include:
    - shortcrust
    - choux
    - flaky/rough puff
    - suet
    - hot-water crust
    - filo pastry
    - puff pastry.

Shortcrust Pastry

- Shortcut pastry uses the rubbing-in method and is used for making pies and tarts.
- The ratio of ingredients is half fat to flour (1:2).
- Soft (plain) flour is used as it contains less gluten.
- Fats – a mixture of 50% lard (shortness) and 50% butter/margarine (colour and flavour) creates ideal shortening.
- Water binds the mixture.
- Salt adds flavour and aids the chemical reaction.
- Fat coats the flour and restricts the amount of gluten formed.
- The texture should be short, crisp and light.

Choux Pastry

- Choux pastry is used for eclairs, choux buns and gougères.
- All the ingredients must be weighed accurately.
- Strong flour is used to form the structure of the choux.
- Water and fat is brought to a rolling boil and the flour is added in one go immediately then mixed vigorously until the paste forms a soft ball (roux). The paste is cooled; beaten eggs are then added gradually to a heavy dropping consistency.
- The pastry is cooked in a hot oven.
- When the choux is baked, the water turns to steam and raises the dough, and the egg protein coagulates to set the structure.

Pasta

- Pasta is made from strong wheat flour called Durum wheat, which has a high gluten content and is usually labelled type '00'.
- The liquid can be olive oil or egg. Ingredients such as spinach, tomato puree, squid ink or beetroot add colour.
- The flour and liquid are mixed then kneaded to develop the gluten content; then the dough is rested.
- The dough is rolled using a machine or by hand until thin and air dried. It can be made into a variety of shapes and filled.

> **Key Words**
>
> gliadin
> glutenin
> gluten
> shortcrust
> choux
> ratio
> rolling boil
> heavy dropping
>   consistency
> rest

> **Quick Test**
>
> 1. What type of flour is used to make bread dough?
> 2. What gas does yeast produce?

Review Questions

Food Provenance and Production Methods

1 What is 'traceability'? [5]

....

....

....

2 Name a more economical method of farming with less environmental impact. [1]

....

3 Give **one** disadvantage of the use of factory ships in a fishing fleet. [1]

....

Food Provenance: Food and the Environment

1 Explain how the fishing industry can ensure sustainability. [3]

....

....

....

2 What is a landfill? [1]

....

Food Provenance: Sustainability of Food

1 Which of these products are Fairtrade products? Tick (✓) the correct answers. [4]

a) Coffee ☐   b) Eggs ☐   c) Chocolate ☐

d) Flour ☐   e) Tea ☐   f) Bananas ☐

2 Products that have a Red Tractor logo on the packaging have a flag also to show the country of origin. [1]

True or **False?** ....

3 Name **one** result of deforestation. [1]

British and International Cuisines

1 Which country would you associate sashimi with? Tick (✓) **one** answer. [1]

a) China ☐   **b)** Japan ☐   **c)** Spain ☐   **d)** China ☐

2 Explain **three** reasons why we now eat foods from other countries in the British diet. Use the following key words to help you.

Multicultural: [1]

Foods available: [1]

Lifestyle: [1]

Food Manufacturing

1 Primary and secondary processing are stages of food manufacturing. Explain what secondary processing is. [2]

2 Give an example of a secondary processed food. [1]

Factors Affecting Food Choice: Sensory Evaluation

1 This is a chart to show the results of testing a pizza.

a) What name is given to this type of chart?

.... [1]

b) Identify the **best** feature of the product tested. [1]

....

c) Identify the two **worst** features (areas to be improved). [2]

....

....

d) What **three** suggestions would you make to improve this product, and why? [6]

I: ....

II: ....

III: ....

Factors Affecting Food Choice

1 Which of the following food outlets would be used by people on a very low income?
Tick (✓) **one** answer. [1]

a) Market stall ☐   b) Supermarket ☐   c) Food bank ☐   d) Grocer ☐

2 Explain what needs to be considered when planning what to feed a family. Use the following headings and give **two** points for each heading.

What to cook: .... [2]

....

How to cook it: .... [2]

....

Food Labelling

1 a) Look at the chart below showing the traffic light labelling system.

Per 100g of food			
	Low	Medium	High
Fat	Less than 3g	3g – 20g	More than 20g
Saturated fat	Less than 1.5g	1.5g – 5g	More than 5g
Salt	Less than 0.3g	0.3g – 1.5g	More than 1.5g
Sugars	Less than 5g	5g – 15g	More than 15g

Adapted from the Food Standards Agency

Explain **six** ways in which the traffic light labelling system helps the consumer to make good food choices. [6]

I: ....

II: ....

III: ....

IV: ....

V: ....

VI: ....

b) Name **three** pieces of information that must be included on pre-packed foods. [3]

I: ....

II: ....

III: ....

c) Explain **three** examples of when nutrition information must be provided on a pre-packed food product. [3]

I: ....

II: ....

III: ....

Practice Questions

Knife Skills

1 Name and describe **two** vegetable knife cuts.

Example: brunoise	Very small dice

[4]

2 Name **three** vegetable cuts that require you to cut the ingredient into vertical strips.   [3]

I: ....   II: ....   III: ....

Prepare, Combine and Shape

1 Which glaze would be most suitable for a batch of Chelsea buns? Tick (✓) **one** answer.   [1]

   a) Egg wash   ☐

   b) Arrowroot   ☐

   c) Sugar and water   ☐

   d) Egg yolk   ☐

Dough

1 What type of wheat is used to make pasta?   [1]

....

2 What are the names of the proteins found in a strong flour?   [2]

....

Review Questions

Factors Affecting Food Choice: Sensory Evaluation

1 Name **three** sensory tasting characteristics. [3]

I: .... II: .... III: ....

2 For each of the following, say which testing method would be the most suitable.

a) To find out which brand of fish fingers is preferred from a range of shops. [1]

....

b) To find out whether people can tell the difference between low-fat cheddar cheese or full-fat cheddar cheese. [1]

....

Factors Affecting Food Choice

1 When feeding a family on a budget, which of the following foods is generally the most expensive to buy? Tick (✓) **one** answer. [1]

a) Chicken ☐ **b)** Potatoes ☐ **c)** Frozen peas ☐ **d)** Bread ☐

2 Explain **two** points about what influences the foods we choose to eat, using the following prompts:

Buying foods in season .... [2]

....

Choosing where to shop .... [2]

....

Cost of food .... [2]

....

Availability of different foods to buy .... [2]

....

Review Questions

Food Labelling

1 **a)** How much does an average serving of this cereal weigh?

.... [1]

b) How much energy does 100 g of this cereal provide?

.... [1]

c) What could you serve with the cereal to make it healthier? [1]

....

...in (19% RDA) and adding a handful of fruit will count as one of your 5-a-Day.		
Typical values	100g contains	45g serving contains
Energy	1570kJ 375kcal	710kJ 170kcal
Protein	10.3g	4.6g
Carbohydrate	73.8g	33.2g
of which sugars	15.0g	6.8g
Fat	2.0g	0.9g
of which saturates	0.3g	0.1g
Fibre‡‡	8.2g	3.7g
Sodium	0.2g	0.1g
Salt equivalent	0.6g	0.3g

‡‡Fibre has been determined by AOAC ...
For guideline daily am...

d) How much of the following nutrients would a serving provide?

Fibre: ....   Saturates: .... [2]

2 Name **four** items on a food label that are important for food safety. [4]

I: ....   II: ....

III: ....   IV: ....

Knife Skills

1 A chef needs to have their own set of knives. Name and describe two different chef knives, giving one possible use for each. [6]

Name of knife	Description	One Possible Use

Prepare, Combine and Shape

1 What type of binding agent is generally used in a sausage mixture? Tick (✓) **one** answer. [1]

a) Breadcrumbs ☐   **b)** Flour ☐   **c)** Egg ☐   **d)** Water ☐

2 Which of these dishes uses three methods of combining, shaping and coating? Tick (✓) **one** answer. [1]

a) Burgers ☐   **b)** Fishcakes ☐   **c)** Chicken goujons ☐   **d)** Koftas ☐

3 What kind of glaze is used on a batch of scones? [1]

....

4 Give **two** examples of foods that can be shaped using a mould. [2]

I: .... II: ....

Dough

1 Complete the following questions to show your understanding of shortcrust pastry.

a) What is the ratio of fat:flour? .... [1]

b) What type of flour should be used? .... [1]

c) What fats should be used?

.... [2]

d) What method should be used? .... [1]

e) What texture should the cooked pastry have? .... [1]

2 What are the functions of each of the following ingredients in bread dough?

a) Yeast .... [1]

b) Sugar .... [1]

c) Fat .... [1]

d) Warm liquid .... [1]

Mixed Questions

1 The best method of cooking a quiche is: [1]

   A by steaming. ☐   **B** by grilling. ☐

   C by microwave. ☐   **D** by baking. ☐

2 Circle **one** answer. On a food product label, RI stands for: [1]

   Requires Improvement   **Reference Intake**   **Radical Impression**

3 Give **three** functions of fat in the diet. [3]

   I: ....

   II: ....

   III: ....

4 When using raising agents, it is important to measure them correctly. Too little raising agent means a lack of rise and gives a close texture. What happens if too much raising agent is measured? [3]

   ....

   ....

   ....

5 When making a sauce it is important to understand heat transfer.

   a) Describe the method of heat transfer from the hob through the saucepan. [1]

   ....

   b) Describe the method of heat transfer through the milk. [1]

   ....

   c) Explain the purpose of stirring (agitating) the milk related to heat transfer. [2]

   ....

   ....

6   Sterilised milk has a longer shelf life. Name **three** other types of milk that also have a longer shelf life and can be stored prior to use out of the fridge. State how each type of milk is packaged.   [6]

I: ....

II: ....

III: ....

7   **a)** Define the term 'coagulation' and describe how it affects the filling of a quiche.   [3]

....

....

....

b) Give another example of coagulation, apart from in a quiche filling.   [1]

....

8   What are fish farms? Explain how they can help to make fish a more sustainable commodity.   [2]

....

....

....

9   Which of the following products would show a use-by date? Circle **one** answer.   [1]

Packet of dried pasta   **Can of soup**   **Pot of yoghurt**   **Jar of jam**

10   Explain intensive animal farming methods.   [5]

....

....

....

....

....

Mixed Questions

11 A yeast batter for rich dough needs to be fermented. Describe the conditions needed to enable fermentation to take place. [4]

_____

_____

_____

_____

12 Obesity is considered a major risk to health. Underline **two** medical conditions that are linked to obesity. [2]

dementia   coronary heart disease   lung cancer

conjunctivitis   diabetes   dermatitis

13 When carrying out a tasting panel on a range of similar food products, which of these tests will decide which is the most popular product? [1]

A Rating test ☐   B Ranking test ☐

C Triangle test ☐   D Paired preference test ☐

14 Which of these proteins is **not** found in meat? Underline **one** answer. [1]

Elastin   Gluten   Myoglobin   Collagen

15 Identify the conditions that food spoilage organisms need in order to grow. [3]

_____

_____

16 Which of the following products is an example of secondary processing? [1]

A Wholemeal flour ☐   B Bread ☐

C Potatoes ☐   D Eggs ☐

17 When filleting a flat fish:

a) What is the first step? _____ [1]

b) What type of knife and chopping board would you need? [2]

....

c) Explain **three** points to show how you would know the fish is fresh. [3]

I: ....

II: ....

III: ....

18 Fruit and vegetables are a good source of dietary fibre. Give **two** reasons why we need plenty of fibre in our diets. [2]

I: ....

II:...

19 Which part of the body produces insulin? [1]

A Stomach ☐ **B** Liver ☐ **C** Pancreas ☐ **D** Spleen ☐

20 Blue veined cheese is one example of a food where microorganisms are used in food production. Name **one** other food, apart from cheese, that uses a microorganism in its production process. [1]

....

21 State **three** methods of preserving food at home. [3]

I: ....

II: ....

III: ....

22 Tick the boxes below to show if the statements are **true** or **false**. [3]

Statement	True	False
Vegetarians eat fish		
Hindus eat pork		
Jewish people don't eat shellfish		

23 Fill in the missing word. [1]

Saturated fats raise the c.. level in the body.

Mixed Questions

24 Fillings and dental extractions in children have been linked to overconsumption of which type of carbohydrate? [1]

....

25 Which of the following statements describes the consistency of choux pastry dough? [1]

A Pouring ☐   B Heavy dropping ☐

C Coating ☐   D Soft ☐

26 a) Name **four** of the joints that can be found in a chicken. [4]

I: ....   II: ....   III: ....   IV: ....

b) What colour of chopping board should be used to cut chicken? .... [1]

c) What is the best choice of kitchen knife to use? .... [1]

d) Explain the process of portioning out a chicken. [5]

....

....

....

....

27 Which of the following nutrients is **not** found in fish? [1]

A Protein ☐   B Vitamin C ☐

C Zinc ☐   D Omega 3 fatty acid ☐

28 What advice would you give an elderly relative who is planning a healthy diet? [2]

....

....

29 Which of the following statements are **true**? [2]

Vegetarians may lack iron in their diet.	
Kosher meat is eaten by Muslims.	
Lacto vegetarians eat honey.	
Coeliac disease is caused by insensitivity to rice.	

30 Fruit and vegetables that are produced without the use of artificial fertilisers are called: [1]

A GM (genetically modified). ☐   **B** sustainable. ☐

C organic. ☐   **D** intensive farming. ☐

31 Explain the importance of using colour-coded equipment when handling and preparing food. [3]

....

....

....

32 Complete the chart below. Provide **three** examples of each type of protein. [6]

High Biological Value (HBV) Protein	Low Biological Value (LBV) Protein

33 Jake is preparing the following family meal: [8]

Chicken curry with rice

Chocolate mousse

Give Jake advice on how the high-risk ingredients in the meal should be prepared and cooked to avoid food poisoning.

....

....

....

....

....

....

....

34 **a)** What is this logo called? [1]

....

....

b) Where would you be likely to find this logo? [1]

....

c) What does this logo tell you? [8]

....

....

....

....

....

....

....

....

35 Give **two** reasons why someone may need to increase their water intake. [2]

I: ....

....

II: ....

....

36 What is the name given to the production of foods using specially developed nutrient-rich liquids rather than soil? [1]

A Seasonal ☐ **B** Biodegradable ☐

C Hydroponics ☐ **D** Genetically Modified (GM) ☐

37 Give **two** functions of vitamin A in the body.   [2]

I: ....

II: ....

38 Name **three** microorganisms that cause food to spoil.   [3]

I: ....   II: ....   III: ....

39 Which of these foods is least harmful to the environment? (Circle) the correct answer.   [1]

Roast beef   **Lamb stew**   **Beef burger**   **Roast chicken**

40 Why is white bread a good source of calcium?   [1]

....

41 Fill in the missing information.   [4]

Method	Details on Main Function of Fat in the Dish
....	Used for foods that are reconstituted as 'instant' foods, e.g. baby foods.
Spray drying	This method is used for some foods that are ....
Accelerated Freeze Drying (AFD)	Food is .... and the temperature is then increased to make the ....

42 Airplanes, lorries and boats are all used to transport food. Which greenhouse gas do they produce?   [1]

....

43 Vitamin C is an antioxidant. Which of the following statements best describes the function of an antioxidant? Underline the correct statement.   [1]

Antioxidants protect us from pollutants in the environment.

Antioxidants protect us from food poisoning.

Antioxidants protect us from dementia in old age.

44 Look at the refrigerator below and label where the following foods should be stored.   [4]

| Eggs | Mango | Raw fish | Chocolate eclairs |

45 Give **one** function of sodium in the diet.   [1]

....

46 Which vitamin can be manufactured in the body by the action of sunlight on the skin?   [1]

....

47 Complete the following table.   [4]

Vitamin	Main Function in the Body	Main Food Sources
Iron		
Calcium		

Total Marks .... / 131

Answers

Page 7 Quick Test
1. **Two from:** Carbohydrates; Protein; B group vitamins; Calcium; Iron; Dietary fibre
2. Incorrect storage can lead to mould developing and bacteria contamination which could cause food poisoning.

Page 9 Quick Test
1. In a fridge; In a freezer
2. **Two from:** Roasting; Baking; Boiling; Shallow/deep frying

Page 11 Quick Test
1. **Two from:** Hard fruits; Soft/berry fruits; Citrus fruits; Stone fruits
2. **Two from:** Fruits and seeds; Flowers; Leaves; Stems; Shoots; Tubers; Roots; Bulbs
3. They are at their best (ripeness, sweetness, flavour), which can mean higher nutritional value.

Page 13 Quick Test
1. High Biological Value
2. **Two from:** To add colour to food; To add flavour; To add a different texture.
3. A heat treatment – heated to a high temperature for a short time and then cooled rapidly.

Page 15 Quick Test
1. Covered, in the bottom of the fridge, so that juices do not drip onto other foods.
2. Animals; poultry; offal; game.
3. To add flavour and to tenderise the meat.

Page 17 Quick Test
1. Oily fish
2. A blue chopping board and a filleting knife.

Page 19 Quick Test
1. The shell, the egg white and the yolk.
2. A very large egg is 73g and over; a small egg is 53g and under.
3. **Three from:** Hen eggs; Duck eggs; Goose eggs; Quail eggs.

Page 21 Quick Test
1. Edamame beans
2. **Three from:** Walnuts; Hazelnuts; Almonds; Pecans; Chestnuts; Pistachios; Any other suitable answer.
3. They are quite high in fat.
4. They can be used in making a variety of dishes and do not require any preparation.

Page 23 Quick Test
1. **Two from:** To marinade foods; To fry foods; To baste food during cooking; To make dressings.
2. They have a low fat, high water content.

Bread, Cereals, Flour and Oats
1. Yeast [1] Water [1]
2. To allow the yeast [1] time to work producing carbon dioxide gas [1], which makes the bread rise [1].

3. a) Freezing [1]
   b) Kept in its plastic wrapper and stored in a cool, dry place [1]
4. a) False [1] b) True [1]

Rice, Potatoes and Pasta
1. **Two from:** White basmati; Brown basmati; Jasmine; Patna; Carolina [2]
2. Skin [1] Fleshy section [1] Core/pith [1]
3. The plastic bag can make the potatoes sweat. [1] This can cause them to go bad/rot. [1]

Fruit and Vegetables
1. **Two from:** Vitamin A; Vitamin C; Vitamin E [2]
2. **Two from:** Canned; Dried; Fresh; Frozen; Bottled [2]
3. **Two from:** Nectarines; Cherries; Apricots; Peaches [2]
4. Spinach [1] Cabbage [1]

Milk, Cheese and Yoghurt
1. Fresh milk has cream on top [1] Homogenised has the cream dispersed throughout the milk. [1]
2. Ultra Heat Treated [1]
3. **Two from:** Cheese will add colour [1] as it can go golden brown when heated/cooked [1]; It can provide a subtle flavour [1] if a mild cheese is used or a sharp/mature flavour [1] if strong cheese is used; It can add a different texture [1] as it becomes very soft and moist when heated and melted [1]; It will help set the quiche [1] as the cheese adds thickness to the filling [1].

Meat
1. b) [1]
2. d) [1]
3. a) **Two from:** Stewing; Braising; Pot-roasting; Casseroling [2]
   b) Grilling [1] Frying [1]
   c) Grilling [1] Frying [1]

Fish
1. c) [1]
2. d) [1]
3. a) **One of:** Cod; Haddock; Whiting; Pollock; Coley [1]
   b) **One of:** Plaice; Sole; Halibut; Turbot [1]
   c) **One of:** Salmon; Sardines; Herring; Mackerel; Tuna; Whitebait [1]
4. Check that the eyes are bright – dull eyes indicate that the fish may still be safe to eat but is not very fresh [1]; Check that the scales are still in place [1]; Check that the gills are bright red – if they are dark red, the fish is not fresh [1]; Smell the fish – does it have a slightly salty smell of the sea? This is an indicator of freshness, a nasty smell will not improve with cooking [1]; Check for a thin layer of clear slime – if the liquid is not clear, the fish has begun to rot [1]; Check the flesh is firm with your finger – if the flesh bounces back, it is fresh [1]. **(1 mark for each point made, up to a maximum of 5 marks.)**

Eggs and Poultry
1. **Two from:** Chicken; Turkey; Duck; Goose [2]
2. The muscle fibres in poultry are shorter than in beef or lamb. [1]

Soya, Tofu, Beans, Nuts and Seeds
1. **Three from:** Soya milk; Miso; Tempeh; Soya flour [3]
2. Tofu is made by curdling the fresh soya milk [1], then removing any liquid which leaves curds [1]. The remaining curds are pressed, forming a set block. [1]
3. Legumes [1]
4. A pulse vegetable is an edible seed that grows in a pod. [1]

Butter, Oils, Margarine, Sugar and Syrup
1. **Shorten:** butter is rubbed into flour [1] for a short, crumbly feel when making pastry [1]. **Aerate:** when making cakes, butter is creamed with sugar [1] to add air and help the cake rise [1].
2. **Two from:** Butter is a dairy product; It is a solid block when stored chilled; When heated, it will melt; Butter has a rich flavour and has a high saturated fat value. [2]
3. Margarine is considered to be a cheaper alternative to butter [1] Margarine might be considered 'healthier' as it provides unsaturated fat not saturated. [1]

Page 31 Quick Test
1. Source of vitamins; Protection for organs; A component of hormones; Energy
2. Amino acids
3. Beans on toast/Hummus and pitta bread

Page 33 Quick Test
1. It provides energy.
2. Excess carbohydrate is converted to fat and is stored under the skin.
3. Non-Starch Polysaccharides (dietary fibre).

Page 35 Quick Test
1. Vitamins A, D, E and K.
2. **Three from:** Citrus fruit; Kiwi fruit; Blackcurrants; Salad and green vegetables; Potatoes
3. Folic acid/folate/vitamin B9

Page 37 Quick Test
1. To replace supplies lost through blood during periods.
2. When bones are at maximum strength.
3. Hormones in the thyroid gland.
4. **Two from:** Milk and dairy foods; Green leafy vegetables; Nuts, seeds and lentils; White bread – calcium is added by law; Wholegrain cereals.

Bread, Cereals, Flour and Oats
1. A cereal is grass [1] with starchy, edible grains or seeds [1].
2. **Two from:** Wheat; Oats; Rye; Barley [2]
3. **Two from:** Wholemeal flour; Self-raising flour; Brown flour [2]

Rice, Potatoes and Pasta
1. Durum [1]
2. If stored correctly it has a long shelf-life [1], which means it will not go off or out of date for an extended period of time. [1]

Fruit and Vegetables

1. They have a higher vitamin C value [1], cooking will reduce the value. [1]
2. **Two from:** Steam; Boil; Roast [2]
3. They are not grown in the UK [1]; To meet demands made by consumers [1]; People want to buy them all year round. [1]

Milk, Cheese and Yoghurt

1. condensed milk [1]
2. High biological value [1]

Meat

1. d) [1]
2. b) [1]
3. a) Pork [1]
   b) Beef [1]
   c) Lamb/mutton [1]
   d) Venison/game meat [1]
   e) **One from:** Chicken; Turkey; Duck; Goose [1]

Fish

1. d) [1]
2. b) [1]
3. **Method: Three of:** Canning; Freezing; Smoking; Salting [3]
   Three of:
   Canning example: One of: Salmon; Tuna; Sardine; Pilchard [1]
   Freezing example: One of: Cod; Haddock; Pollock; Coley [1]
   Smoking example: One of: Salmon; Haddock; Mackerel [1]
   Salting example: One of: Cod; Herring [1]
4. Smoking [1] Salting [1]
5. **Four from:** Protein; Minerals; Iron; Zinc; Iodine; Vitamins; Vitamin A; Vitamin D; Omega 3 fatty acids [4]

Eggs and Poultry

1. **Two from:** Away from strong smelling foods as they absorb the odours/flavours; In a refrigerator; They should be placed pointed end downwards. [2]

Soya, Tofu, Beans, Nuts and Seeds

1. **Any seed from:** Pumpkin; Sunflower; Chia; Poppy; Sesame. [1]
   Explanation: One from: They can be sprinkled on a glazed loaf of bread or rolls during baking; Mixed into a bread dough and baked; Eaten as a healthy snack; Added to salads for extra crunch; Sunflower seeds are used for the making of oils. [1]
2. A fruit inside a dry shell [1]
3. Iron [1] Zinc [1]

Butter, Oils, Margarine, Sugar and Syrup

1. Sugar beet is a root crop [1]; Sugar cane is a large bamboo type of grass [1]
2. Caster sugar – A finer crystal sugar; Demerara sugar – Coarse crystals made from raw sugar; Icing sugar – A powder sugar [2 for all correct]

Protein and Fat

1. b) [1]
2. **One of:** Beans on toast; Lentil soup with bread; Hummus and pitta bread; Any other suitable answer [2]
3. b) [1]
4. **Two from:** Full fat milk; Hard margarine; Coconut oil; Palm oil; Butter; Eggs; Cheese; Cream; Cakes; Biscuits; Chocolate; Pastries; Meat products; Beef fat/dripping/lard; Any other suitable answer [2]

Carbohydrates

1. c) [1]
2. **Two from:** They are the main source of energy in the body for movement; For digestion; For growth [2]
3. Non Starch Polysaccharides [1]
4. **Three from:** Wholegrain cereals; Wholegrain breakfast cereals, e.g. Weetabix, bran flakes, porridge oats, shredded wheat; Wholemeal bread; Wholemeal pasta; Wholemeal flour; Fruit; Vegetables; Dried fruit; Nuts; Seeds; Beans; Peas; Lentils; Any other suitable answer [3]

Vitamins

1. Vitamin B group [1] Vitamin C [1]
2. c) [1]
3. Fat-soluble vitamins [1]
4. From the action of sunlight on the skin [1] which enables the body to make vitamin D [1].

Minerals and Water

1. b) [1]
2. Iron supports the production of haemoglobin in red blood cells [1] which transports oxygen around the body [1].
3. **Two from:** Red meat – liver; Lentils; Dried apricots; Cocoa; Chocolate; Corned beef; Curry spices; Green leafy vegetables; Fortified breakfast cereals; Any other suitable answer [2].
4. **Two from:** Cheese or a named cheese; Cream; Yoghurt; Bread; Fish or fish where the bones are eaten; Leafy green vegetables or named vegetable; Nuts or named nut; Seeds or named seed; Dried fruit; Any other suitable answer [2].
5. **Three from:** Water is essential for normal brain function; Drinking enough water decreases the risk of kidney problems; Drinking the right amount of water helps to maintain normal blood pressure; Water aids bowel movements; Water helps to maintain cell function/healthy skin; The right amount of water in the body regulates temperature; Water is needed to maintain hydration; Water aids digestion; Water is needed to make body fluids, e.g. blood, saliva and mucus membranes [3].

Page 45 Quick Test

1. **Three from:** Base your meals on starchy carbohydrates; Eat lots of fruit and vegetables (5–7 portions per day); Eat plenty of fish, including oily fish; Cut down on saturated fat and sugars; Eat less salt – no more than 6g a day for adults; Get active and be a healthy weight; Don't get thirsty (drink six to eight glasses of water a day); Don't skip breakfast.
2. For the development of the neural tube of the foetus.
3. The first breast milk, (full of antibodies)
4. Weaning

Page 47 Quick Test

1. A condition where bones become brittle and break easily.
2. **Two from:** Lack of energy; Pale complexion; Shortness of breath; Tiredness

Page 49 Quick Test

1. Judaism and Islam
2. A vegan does not eat honey.
3. Foods that contain gluten, e.g. wheat, barley, rye, oats.

Protein and Fat

1. chicken; milk; soya [3]
2. Protein complementation [1]
3. The level of cholesterol [1]

Carbohydrates

1. pasta; potato; oats [3]
2. lentils; cabbage; apples; shredded wheat [4]
3. Sugar [1]

Vitamins

1. Kiwi fruit; lemons; cabbage [3]
2. Folate (folic acid) reduces the risk of neural tube defect (Spina Bifida) in babies [1].
3. **Two from:** Vitamin C and vitamin B are destroyed by heat so vegetables that are not subjected to heat retain these vitamins; Vitamin C is destroyed on exposure to oxygen therefore after it has been cut, before cooking, there are losses; Vitamin C and vitamin B are water-soluble so will leach into water during the cooking process [2]
4. Ascorbic acid [1]

Minerals and Water

1. haemoglobin [1] red blood [1] oxygen [1]
2. Due to monthly menstrual blood loss [1]
3. The body's metabolic rate [1]
4. **Two from:** In hot weather to replace water lost by excess sweating; After physical exertion to replace water lost by excess sweating; Lactating mothers need an increased supply of water for the production of milk; People suffering from sickness and diarrhoea need to increase their intake of water in order to keep hydrated due to loss of water via the sickness and diarrhoea [2].

Making Informed Choices

1. **Three from:** Eat less sugar; Eat more fibre; Eat more starchy food; Eat at least five portions of fruit and vegetables daily; Don't skip breakfast; Eat the right amount to stay a healthy weight; Follow the Eatwell Guide; Drink plenty of water. [3]
2. Weaning [1]
3. Carbohydrates [1]
4. 6–8 glasses of water [1]
5. Older people do not need as many calories per day [1] (they will eat smaller portions). Reason: They are not so active/they do less exercise/their basic metabolic rate will go down. [1]

Diet, Nutrition and Health

1. b) **[1]**
2. **Two from**: Coronary heart disease; Type 2 Diabetes; Some types of cancer; High blood pressure; Risk of stroke; Arthritis; Breathing problems **[2]**
3. Insulin **[1]**
4. **Three from**: Weight gain/obesity; Can produce high/bad cholesterol; Can block arteries; Angina; Coronary Heart Disease (CHD)/heart disease/heart attack; Trans fats/ higher risk of cancer **[3]**
5. BMR is the body's basic energy rate if the person is at complete rest **[1]** BMR is the energy needed by the body just to function, with no movement except breathing/ natural functions at rest **[1]**
6. Energy density is the amount of energy calories (kcal) or kilojoules (kJ) a food contains **[1]** per gram, e.g. Fat = 9 kcal/g **[1]**

Food Choices

1. c) **[1]**
2. an epi-pen **[1]**
3. Iron **[1]**; vitamin D **[1]**; Vitamin B12 **[1]**

Pages 54-63 **Revise Questions**

Page 55 Quick Test

1. True
2. Convection
3. Water-based; Fat-based; Dry
4. Conduction; Convection; Radiation

Page 57 Quick Test

1. Enzymes
2. Coagulation/Denaturation

Page 59 Quick Test

1. Gelatinisation
2. Radiation/grill
3. True

Page 61 Quick Test

1. Shortening
2. True
3. Creaming

Page 63 Quick Test

1. Air is the raising agent
2. Air expands when heated
3. By forming a foam
4. By turning to steam

Pages 64-65 **Review Questions**

Making Informed Choices

1. chocolate **[1]** beef **[1]** apricots **[1]**
2. c) **[1]**
3. iron **[1]** liver **[1]**

Diet, Nutrition and Health

1. a) **[1]**
2. milky drinks **[1]** cheese **[1]** yoghurts **[1]**
3. Diabetes is controlled by careful management of sugar in the diet. **[1]** In addition, insulin medication may be frequently injected **[1]**
4. c) **[1]**
5. A condition where bones become weak and brittle and are more likely to break – this usually occurs in old age. **[1]**

Food Choices

1. d) **[1]**
2. Anaphylaxis (or anaphylactic shock) **[1]**
3. Lactose is a sugar **[1]**
4. a) People over 40 **[1]** People who are overweight **[1]**
   b) Healthy diet **[1]** Increased physical activity **[1]**

Pages 66-69 **Practice Questions**

Cooking of Food, Heat Transfer and Selecting Appropriate Cooking Methods

1. a) microorganisms **[1]**
   b) shelf life **[1]** keep quality **[1]**
   c) variety **[1]**
   d) digest **[1]**
2. Conduction **[1]** Convection **[1]** Radiation **[1]**
3. **Water-based methods: Two from:** Boiling; Stewing; Steaming; Poaching; Braising; Pressure cooking **[2]**
   Dry cooking methods: Two from: Baking; Grilling; Roasting; Barbecuing; Dry-frying **[2]**.
   Fat-based methods: Two from: Shallow frying in fat; Deep-fat frying; Stir frying **[2]**.

Proteins and Enzymic Browning

1. Heat **[1]** Reduction of pH **[1]** Enzymes **[1]** Mechanical actions **[1]**
2. a) It changes from being runny to being set **[1]**
   b) Due to coagulation **[1]** Due to the effect of heat **[1]**
3. a) Gluten **[1]**
   b) Strong flour contains more protein than plain cake flour. **[1]**
4. a) Water must be added **[1]** Kneading must take place **[1]**
   b) Gliadin **[1]**
5. a) Enzymic browning **[1]**
   b) **One of**: Inactivate enzymes by using an acid such as lemon juice; Remove the presence of air, e.g. place in water; Cook **[1]**.

Carbohydrates

1. liquid **[1]** gelatinisation **[1]** heated **[1]** stirred **[1]** boiling point **[1]**
2. a) **Colour:** The bread turns golden **[1]**
   Flavour: The bread tastes sweeter **[1]**
   Texture: The bread becomes crisp **[1]**
   b) Dextrinisation **[1]**
   c) Hygroscopic **[1]**
   d) The toast becomes less crisp **[1]**

Fats and Oils

1. a) **[1]**
2. a) **Functions:** Aerate mixture **[1]** Trap air **[1]**
   Characteristics: Cake rises **[1]** Increased volume **[1]**
   b) **Function:** Shorten the dough **[1]**
   Characteristic: Crumbly short texture **[1]**

Raising Agents

1. To increase volume **[1]** To make a light texture **[1]** To raise mixtures **[1]**
2. a) Air **[1]**
   b) The raising agent is incorporated by whisking air into the sponge mixture, either by hand or with an electric mixer **[1]**

c) **One of:** Baking powder; Bicarbonate of soda; Cream of tartar **[1]**.
d) Carbon dioxide **[1]**
e) During baking the heat of the oven causes the raising agents to be active and produce the gas. **[1]** The gas swells with heat and raises the scone **[1]**.

Pages 70-81 **Revise Questions**

Page 71 Quick Test

1. Bacteria
2. Between 5 °C and 63 °C – this is known as the 'danger zone'
3. Eat food as soon as possible after making/ cooking, if not cool down as quickly as possible and store in the fridge or freezer.
4. **Possible answers:** Bread; Wine; Beer

Page 73 Quick Test

1. Lactobacillus
2. Mould
3. Safeguard the immune system; Improve digestion; Keep the body's intestine balanced

Page 75 Quick Test

1. **Any or all of the following are possible:** Stomach pains; Diarrhoea; Vomiting; Nausea (feeling sick); Fever
2. **Three from**: Salmonella; Staphylococcus Aureus; Clostridium perfringens; Clostridium Botulinum; Bacillus cereus; E-Coli; Listeria; Campylobacter; Norovirus
3. Raw food; Bacteria passed on from people; Bacteria carried in air and dust; Bacteria on equipment and utensils; Soil; Pests; Contaminated water; Degrading food waste
4. Very young children and babies; Elderly people; People who have a serious illness or are recovering from a serious illness; Pregnant women and nursing mothers; People who have allergies

Page 77 Quick Test

1. The 'Use-by' and 'Best before' dates
2. Between 1 °C and 4 °C to make sure that food is held below 5 °C
3. False
4. −18 °C or below
5. Ice crystals remain at the centre; Cooking will melt the ice but the correct core temperature may not be achieved and bacteria may survive

Page 79 Quick Test

1. **Four from**: Before preparing food; Between handling raw and high-risk or ready-to-eat foods; After you have been to the toilet; After sneezing or coughing; After changing a waterproof plaster; After using cleaning fluids; After handling food waste or rubbish; After handling known allergens
2. The thickest part of the food (core) should reach 75 °C, or 70 °C for two minutes.

Page 81 Quick Test

1. Vitamins A, C, E, and K
2. Six months
3. Vacuum has oxygen removed and MAP has oxygen removed and replaced with another gas

Cooking of Food, Heat Transfer and Selecting Appropriate Cooking Methods

1. **In the following order:** flavours [1] mouthfeel/texture [1] texture/mouthfeel [1] bulk [1] colour [1]

2. Conduction occurs as heat transfers through the pan [1] This heat comes from the heat source [1] Convection takes place in water in a pan during boiling [1] Heat passes through the potato by conduction. [1] Boiling uses two methods of heat transfer, the first method is conduction [1] The second method is convection [1].

Proteins and Enzymic Browning

1. **Meaning:** Protein denaturation means the functional properties [1] of a protein change [1].
   Example, possible answer: Cooked egg white [1] It is denatured and therefore it will not whip to a foam [1].

2. **In the following order:** gluten [1] elastic [1] kneading [1] short [1] structure [1]

Carbohydrates

1. The solution becomes viscous when water and sugar are heated together [1] The colour of this liquid becomes increasingly golden [1]

2. **a) Choice:** Recipe B [1]
   b) Explanation: The amount of flour would thicken the milk [1] To make a smooth coating sauce [1] The amount of flour in Recipe A would not [1] be enough, the sauce would remain runny [1].

Fats and Oils

1. The rubbing-in method [1]

2. **a)** The margarine/butter [1] and the caster/baking sugar [1]
   b) The mixture becomes paler as the fat and sugar are creamed together [1]
   c) Trapping air (aeration) [1] Causes a paler coloured air-in-fat foam to form [1]
   d) During baking the trapped air would expand [1] This makes the cakes rise [1]

Raising Agents

1. I: A warm temperature is needed [1] Of 25 °C–35 °C [1]
   II: Moisture is needed [1] This is supplied from the liquid in the recipe [1]
   III: The yeast requires food [1] This is supplied by the flour or the added sugar [1]
   IV: Time is needed [1] To produce the gas that raises the mixture [1]

2. Raising agents are active ingredients that make food products rise or processes that make food products [1] and have open airy textures [1] Raising agents can be biological, chemical or physical [1]

Microorganisms, Enzymes and Food Spoilage

1. Enzymes are molecules that control chemical reactions in food [1]

2. Enzymic browning [1]

3. Apple/banana [1]

4. **One of:** Coat the fruit in an acid such as lemon/lime juice; Coat the fruit in sugar to halt/prevent browning; Stop oxygen from turning the fruit brown by immersing the fruit in water or juice [1]

Microorganisms in Food Production

1. b) [1]
2. Lactic acid [1]
3. False [1]

Bacterial Contamination

1. True [1]
2. a) [1]
3. It means that the food is safe to eat up until the date marked on the food product or its packaging [1]

Buying and Storing Food

1. True [1]
2. a) cooked [1]
   b) perishable [1]
   c) 0 °C and 4 °C, below 5 °C [1]
   d) −18 °C and below [1]

Preparing and Cooking Food

1. c) [1]
2. If food is not reheated properly, the bacteria in it may survive and multiply – every time food is reheated the chances of this happening are increased [1]
3. cooked rice [1] cooked chicken [1]

Food Preservation

1. **Three from:** Canning; Irradiation; Pasteurisation; Sterilisation; Ultra heat treatment [3]

Page 89 Quick Test

1. So that if a risk is identified, the source can be quickly isolated and consumers can be protected.

2. Animals have access to the outdoors as they would in nature; They can behave and feed naturally; The resulting product is better quality as the animal has not suffered stress.

3. Hydroponic farming requires large areas of glasshouses, with controlled systems where the products grow in nutrient-rich liquids, without soil.

Page 91 Quick Test

1. Food miles are the distance that food travels from its origin to your plate.

2. Recycling can use more energy, and some solutions used to clean recycled products are polluting.

3. **Two from:** Restrict catch sizes; Have minimum sizes of fish allowed to be kept for sale; Widen the selection of fish being eaten to more species; Put caught young fish back in the sea so they can go on to breed and reproduce.

Page 93 Quick Test

1. The Red Tractor logo flag shows the country of origin of the food product.

2. Fairtrade products give a realistic income to the farmer; Fair prices for the goods; Local investment; Better working conditions

3. To make way for growing crops and animal grazing

4. Methane and CO_2

Page 95 Quick Test

1. **Possible answers:** Cornish Blue (from Cornwall), Lanark Blue (from Scotland), Caerphilly (from Wales)

2. Roast meat, beans, pulses and fish all provide protein. Roast potatoes (starchy carbohydrate) and accompanying vegetables provide at least two of the five recommended portions of vegetables per day.

3. The crimped edge of a Cornish pasty provided a 'baked-in' handle for tin miners to hold while they ate the pasty. Sometimes they threw the 'handle' away and sometimes they ate it.

Page 97 Quick Test

1. A food that cannot be eaten in its original condition – it needs to be prepared or changed before it can be eaten.

2. **Two from:** Clotted; Single; Whipping; Double; Extra thick; Soured cream; Crème fraiche

3. **One from:** Colourings; Flavour intensifiers; Preservatives; Stabilisers; Emulsifiers

4. To replace colour lost during processing or to make the food look more appealing.

Microorganisms, Enzymes and Food Spoilage

1. **Two from:** Yeast; Mould; Fungi/fungus [2]

2. **Three from:** The length of time exposed – the longer the exposure, the greater the growth; Temperature – the higher the temperature, the faster and greater the growth; Moisture – the higher the level of moisture the greater the growth; The amount of microorganisms originating in the food itself influence growth – the more microorganisms there are to begin with, the more rapid their growth; Level of oxygen/air/air flow – the more exposure to oxygen, the greater the chance of growth; Neutral pH [3]

3. **Three from:** Milk/yoghurt; Meat/poultry; Fish/shellfish; Eggs; Vegetables; Salad; Fruit; Bread; Cream; Any other suitable answer [3]

4. b) [1]

Microorganisms in Food Production

1. **Three from:** Bread dough is mixed and kneaded, millions of air bubbles are trapped and distributed through the dough; The yeast in the dough provides microorganisms, which absorb the starches and sugars in the flour, turning them into alcohol and carbon dioxide gas; This gas expands the air bubbles, causing the bread to rise; During rising, the yeast divides and multiplies, producing more carbon dioxide. As long as there is ample air and food (carbohydrates) in the dough, the yeast will multiply until its activity is stopped by the heat of the oven [3].

2. A culture is used to develop taste and texture [1].

3. Probiotic cultures offer health benefits such as helping to improve digestion [1] Safeguarding the immune system [1] Keeping the body's intestinal flora in balance [1].

4. The cheese is treated with mould, which contains microorganisms, and these microorganisms develop as the cheese matures [1] The mould continues to develop throughout the process, imparting the blue-veined appearance of the cheese and giving flavour [1].

Bacterial Contamination

1. **Two from**: Poultry – chicken/duck/turkey/goose; Meat – beef/lamb/pork/sausages/burger; Offal – liver/kidneys; Fish/shellfish; Eggs; Dairy Products – cream/milk/yoghurt; Cooked rice **(no marks awarded for 'rice' only)**/reheated rice; Custards/sauces/gravy; **Credit will also be given for a named food product, e.g. chicken curry containing fresh cream [2]**.

2. **Eight from**: The presence of excess microorganisms in food are a major cause of food poisoning – usually bacteria but sometimes viruses; Food that has not been cooked properly, e.g. eggs that are still raw/undercooked products, i.e. meats; Food that has not been stored properly, e.g. where cross contamination has taken place between raw and cooked meats; Food poisoning takes place when microorganisms are allowed to multiply at a high rate, this is when they produce toxins/poisons/waste products (microorganisms cause the symptoms of food poisoning); A lack of knowledge and understanding about how to store, cook and prepare foods in the home and/or in industry can lead to food poisoning; Intensive farming methods can lead to disease spreading easily in perishable foods such as poultry or seafood, thus leading to food poisoning; Dirty water can be a cause of food poisoning as the water can carry bacteria into the body; Pests/animals can transmit food poisoning via bacteria/pests; Poor standards of food hygiene in people handling food can transmit food poisoning to themselves and to others; Dust and soil can carry food poisoning onto or into food **[8]**.

Buying and Storing Food

1. **a)** 100 °C. **[1]**
   b) –18 °C. **[1]**
   c) 5 °C; 63 °C. **[1]**
   d) 75 °C. **[1]**
2. **a)** False **[1]**
   b) False **[1]**
   c) True **[1]**
3. **Four from**: Ensure the food is cooled before refrigerating or freezing it as the microorganisms will continue to multiply. If the food is hot, then it heats the fridge or freezer and therefore puts all the food within the danger zone; Ensure the food is kept in the refrigerator (between 0 and 5 °C) so that it is out of the 'danger zone' where microorganisms are most active; Cool food quickly as this limits microorganism growth time, ensuring less time in the 'danger zone'; Do not leave food out for long periods of time as this encourages the growth of microorganisms; Keep food out of the 'danger zone' of 5–63 °C because this is where the microorganisms are most active – out of this range the microorganisms remain inactivated; Use the food within a few days of cooking/opening because exposure to air and temperatures once open encourages food to deteriorate and microorganisms to multiply; Transfer food to containers from tins and cans because open cans encourage microorganism activity and can lead to poisoning from the can oxidising **[4]**.

Preparing and Cooking Food

1. **a)** 5 °C **[1]**
   b) 75 °C **[1]**
2. **Reheating cooked foods**: 75 °C (**accept 72 °C–75 °C**) **[1]**
   Storing chilled foods: blast chilling 4 °C is within range (**accept 0–4 °C or 'below 5 °C'**) **[1]**
3. A food or temperature probe **[1]** ('thermometer' will not be accepted)
4. Sterilise/clean with antibacterial wipe (**clean not acceptable unless qualified, 'disinfect' will not be accepted**)/make sure sterile before and after use **[1]** Check reading before start (ideally room temp), do not touch container/baking tin with probe, then place into centre of food/core temperature **[1]** Keep in place for two minutes **[1]** Check temperature is 75 °C or over **[1]** Remove from food/take the reading when it is stable/after two minutes **[1]** If not at correct temperature continue cooking food and re-apply later **[1]**.

Food Preservation

1. Vitamin B6 **[1]** Vitamin C **[1]**
2. There is usually no change to food or nutrient content. **[1]**

Pages 102-103 Practice Questions

Food Provenance and Production Methods

1. **c)** **[1]**
2. Less methane being produced by animals **[1]** More land available to grow high-protein crops, e.g. soya **[1]**.
3. low cost **[1]**
4. **Three from**: Grown naturally; No chemical or synthetic treatments; No antibiotics; Natural manure and compost only as fertilisers; Must be GM-free **[3]**.

Food Provenance: Food and the Environment

1. **a)** carbon dioxide **[1]**
   b) your table **[1]**
   c) more **[1]**
   d) front **[1]**
2. Packaging that rots naturally **[1]** Packaging that rots quickly **[1]**.
3. The body gets delivery of the correct nutrients for that time of year **[1]** also trace elements and minerals for the correct time of year **[1]**.

Food Provenance: Sustainability of Food

1. **c)** **[1]**
2. **Four from**: Farmers in developing countries get realistic incomes; Investment in local community; Better working conditions; Fair price for goods; Sustainable production **[4]**.

British and International Cuisines

1. **b)** **[1]**
2. Its colour **[1]** Its texture **[1]** Its flavour **[1]** Ingredients from the region that produces the cheese **[1]**

Food Manufacturing

1. **Example answers**: Peeling and slicing raw carrots; Washing salad leaves; Making wheat into flour (milling); Heating and cooling milk to make pasteurised/semi-skimmed milk. **[2]**

Pages 104-115 Revise Questions

Page 105 Quick Test

1. Texture
2. On your tongue
3. So that the tester is not influenced by brand loyalty

Page 107 Quick Test

1. PAL stands for Physical Activity Level
2. The Eatwell Guide
3. A variety of textures, flavours and colours

Page 109 Quick Test

1. 100 g
2. European Union
3. The following must also be included: Kilocalories and kilojoules; Protein; Sugars

Page 111 Quick Test

1. With the point facing downwards
2. No
3. To avoid the food moving and the knife slipping
4. Bridge hold; claw grip

Page 113 Quick Test

1. By hand
2. A mould or your hands
3. Sugar and water

Page 115 Quick Test

1. Strong flour
2. Carbon dioxide

Pages 116-117 Review Questions

Food Provenance and Production Methods

1. The ability to track any food **[1]**, animal feed **[1]**, food-producing animal **[1]** or substance **[1]** that will be used for consumption through all stages of production, processing and distribution **[1]**.
2. Organic/free range **[1]**
3. They strip the seabed bare of every living creature for miles **[1]**.

Food Provenance: Food and the Environment

1. **Three from:** Restriction on the sizes of catches allowed; Ensuring that fish caught must be returned if they don't meet a minimum size requirement; Encouraging the public to eat a wider variety of fish; Returning young fish to the water **[3]**
2. A site where rubbish is dumped and buried **[1]**.

Food Provenance: Sustainability of Food

1. **a) c) e) f)** **[4]**
2. True **[1]**
3. **One from**: CO$_2$ builds up, which contributes to global warming; Animals lose their natural habitat, putting them in danger; Deforested land suffers from soil erosion and becomes infertile **[1]**.

British and International Cuisines

1. **b)** **[1]**
2. **Multicultural:** Due to the influence of people originally from other countries (or previous generations of their families) now living in the UK **[1]**.
   Foods available: One of: Specialist food shops that cater to particular cuisines or ethnic groups increase the diversity of food available; International foods are now

available to buy online and in supermarkets; Recipe books that expain how to make food from all over the world are readily available and relatively cheap to buy from bookshops or online; Free recipes from all over the world are available online **[1]**.
Lifestyle: One of: People now routinely take holidays to other countries, where they are exposed to different cuisines – they may take the new ingredients and recipes home with them; We have a diverse range of takeaways/restaurants that sell the cuisines of other countries **[1]**.

Food Manufacturing
1. Secondary processing is a follow on from primary processing **[1]** It is a further process that can take place using a primary processed product to make a new food product. **[1]**
2. **One from:** Cream; Butter; Yoghurt; Cheese; Pasta; Bread **[1]**

Pages 118-120 **Practice Questions**

Factors Affecting Food Choice: Sensory Evaluation
1. **a)** Star profile/Radar diagram **[1]**
   b) Pizza base texture **[1]**
   c) Taste of cheese **[1]** Golden brown cheese **[1]**
   d) Use stronger cheese **[1]** to improve the taste of the pizza **[1]** More cheese when cooked **[1]** would improve both colour and flavour **[1]** Cook pizza for longer **[1]** until the cheese browns in the oven **[1]**.

Factors Affecting Food Choice
1. **c)** **[1]**
2. **What to cook: Two from**: What do people in the family like?; What ingredients are needed?; How many people are you catering for? **[2]**
   How to cook it: Two from: Equipment available; Skill needed; Recipe **[2]**

Food Labelling
1. **a)** **Six from:** Traffic light labelling educates consumers so that they can make informed choices; Traffic light labelling identifies the nutritional content levels of the food; Traffic light labelling is easy to read/interpret; Red – poor choice for healthy eating; Amber – caution in quantities eaten; Green – free to eat in high quantities; Should aim for more green, less red and moderate amounts of amber foods **[6]**
   b) **Three from:** Energy value in kilojoules (kJ); Energy value in kilocalories; Amount in grams of fat; Amount in grams of saturates; Amount in grams of sugars; Amount in grams of protein; Amount in grams of salt **[3]**
   c) **Three from:** When the supplier makes a nutrition claim for the food product; When the supplier makes a health claim for the food product; If vitamins are added to the food product; If minerals are added to the food product **[3]**

Knife Skills
1. **Two from**: Jardinière **[1]** – baton shaped lengths **[1]**; Julienne **[1]** – matchstick sized

strips **[1]**; Macedoine **[1]** – medium sized dice **[1]**; Chiffonade **[1]** – fine shreds of leafy vegetables **[1]**; Battonet **[1]** – Square shaped lengths **[1]**; Turning **[1]**; – barrel shaped **[1]**
2. Julienne **[1]** Battonet **[1]** Jardinière **[1]**

Prepare, Combine and Shape
1. c) **[1]**

Dough
1. Durum wheat **[1]**
2. Glutenin **[1]** Gliadin **[1]**

Pages 121-123 **Review Questions**

Factors Affecting Food Choice: Sensory Evaluation
1. **Three from:** Sweetness; Flavour; Colour; Texture; Appearance; Aroma **[3]**
2. **a)** Ranking test **[1]**
   b) Triangle test **[1]**

Factors Affecting Food Choice
1. **a)** **[1]**
2. **Buying foods in season:** In-season food has more flavour **[1]** In-season food has more nutritional value **[1]**
   Choosing where to shop: Two from: Type of shops available; Income available; Access – transport **[2]**
   Cost of food: Two from: What income is available; Quality v cost; Cost of seasonal food; Taking advantage of special offers **[2]**
   Availability of different foods to buy: Two from: Multi-cultural influences; Organic food choices; Gluten-free options; Dairy-free options **[2]**

Food Labelling
1. **a)** 45 g **[1]**
   b) 1570 kJ/375 kcal **[1]**
   c) Handful/portion of fruit **[1]**
   d) Fibre: 3.7 g **[1]** Saturates: 0.1 g **[1]**
2. **Four from:** Allergen information; Date mark; Cooking instructions; Storage instructions; Batch mark **[4]**

Knife Skills
1. **Name of knife: Two from**: Cook's; Paring; Boning; Filleting; Carving; Bread; Palette **[2]**
   Description: Cook's: Come in different sizes and their strong, ridged blades make them suitable for a wide range of tasks **[1]**
   Paring: A small knife with a thin and slightly flexible blade **[1]**
   Boning: A very strong blade that will not bend or break easily, can be straight or curved **[1]**
   Filleting: Thin-bladed, flexible and very sharp knife **[1]**
   Carving: Long blades with a serrated or plain edge, can be rounded or pointed **[1]**
   Bread: Long serrated edge **[1]**
   Palette: Flexible blade, rounded at the top **[1]**
   One possible use: Cook's: One from: Dicing; Chopping and trimming vegetables; Chopping and trimming meat and poultry; Chopping fresh herbs **[1]**
   Paring: Fruit and vegetable preparation **[1]**
   Boning: Removing bones from meat joints and poultry **[1]**
   Filleting: Filleting fish **[1]**
   Carving: Carving meat joints or cooked hams **[1]**

Bread: Slicing loaves and other bread products, sandwiches **[1]**
Palette: One from: Icing cakes; Turning food over during cooking; Moulding and smoothing food **[1]**

Prepare, Combine and Shape
1. **a)** **[1]**
2. **b)** **[1]**
3. A milk glaze **(egg glaze also acceptable)** **[1]**
4. **Two from:** Loaf; Cake; Jelly; Burger; Mousse **[2]**

Dough
1. **a)** 1:2 **[1]**
   b) Plain flour **[1]**
   c) Mixture of lard **[1]** vegetable fat/butter **[1]**
   d) Rubbing-in **[1]**
   e) **One from**: short/crisp/light **[1]**
2. **a)** Acts as a raising agent **[1]**
   b) Feeds the yeast **[1]**
   c) Increases shelf-life/can add colour and flavour **[1]**
   d) Provides the yeast with moisture/helps to form gluten **[1]**

Pages 124-132 **Mix it Up Questions**

1. D **[1]**
2. Reference intake **[1]**
3. **Three from**: Used for energy; Helps insulate the body/keep warm; Provides the body with fat-soluble vitamins A, D, E and K; A component of hormones **[3]**.
4. **Three from**: A coarse texture results; Over-rise takes place; Collapse/sink in product's structure; Unpleasant taste **[3]**.
5. **a)** Heat is transferred from the hob through the saucepan by conduction **[1]**.
   b) Heat is transferred through the milk by convection **[1]**.
   c) Stirring (agitating) the milk distributes the heat throughout the milk **[1]**; preventing lumps **[1]**.
6. **Three from**: Condensed milk in tins; Evaporated milk in tins; Dried milk in card containers; UHT milk in card cartons **[6]**.
7. **a)** Coagulation is the denaturation of protein **[1]**; It can be caused by heat during cooking **[1]**; It makes a quiche filling set **[1]**.
   b) **One example of cooked egg:** Cakes; Puddings; Omelette **[1]**.
8. They may be tanks on land or nets floating in seawater or fresh water **[1]**; Fish stocks are controlled, but still within a semi-natural environment **[1]**.
9. Pot of yoghurt **[1]**
10. **Five from**: Large farms; Large numbers of animals in crowded buildings; Massive buildings; No access to natural resources for the animals, e.g. daylight; Very few farm workers needed to run computerised feeding systems; Antibiotics used on the animals; Growth enhancers used on the animals **[5]**.
11. **Conditions required are:** Food – from sugar or flour **[1]**; Time – to allow doubling of dough size **[1]**; Moisture – the liquid in the recipe **[1]**; Warmth – 20–25 °C **[1]**.
12. coronary heart disease **[1]**; diabetes **[1]**
13. B **[1]**
14. Gluten **[1]**

15. **Three from**: Warm temperature/ 37 °C; Moisture; Food; Time; Neutral pH; May need oxygen **[3]**.
16. B **[1]**
17. a) Remove the head **[1]**
    b) Filleting/Cook's knife **[1]**; Blue board **[1]**
    c) **Three from**: Eyes are bright and not dull; Scales are in place; Gills are bright red; Slightly salty smell of the sea; Thin layer of slime; Flesh is firm **[3]**.
18. **Two from**: To make food passing through digestive system soft and bulky; Helps prevent constipation; Helps prevent diverticular disease and some forms of cancer **[2]**.
19. C **[1]**
20. **One of**: Bread or named bread; Yoghurt or named yoghurt **[1]**.
21. **Three from**: Making jams/jellies/ crystallising; Pickling/chutneys; Bottling; Drying; Freezing; Salting; Smoking **[3]**.
22. Vegetarians eat fish: False **[1]**; Hindus eat pork: False **[1]**; Jewish people don't eat shellfish: True **[1]**
23. cholesterol **[1]**
24. Sugar **[1]**
25. B **[1]**
26. a) **Four from**: Breast; Leg; Wing; Drumstick; Thigh **[4]**
    b) Red **[1]**
    c) Boning knife/Cook's knife **[1]**
    d) Remove legs **[1]**; Separate the drumstick and the thigh **[1]**; Remove wings **[1]**; Find the wishbone at the front of the bird, release the wishbone **[1]**; Cut through the knuckle at the base, then carefully remove the breasts from the carcass **[1]**.
27. B **[1]**
28. **Two from**: Follow the Eatwell Guide; Eat smaller portions; Drink plenty of water; Make sure that your diet contains plenty of calcium-rich foods to help prevent osteoporosis **[2]**.
29. **True statements:** Vegetarians may lack iron in their diet **[1]**; Lacto vegetarians eat honey **[1]**.
30. C **[1]**
31. **Three from**: To avoid cross contamination; To keep raw foods and cooked foods apart; To avoid bacteria transfer; Reference to named bacteria **[1 mark per bacteria, up to three bacteria]**; Examples – chopping boards/knives/storage containers can be colour coded **[1]**; Colours used to identify equipment – Raw meat – red/Salad and fruit – green/Fish – blue/Vegetables – brown/Cooked meat – yellow/Bakery and dairy – white **[1]**.
32. **High biological value (HBV) protein, three from**: Meat; Fish; Eggs; Cheese; Milk; Soya **[3]**.
    Low biological value (LBV) protein, three from: Nuts; Seeds; Lentils; Pulse vegetables; Bread **[3]**.
33. **Eight from**: Identification of chicken as a high-risk ingredient; Identification of eggs as a high-risk ingredient; Identification of cream as a high-risk ingredient; Identification of rice as a high-risk ingredient; Cross contamination should be avoided; Correct storage temperatures should be observed; Food hygiene and cleaning procedures must be applied to hands, hair, etc. and equipment; Correct reheating temperatures must be observed; Correct cooking temperatures must be achieved; Storage after cooking should meet the correct standards **[8]**.
34. a) The Red Tractor logo (controlled and monitored by Assured Food Standards (AFS)) **[1]**
    b) On food labels or on food packaging **[1]**
    c) That the food has been produced, processed, and packed **[1]** to Red Tractor standards **[1]** The flag on the logo shows the country of origin **[1]** The logo assures high standards of food hygiene and safety **[1]** The logo assures high standards of equipment used in production **[1]** The logo assures high standards of animal health and welfare **[1]** The logo assures high standards in environmental issues and the responsible use of pesticides **[1]** Any product with this logo can be traced from farm to fork **[1]**.
35. **Two from**: In hot weather to replace water lost by excess sweating; After physical exertion to replace water lost due to excess sweating; Lactating mothers need an increased supply of water for the production of milk; People suffering from sickness and diarrhoea need to increase their intake of water due to water loss through sweating/vomiting/excess excretion **[2]**.
36. C **[1]**
37. **Two from**: Maintenance of normal iron metabolism; Maintenance of normal vision; Maintenance of skin and the mucus membranes **[2]**.
38. Moulds **[1]**; Yeast **[1]**; Bacteria **[1]**
39. Roast chicken **[1]**
40. Calcium is added to white bread by law (fortified) **[1]**
41. **Method:** Roller drying **[1]**
    Details, spray drying: This method is used for some foods that are damaged by dry heats **[1]**.
    Details: Food is frozen **[1]** and the temperature is then increased to make the ice vaporise **[1]**.
42. Carbon dioxide **[1]**
43. Antioxidants protect us from pollutants in the environment **[1]**.
44. Eggs – in the door **[1]**; Mango – in the salad drawer **[1]**; Raw fish – on the bottom shelf or below the chocolate éclairs **[1]** **[the raw fish must be below the chocolate éclairs, fish in the salad drawer will not be accepted]**; Chocolate eclairs – on the first shelf or second shelf **[1]** **[must be above the raw fish]**.
45. **One of**: Sodium regulates the amount of water in the body; Sodium assists the body in the use of energy; Sodium helps to control muscles and nerves **[1]**.
46. Vitamin D **[1]**
47. **Iron, main function in the body:** Manufacture of haemoglobin in red blood cells **[1]**.
    Iron, main food sources: Red meat, especially liver **[1]**.
    Calcium, main function in the body: Strengthening of bones and teeth **[1]**.
    Calcium, main food sources: Milk and dairy products **[1]**.

Glossary

A

additive substances added to foods to extend the shelf life, or enhance the taste and appearance

aeration processes in food preparation that incorporate air to give light, open textures or assist rising

allergy condition, such as itchy skin or restricted breathing, caused by sensitivity to something in the environment or to a food

allergen a food that causes a bad chemical reaction

amino acids small molecules that form long chains in proteins

anaemia if there is a deficiency of iron in the blood, it is called anaemia; symptoms include tiredness

anaphylaxis an acute allergic reaction to a food, e.g. nuts, that can, in extreme cases, lead to death

antioxidants these help to protect cell membranes and to maintain healthy skin and eyes; vitamin E is an antioxidant

ascorbic acid another name for vitamin C

B

bacteria single-celled organisms that are able to reproduce rapidly (also called microorganisms); bacteria are sometimes useful and are used to help make food, e.g. cheese, and are sometimes harmful (pathogenic) and can cause food poisoning

barn-reared animals animals bred and housed in a large barn, rather than fully outdoors or in cages

Basal Metabolic Rate (BMR) the energy needed by the body to power your internal organs when completely at rest

baste during the cooking of meat, e.g. roasting chicken, the cooking juices in the pan such as oil/butter or a marinade are brushed on the meat, or spooned over the chicken covering the surface to add flavour and moistness

batch the quantity of food products made in one operation, e.g. scones, bread rolls

best-before date a safety date found on foods and their packaging; best-before dates usually appear on foods that have a long shelf life such as canned, dried and frozen food products

binding various ingredients, such as water, egg, flour or breadcrumbs, are used to 'bind' other ingredients together

bland when food is lacking a strong taste; can make it unappealing because it does not have a distinguishing taste or flavour

Body Mass Index (BMI) a measure that adults can use to see if they are a healthy weight for their height; the ideal healthy BMI is between 18.5 and 25

bridge hold a knife skill technique where the food being cut is secured with one hand held in the shape of a bridge, while the free hand slices beneath 'the bridge' with the knife

C

caramelisation change of colour and flavour when heating sugar or a sugar solution

carbon footprint the total amount of greenhouse gas emissions something causes – the 'something' can be an individual, a country, an event, a journey, etc.

cardiovascular anything that relates to the heart and blood vessels

chemical preservation any chemical that is added to a food product in order to extend its shelf life; chemical preservation usually inhibits the growth of bacteria

chemical raising agents food-safe chemicals that produce carbon dioxide gas, e.g. bicarbonate of soda, baking powder

chilled food food that must be stored at a temperature of below 5 °C

cholesterol a type of fat found in the blood, which is made in the liver and is also obtained from the food you eat; there is 'good'

cholesterol (called HDL, high-density lipoprotein) that helps to break down fat and 'bad' cholesterol (called LDL, low-density lipoprotein) that clogs up blood vessels

chopping to cut something up using a knife

choux a type of pastry used for eclairs, choux buns and gougères

claw grip a knife skill technique where the food being cut is secured with one hand held in the shape of a claw, while the free hand slices the food with the knife

climate change a change in global or regional temperatures caused by increased levels of carbon dioxide due to the intensive use of fossil fuels such as coal and oil

coagulate protein denaturation by heat

coating a covering of one type of food product by another, e.g. fish coated in breadcrumbs

cobalamin another name for vitamin B12

coeliac coeliac disease is caused by the body's immune system mistaking substances in gluten (a protein found in wheat, barley, rye, and also oats, which contain a similar substance to gluten), as a threat and attacking them; Coeliacs cannot absorb nutrients if they eat gluten – this causes severe pain and can lead to anaemia and malnutrition

collagen the name of the main structural protein in connective tissue

colostrum the first milk produced by a lactating mother; it is full of antibodies that are useful to the new-born baby

combining to mix ingredients together, either by hand or with a machine such as a hand mixer

composting to make a compost out of decayed plant matter that can be used to fertilise new plants

condensed a liquid such as milk that has been evaporated, has not been sterilised, and has had sugar added to it

conduction heat transfer from one molecule to another

connective tissue tissues made of fibres that form a framework in the body to bind or separate other tissues and organs

constipation when faeces become difficult to expel from the body because they are hard and small

consistency mouthfeel sensory term related to thickness and smoothness of a mixture

contamination when a food product has become impure via contact with a harmful material, e.g. bacteria

convection heat transfer by rising and falling currents in a liquid or air

core temperature the temperature at the centre of cooked food; reheated food should reach a core temperature of 75 °C

creaming beating together yellow fat and caster sugar to aerate it

crop rotation the practice of growing different crops every year in the same field – switching the type of crop grown helps to keep the soil fertile

cross-contamination transferring bacteria from one place to another

crustacean crabs, lobsters, prawns, crayfish, shrimp and squid are all crustaceans

cuisine a style or method of cooking characteristic of a particular country, region or establishment

curdling the separation of a food ingredient because of overheating or because an acidic ingredient has been added, e.g. lemon juice added to a milk

D

danger zone 5 °C–63 °C; the temperature zone that food must be kept out of because it is the zone in which bacteria will multiply and contaminate foods

dehydration the process of the removal of water

denaturation   changing protein function by heat (cooking), acids, or mechanical actions

dextrinisation   browning due to dry heat, charring food

diabetes   a medical condition caused by the inability of the pancreas to produce any, or enough, insulin to control the amount of sugar in the blood

dicing   to cut food into cubes

dietary fibre (NSP)   a type of carbohydrate; it cannot be digested to provide energy but is needed to keep the digestive system healthy (non-starch polysaccharides)

disaccharides   complex sugars that are formed when two monosaccharides join together

diverticular disease   when pouches form in the intestines that then become infected with bacteria

dried   without moisture. Dried milk is a manufactured dairy product that is made by evaporating most of the moisture from the milk.

drying   to remove most or all of the moisture from a food; usually done to extend the shelf life of the food

E

Eatwell Guide   a guide that shows the proportions in which different groups of foods are needed in order to have a well-balanced and healthy diet.

elastin   a protein found in connective tissue that functions together with collagen; elastin can recoil like a spring and is found in parts of the body that have elasticity, e.g. the skin

emulsification   mixing liquids that do not normally mix, e.g. oil and water

emulsifiers   a substance that will act as a stabiliser for emulsions, preventing liquids that do not mix from separating. Lecithin found in egg yolk is an emulsifier

energy density   the amount of energy calories (cal) or kilojoules (kJ) a food contains per gram

enriched dough   basic bread dough with the addition of sugar, butter and sometimes egg

enrobed   to cover a food stuff in a coating, e.g. breadcrumbs around fish

enzymes   biological catalysts found in all cells, usually made from protein; enzymes break down plant and animal tissues causing fruit to ripen, meat to tenderise and enzymic browning (also known as oxidation) to speed up

enzymic browning   browning of food due to enzymes in cut fruits and vegetables

essential amino acids   the eight amino acids that need to be provided in the diet for good health

Estimated Average Requirements (EARs)   tables used by nutritionists that provide guidelines to the energy needs of individuals at various stages of life

ethical   decisions or actions taken on the basis of strongly held moral beliefs or intellectual principles

evaporated   when a liquid is heated so that water is removed

F

Fair trade   an organisation dedicated to securing fair working, social and environmental conditions, sale prices and trade deals for farmers and manufacturers in developing countries

fat-soluble vitamins   these are vitamins A, D, E and K and they are stored in the body for longer periods than water-soluble vitamins

fatty acids   fat is made up of fatty acids and glycerol

field to fork   the name given to the food chain from the start of agricultural production to final consumption

filleting   a thin-bladed, flexible and very sharp knife used to fillet fish

fish farms   places where fish are commercially farmed

foam   the incorporation of a gas or air in a liquid, e.g. egg white foam

foetus   a baby still in the womb

folate (folic acid)   another name for vitamin B9

food miles   the distances food travels from its point of origin to your table

food waste   food that is wasted by not being eaten or by being discarded; food can be discarded for many reasons, e.g. during production due to contamination or in supermarkets due to the expiration of use-by dates

fortified   strengthening the nutritional content of a food by adding vitamins and minerals

free range farming   farming where the animals reared can roam freely outdoors for a portion of the day rather than being confined in a small space indoors 24 hours a day

G

gelatine   a water-soluble protein that comes from collagen and is used in food preparation; it is colourless and tasteless

gelatinisation   chemical term for thickening by starch and starchy foods

glaze   to coat a food with a substance, e.g. brushing pastry with beaten egg to give colour and shine when baked

gliadin   one of the two main components of the gluten fraction of the wheat seed (the other component is glutenin)

gluten   a protein found in wheat flour

glutenin   one of the two main components of the gluten fraction of the wheat seed (the other component is gliadin)

glycerol   part of a fat molecule

goujons   strips of chicken or fish that are deep-fried

Greenhouse Gas (GHG)   any of a number of gases that absorb solar gases that contribute to the greenhouse effect, which contributes to global warming and climate change; examples include carbon dioxide, fluorocarbons, and methane

Genetically Modified (GM)   foods that have had changes introduced into their DNA using genetic engineering; GM foods can be manipulated to emphasise certain traits or to extinguish negative characteristics

H

haemoglobin   a red protein (it gives blood its colour) that transports oxygen around the body via red blood cells

halal   meat that can be eaten by Muslims because it has been killed in accordance with Islamic law

hatcheries   buildings/pools where fish or poultry eggs are artificially controlled and then hatched

heavy dropping consistency   when a mixture drops heavily from a spoon, rather than flowing from the spoon in a liquid or sticking to it in a lump

High Biological Value (HBV)   food sources, such as animal proteins, that contain all the essential amino acids required by the body

high-risk foods   foods that have a high risk of harbouring harmful bacteria, e.g. raw meat, raw seafood, cooked rice

homogenised   milk that is forced through tiny holes in a machine; this breaks up the fat and disperses it, and it doesn't reform as a layer

hydrogenation   making solid fat from a liquid oil

hydroponics   the name given to the process of growing plants without soil but in sand, gravel or liquid with nutrients added to stimulate growth

hygiene   the practice of preventing contamination by following strict cleanliness procedures

I

intensive farming   commercial agriculture on an industrial scale designed to maximise yields and profit; this type of farming relies on heavy use of pesticides and chemical fertilisers

iron deficiency anaemia   a common condition in teenage girls who have started menstruating (the blood loss incurred by menstruation causes iron deficiency)

K

kosher food that conforms to Jewish dietary law

kwashiorkor a severe form of protein malnutrition

L

lactating the production of milk by women from the mammary glands to feed new-born babies (all mammals lactate)

lacto vegetarian a person who eats only dairy foods, no eggs, meat or fish

lactose intolerance a condition where someone is intolerant of lactose, which is a natural sugar found in milk; lactose intolerance causes stomach upset

Low Biological Value (LBV) protein from plant sources is of Low Biological Value (LBV) and lacks some essential amino acids; the exception is soy, which is a plant protein of HBV

M

Maillard reaction the browning of meat, caused by a reaction with natural sugars and proteins, which produces a dark colour; also known as non-enzymic browning

malnutrition a significant lack of proper nutrition

manufacturer a company producing large quantities of food for sale to the public

marinade a mixture created to tenderise and flavour meat, fish and alternatives

menstruation the monthly process the human female body goes through to discharge the lining of the uterus; takes place from puberty to menopause

microorganisms another name for bacteria

milling the process whereby wheat is made into a flour; wheat grains are blended with other varieties and washed to remove grit and dirt, then huge rotating rollers crush the grains at varying speeds – the crushed grain is sieved and this produces flour

mollusc oysters, mussels, scallops, winkles and cockles are all molluscs

monosaccharides the simplest form of carbohydrate structure

moulds a type of fungus that can settle on food and grow into a visible plant; a sign of food that is not fresh

multicultural foods from a variety of countries, regions and cultures

muscle fibre cells that give structure to muscles; different structures of muscle fibre indicate different types of muscle

myoglobin a protein found in most mammals that is oxygen-binding and protein-binding

N

niacin another name for Vitamin B3

non-enzymic browning browning due to caramelisation or dextrinisation, not caused by enzymes

Non–Starch Polysaccharide (NSP) the correct scientific name for dietary fibre

nutrition labelling labels that show which nutrients a food product contains

O

olfactory relating to the sense of smell

organic food that is grown or produced without using chemical fertilisers or pesticides

origin where something first comes from

osteomalacia the name of the medical condition where bones become soft due to a lack of calcium or vitamin D

osteoporosis the name of a medical condition where bones become weak, brittle and break easily

ovo-lacto vegetarian vegetarians who eat eggs and dairy products (but only cheese that has been made with vegetable rennet)

oxidation changes in food such as colour change or flavour change due to exposure to oxygen

P

packaging the items used to wrap around foodstuffs; designed to protect and preserve

palatability to make food appealing through its appearance, colour, flavour, texture and smell

palate a person's ability to be able to distinguish between, and appreciate, different flavours

paring a small knife used to prepare fruit and vegetables

pasteurised a process of part sterilisation conducted via heat treatment or irradiation; pasteurisation makes food safer to eat and lengthens its shelf life

pathogens bacteria/microorganisms that cause disease

peak bone mass when bones reach their maximum strength

pH level the level of acidity or alkalinity of a food

Physical Activity Level (PAL) the energy needed by the body for movement of all types

physical raising methods using air, steam or water vapour to lighten and raise mixtures

plasticity how fat properties change over a range of temperatures

polysaccharides polysaccharides are made up of many monosaccharide units joined together

pre-packed food that has been packed before the customer buys it

preservation the process of altering a foodstuff so that it can be kept for as long as possible, e.g. canning, pickling

primary processing the conversion of foods in their raw state into a usable food

probiotic probiotic cultures are carefully selected strains; there is good evidence that they help improve digestion, safeguard the immune system, and keep the body's intestinal flora in balance

proportions the parts of a food stuff comparative to the whole amount

protein complementation when LBV foods are eaten together to provide all the essential amino acids, e.g. beans on toast

proving the last stage of rising that bread goes through prior to baking

puberty the stage of life when adolescents mature and become capable of sexual reproduction

R

radiation heat transfer method, a type of electromagnetic radiation that involves waves, e.g. grill

rancid when food has an unpleasant, stale smell or sour taste

rating assessing something in terms of quality, quantity or a combination of both

ratio proportion of ingredients in a basic recipe

recycling re-using/converting waste materials, including food

Red Tractor a logo that tells the consumer that the food has been produced, processed and packed to Red Tractor standards; it assures standards of food hygiene and safety; equipment used in production; animal health and welfare; environmental issues and responsible use of pesticides

Reference Intake (RI) the approximate amount of a nutrient provided by a portion of food

reheating to heat something again; reheated food should reach a core temperature of 75 °C

rest when a dough is left, usually in a fridge or similar cold location, for a period of time before it is baked

riboflavin another name for vitamin B2

rickets a childhood disease caused by a lack of vitamin D; it causes softening of the bones, which results in bow legs

rolling boil when something is boiling all over the surface (both middle and sides) with great energy

rubbing-in incorporating fat into flour when making pastry

S

salting the process of adding salt to a foodstuff to remove its moisture; food-poisoning bacteria cannot survive without moisture

saturated fats come mainly from animal food products, e.g. lard, and they are solid at room temperature; saturated fats raise your cholesterol level – too much bad cholesterol can lead to health problems

seasonal the time of year when fruits and vegetables are naturally at their best or at their peak for harvest time

secondary processing the processing of primary processed products into other food products

semi-skimmed pasteurised milk that has had some of the cream removed

senses perception of a food using hearing, sight, touch, smell and taste

sensory analysis the application of sight, smell, taste, touch and hearing to evaluate test foods

sensory characteristic using the senses to evaluate characteristics of food products, e.g. aroma, texture

serrated a type of knife blade that is jagged; often used to carve joints of meat

shortcrust a type of pastry used for pies and tarts

shortening mouthfeel, such as short or crumbly, produced by short gluten strands

skimmed pasteurised milk that has had all or most of the cream removed

smoking the name given to the process of smoking a foodstuff to a temperature of 76 °C or above; this removes the moisture, extends shelf life, and imparts a distinctive flavour

spina bifida a defect of the lower spine that can result in paralysis in the legs and feet and is sometimes accompanied by learning difficulties

starter culture a mixture of flour and water that ferments with bacteria; a starter culture aids fermentation in bread making

sterilised subjecting a food to a high temperature to kill any bacteria that may be present; typically heating to between 110 °C and 135 °C takes place for 15–20 minutes

sustainable food food that will continue to be available for many years to come

T

temperature a measure of intensity of heat or cold

texture properties of a food sensed by mouthfeel

thiamin another name for vitamin B1

thyroid this is a gland at the front of your neck, just below the Adam's apple; it produces two hormones that control the body's metabolic rate

toxic contains a harmful or poisonous substance

traceability knowing the history of a foodstuff from the place of its birth/planting all the way through its manufacturing journey to the consumer

trans fats trans fats can be formed when oil goes through the process of hydrogenation to form a solid; this process occurs as the molecules flip and rotate

transportation moving items or people from one place to another using various forms of transport, e.g. plane, lorry, boat

U

Ultra-Heat Treated (UHT) the process of heating food above a temperature of 135 °C; this sterilises the food and lengthens its shelf life

unsaturated fats come from plants, e.g. olive oil, and some animals; they are liquid at room temperature

use-by date a safety date found on foods and their packaging – the food must be eaten by the date on the packaging; found on highly perishable packaged food, e.g. meat

V

vegan a person who does not eat any animal or animal products

vegetarian a person who chooses not to eat foods that involve killing animals or fish

viscosity resistance to flow; thickness of a sauce or mixture

volume the amount of liquid in a container, e.g. milk in a measuring jug

W

weevils a very small black type of beetle that can live and breed in flour

Y

yeast a biological raising agent that ferments to produce carbon dioxide

Index

Collins

WJEC Eduqas

GCSE 9-1

Food Preparation and Nutrition

Workbook

Kath Callaghan, Fiona Balding, Jacqui Keepin, Barbara Monks, Barbara Rathmill and Suzanne Gray with Louise T. Davies

Contents

Contents

1 Name **one** type of flat bread. [1]

_____

2 Explain why bread should not be stored in a refrigerator. [2]

_____

_____

3 Tick (✓) **two** nutrients provided by cereals. [2]

a) Vitamin C ☐   b) Protein (LBV) ☐

c) Vitamin D ☐   d) Vitamin E ☐

4 Bread is made using strong flour. Explain why this type of flour should be used. [4]

_____

_____

_____

_____

5 Explain what the term 'extraction rate' means and state the extraction rate for white flour. [2]

_____

_____

White flour extraction rate: _____

6 a) Oats provide energy when eaten. State the type of energy that is provided. [1]

_____

b) Explain the benefits of eating an oat-based breakfast. [3]

_____

_____

_____

Total Marks _____ / 15

1 Name **two** different types of rice. [2]

I: _____   II: _____

2 State what is removed from rice during the processing stage. [1]

_____

3 Name **two** different methods that could be used for the cooking of rice. [2]

I: _____   II: _____

4 Name **one** vitamin that is found in potatoes. [1]

_____

5 Complete the sentences below using the words in the boxes below. [4]

| staple | Edward | main | King |

One variety of potatoes grown in the UK is _____

Potatoes are regarded as a _____ food; this means they form a _____ part of many meals.

6 Explain what can happen to potatoes if they are stored in a light environment. [2]

_____

_____

7 Name **two** different types of pasta. [2]

I: _____   II: _____

8 Pasta will provide iron for the body. Name the ingredient used in the making of pasta that supplies the iron. [1]

_____

Total Marks _____ / 15

1 Tick (✓) **two** examples of citrus fruits. [2]

Strawberries ☐   Limes ☐   Plums ☐   Grapefruits ☐

2 Name **two** examples of hard fruits. [2]

I: ....   II: ....

3 **a)** State the recommended number of fruit and vegetable portions that should be eaten per day.

.... [1]

b) Explain why we should aim to eat this recommended amount on a daily basis. [2]

....

....

4 Name a mineral that is found in bananas. [1]

....

5 Complete the sentence below by filling in the missing word. [1]

Soft berry fruits like strawberries should be stored in the ....

6 Tick (✓) **two** examples of vegetables from the stems group. [2]

Peppers ☐   Asparagus ☐   Celery ☐   Broccoli ☐

7 Explain how different types of vegetables can be grown. [2]

....

....

8 Name which type of short term storage is best for fresh green vegetables and explain why the vegetables should be stored this way. [3]

Type of storage: ....

Explanation: ....

....

Total Marks .... / 16

1 Name **two** different types of fresh milk. [2]

I: _Whole_ II: _skimmed_

2 Tick (✓) the correct type of protein found in milk. [1]

High biological value (HBV) ✓   Low biological value (LBV) ☐

3 Explain the form of carbohydrate found in animal milk. [2]

Milk contains a carbohydrate known as lactose. It is a sugar.

4 Name **two** alternative milks that people with an intolerance to animal milk could use. [2]

I: _Almond_ II: _Oat_

5 Explain what happens during the processing of homogenised milk. [2]

The milk is forced through tiny holes in a machine. This breaks up the fat so that it doesn't reform as a layer.

6 Name the main mineral found in cheese. [1]

Calcium

7 a) Name **one** type of soft cheese _cream cheese_ [1]

b) Name **one** type of blue veined cheese _stilton_ [1]

8 Explain why we should not consume too much cheese on a daily basis. [3]

Cheese can have a high saturated fat content. This fat can be stored in the body & cause weight gain, cholestrol & heart problems.

9 Complete the sentence below using the words in the boxes below. [4]

| milk | culture | friendly | yoghurt |

Yoghurt is made from _milk_ which has a _friendly_ bacteria _culture_ added to it.

Total Marks ____ / 19

1 Which of these nutrients is **not** found in meat? Tick (✓) **one** answer.

a) Fat ☐   b) Vitamin B6 ☐   c) Protein ☐   d) Vitamin C ☑   [1]

2 Which meat is classed as offal? Tick (✓) **one** answer.

a) Pork ☐   b) Poultry ☐   c) Liver ☑   d) Goose ☐   [1]

3 What is meat? Complete the following sentence using the words in the boxes below.

muscle	connective tissue	fibres

Meat is a _muscle_ composed of cells consisting of

fibres, held together by _connective tissue_.   [3]

4 Name **one** part of an animal that is likely to be tougher to eat.

Thighs   [1]

5 Name **two** slow methods of cooking that are suitable for tough cuts of meat.

I: _Stewing_   II: _Braising_   [2]

6 Complete the following sentences about what happens when meat is cooked. Use the words in the boxes below.

Maillard	gelatine	coagulate	browning	sugars

The _Browning_ of meat is caused by a reaction with natural _sugars_ and

proteins to produce a dark colour. This occurrence is called the _Maillard_ reaction or

non-enzymic browning.

As the meat cooks, the proteins _coagulate_ and produce a firm texture. Collagen is

broken down into _gelatine._   [5]

Total Marks _____ / 13

1 Which of the following fish would you expect to find preserved in a can? Tick (✓) **one** answer.

a) Cod ☐   b) Plaice ☐   c) Sardine ✓   d) Halibut ☐   [1]

2 Which of the following fish is a mollusc? Tick (✓) **one** answer.

a) Oyster ✓   b) Crab ☐   c) Shrimp ☐   d) Lobster ☐   [1]

3 Name **two** terms that can be used to describe how fish can be protected when cooked in hot fat.

I: _encobed in batter_   II: _coated with breadcrumbs_   [2]

4 Complete the following statements using the words in the boxes below.

collagen	60 °C	coagulate	muscle	gelatine	connective tissue

Fish cooks quickly because the _muscle_ is short and the

connective tissue is thin.

The connective tissue is made up of _collagen_ and will change into

gelatin and _coagulate_ at

_60° C_.   [6]

5 The picture below shows a fish being filleted. Complete the table below.

	Classification of the fish shown:	What is the chef showing?
	Round fish [1]	The chef is demonstrating a round fish being filleted. The backbone is being detached from head to tail.
	One example of this type of fish: _tuna_ [1]	[2]

Total Marks _____ / 14

1 State **three** different ways of cooking eggs. [3]

I: .... II: .... III: ....

2 Name **two** different types of birds that produce eggs to be used for cooking. [2]

I: .... II: ....

3 Eggs can be used to glaze products before baking.

a) Name a product that could be glazed. .... [1]

b) Explain how the glaze changes the product. [2]

....

....

4 Explain why some people may choose to purchase free range eggs rather than enriched cage farm eggs. [4]

....

....

....

....

5 Complete the following statements using words in the boxes below. [6]

colour	nutritional	enrich	increase	yellow	flavour

Eggs can .... a bread dough. The ....

of the dough is deeper, more ....

The .... of the dough is further developed.

Eggs will .... the .... value of the dough.

6 Identify **one** detailed disadvantage of a hen's egg having a porous shell. [2]

....

....

Total Marks .... / 20

Soya, Tofu, Beans, Nuts and Seeds

1 Tick (✓) **one** food that soya beans are made into. [1]

Sugar ☐   Apples ☐   Flour ☐

2 Soya milk is used to make tofu. State the other name by which tofu is known. [1]

....

3 Complete the following statements using the words in the boxes below. [4]

alternative	tofu	meat	protein

Soya beans and .... will provide a rich source of

....(HBV).

They are regarded as an excellent .... to ....

4 Miso is made using soya beans. Explain what Miso is and why it is used. [2]

....

....

....

5 Name **two** different types of beans. [2]

I: ....   II: ....

6 Explain why beans would be a good food for a vegetarian to consume. [3]

....

....

....

7 Almonds are one variety of nuts. Name **two** others. [2]

I: ....   II: ....

8 Suggest **two** different uses for nuts. [2]

I: ....

II: ....

9 State the name of a seed that is used to make oil. [1]

....

Total Marks .... / 18

1 Fill in the missing word to complete the sentence below. [1]

Butter is classed as a .... product.

2 Give one reason why the amount of butter we eat should be monitored. [1]

....

3 Tick (✓) the statement that identifies what can happen to butter if not covered when stored. [1]

It ferments ☐   It coagulates ☐   It goes rancid ☐   It gelatinises ☐

4 Explain how butter is made. [3]

....

....

....

5 Give the name of a nut that can be used to make oil. [1]

....

6 Tick (✓) the **two** vitamins that have to be added to margarine. [2]

Vitamin A ☐   Vitamin B ☐   Vitamin C ☐   Vitamin D ☐

7 When using the creaming method for cake making, describe the function of sugar. [2]

....

....

8 Explain why we are advised to reduce our intake of sugars and sugary foods. [3]

....

....

....

9 Name **two** types of sweet syrup. [2]

I: ....   II: ....

Total Marks .... / 16

Protein and Fat

1 Fill in the missing words.

The body needs protein for g.., maintenance and r... [2]

2 Give **two** different protein foods suitable for a lacto-vegetarian.

I: .... II: .... [2]

3 Give **three** examples of protein foods that have a High Biological Value (HBV).

I: .... II: .... III: .... [3]

4 Underline the food that is a good example of protein complementation.

Jam sandwich   **Lentil soup and bread**   **Tomato and basil salad**   **Sausage roll** [1]

5 What is the name of the protein deficiency disease? Tick (✓) **one** answer.

a) Beri-beri ☐   **b)** Scurvy ☐   **c)** Kwashiorkor ☐   **d)** Dermatitis ☐ [1]

6 Give **one** example of a fat in liquid form.

.... [1]

7 Which of the following are functions of fat in the diet? Underline **two** answers.

Provides concentrated energy   **Strengthens teeth**

Makes red blood cells   **Provides body with vitamins A, D, E and K**

Promotes growth [2]

8 Which **two** components is fat made up of?

I: .... II: .... [2]

9 What is hydrogenation?

....

.... [1]

Total Marks .... / 15

1 Name the **three** different types of carbohydrates.

I: .... II: ....

III: .... [3]

2 Give an example of a monosaccharide.

.... [1]

3 Fill in the missing words.

Sugars are d .... very quickly in the body, providing instant e .... [2]

4 Most people in the UK do not eat enough dietary fibre. Suggest a similar food that is higher in dietary fibre to replace each of those listed below.

a) White bread ....

b) Cornflakes ....

c) Mashed potato .... [3]

5 Sugar, sweets and sugary drinks are associated with which type of decay in the body?

.... [1]

6 What would be the results of not eating enough carbohydrate?

....

.... [2]

7 Fill in the missing words using the words in the boxes below.

| sugars | starches | fast | energy | slow |

.... have to be digested into .... before

absorption – this is .... release. [4]

8 What is the name of the common medical condition frequently caused by a lack of dietary fibre (NSP) in the diet?

.... [1]

1 Name **two** dietary sources of vitamin A.

I: _____ II: _____ [2]

2 The B group vitamins and vitamin C (ascorbic acid) belong to which vitamin group?

_____ [1]

3 What is rickets and what vitamin deficiency is it associated with?

_____

_____ [2]

4 A deficiency of vitamin B2 Riboflavin can cause what deficiency symptoms? <u>Underline</u> **one** answer.

Broken and split nails   Sore throat   Vomiting   Skin cracking around the mouth . [1]

5 One of the functions of vitamin C (ascorbic acid) is to act as an antioxidant. What do antioxidants do?

_____ [1]

6 What is cholecalciferol?

_____

_____ [2]

7 Which vitamin deficiency can cause night blindness? Tick (✓) **one** answer.

a) Vitamin K ☐

b) Vitamin A ☐

c) Vitamin D ☐

d) Vitamin B1 ☐   [1]

Total Marks _____ / 10

Minerals and Water

1 Which vitamin helps the body to absorb calcium? Tick (✓) **one** answer.

a) Vitamin A ☐   **b)** Vitamin C ☐

c) Vitamin K ☐   **d)** Vitamin D ☐   [1]

2 Give **one** reason why calcium is needed in the body.

.... [1]

3 Name a condition that an excess of sodium (salt) in the diet is linked to.

.... [1]

4 What is salt mainly used for in food preparation?

.... [1]

5 Fill in the missing words.

A lack of iron in the diet can cause iron-deficiency a... and symptoms include

t.. .   [2]

6 What is the daily recommended intake of water?

.... [1]

7 What is the function of fluoride in the diet?

....

.... [1]

8 Iodine supports the correct functioning of which gland in the body? Tick (✓) **one** answer.

a) Thyroid ☐   **b)** Pituitary ☐

c) Saliva ☐   **d)** Adrenal ☐   [1]

Total Marks .... / 9

1 Name the **five** sections of the Eatwell Guide.

I: ....

II: ....

III: ....

IV: ....

V: .... [5]

2 Fill in the missing words.

H.. m... provides babies with all their nutritional

requirements, except for i.. . Babies are born with a supply of this stored in

their l.. . [3]

3 What is colostrum?

.... [1]

4 During pregnancy, why is a good supply of folate (folic acid) required?

....

.... [2]

5 Why are older people advised to eat lots of calcium-rich foods? Tick (✓) **one** answer.

a) To help prevent dementia ☐   b) To keep them hydrated ☐

c) To help strengthen bones ☐   d) To give them a better appetite ☐ [1]

6 Fill in the missing words.

The E.. G... shows the proportions of food groups that

should be eaten daily for a w...-b............................... diet. [2]

7 What would you advise a pregnant woman who is suffering from constipation to do?

....

.... [2]

Total Marks .... / 16

Diet, Nutrition and Health

1 Fill in the missing words.

C............................... H............................... D............................... is linked to diets high

in s............................... fats, which make c............................... in

the blood.

[3]

2 Tick (✓) **one** answer. Symptoms of iron deficiency anaemia include:

a) blurred vision and cataracts. ☐   **b)** sickness and diarrhoea. ☐

c) tiredness, weakness and lack of energy. ☐   **d)** a sore throat. ☐   [1]

3 Fruit and vegetables form part of a balanced diet. How many portions of fruit and vegetables are we advised to eat every day?

.... [1]

4 List **three** different health problems that may be linked to a high consumption of fat in the diet.

I: ....

II: ....

III: ....   [3]

5 Circle the correct option from the words in bold.

In Type 2 diabetes, too little or no **insulin/NSP** is produced, resulting in high levels of

salt/sugar in the **bones/blood**.   [3]

6 What is osteoporosis? Tick (✓) **one** answer.

a) Stiff neck ☐   **b)** When bones become weak and break easily ☐

c) Weak connective tissues ☐   **d)** Persistent nose bleeds ☐   [1]

7 An individual's BMR depends on **three** things. What are these three things?

I: ....   II: ....   III: ....   [3]

Total Marks .... / 15

Food Choices

1 Tick (✓) the boxes below to show if each statement is **True** or **False**.

Statement	True	False
Vegetarians eat fish.		
Buddhists eat pork.		
Sikhs don't eat beef.		

[3]

2 Which part of the body produces insulin? Tick (✓) **one** answer.

a) Stomach ☐   **b)** Liver ☐   **c)** Pancreas ☐   **d)** Spleen ☐   [1]

3 Coeliac disease is caused by the body's immune system reacting to:

a) sucrose. ☐   **b)** thiamin. ☐   **c)** gluten. ☐   **d)** collagen. ☐   [1]

4 State **three** reasons why a person may be a vegetarian.

I: ....

II: ....

III: .... [3]

5 Explain the difference between a lacto-vegetarian and a vegan in terms of the foods that each does not eat. Explain why the diets differ.

a) Lacto-vegetarian diet

....

....

....

.... [3]

b) Vegan diet

....

....

....

.... [3]

Total Marks .... / 14

1 What does heat transfer in liquids and in air cause? Tick (✓) **one** answer.

a) Halogen currents ☐

b) Conduction currents ☐

c) Convection currents ☐

d) Induction currents ☐ [1]

2 What is cooking?

....

....

.... [3]

3 Cooking methods can change the nutritional value of a food. Fill in the blanks to complete the chart.

Cooking Method	Change to Nutritional Content	Example
Dry method	....	Grilling sausages
Water-based (moist) method	....	....

[3]

4 This question is about selecting appropriate cooking methods. Use the words in the boxes below to complete the sentences correctly.

| moist | | hot | | conserve | | sensory | | add | | tough | | quick |

Cooking methods can alter the .... properties of food by adding crispness or softening.

The right cooking methods can .... vitamins, or .... energy value.

When meat needs cooking, long, slow .... cooking is best for

.... cuts of meat.

If the meat is tender a .... and .... method of cooking such as grilling can be used. [7]

Total Marks .... / 14

1 Tick (✓) **one** answer. The main function of eggs in a quiche tart is:

a) to aerate the filling. ☐

b) to add flavour. ☐

c) to set the filling. ☐

d) to reduce the number of calories. ☐ [1]

2 Food preparation before cooking, for example marinating, is a requirement of some recipes.

a) What is a marinade?

....

....

.... [3]

b) Explain why a marinade is used in cooking.

....

....

....

.... [3]

c) What might be the advantages of using a marinade for chicken kebabs?

....

....

....

.... [4]

d) Name **two** quick cooking methods that could be used to cook chicken kebabs.

I: .... II: .... [2]

3 Gluten is a protein found in wheat. Which statements about gluten are **true** and which are **false**? Circle **one** answer for each of the parts **a)–d)**.

a) Gluten makes dough stretchy and elastic. **True/False** [1]

b) Gluten forms the structure of a baked loaf of bread. **True/False** [1]

c) Salt causes gluten to be weakened. **True/False** [1]

d) Gluten helps pasta hold its shape when cooked. **True/False** [1]

Total Marks .... / 17

1 Which one of the following is **not** a sauce making method? Tick (✓) **one** answer.

a) Creaming method ☐   b) All-in-one method ☐

c) Roux method ☐   d) Blending method ☐   [1]

2 Carbohydrates are useful functional ingredients. Which of the following is **not** a function of carbohydrate? Tick (✓) **one** answer.

a) Caramelisation ☐   b) Coagulation ☐

c) Dextrinisation ☐   d) Gelatinisation ☐   [1]

3 A café needs to make macaroni cheese for lunch service. The chef uses the ingredients listed below. Give **one** main function of each of these ingredients in the macaroni cheese.

semi-skimmed milk ....

wheat flour ....

margarine ....

seasoning ....

Red Leicester cheese ....

macaroni .... [6]

4 Describe six stages of making macaroni cheese.

1 ....

2 ....

3 ....

4 ....

5 ....

6 .... [6]

5 How does the cheese sauce become thick and smooth?

....

....

....

.... [5]

Total Marks .... / 19

Fats and Oils

1 Tick (✓) **one** answer. The main function of fat in pastry is:

a) to combine other ingredients. ☐   b) to shorten the texture. ☐

c) to spread easily. ☐   d) to add bulk to the mix. ☐   [1]

2 This question is about understanding emulsified sauces.

> **Basic recipe for Hollandaise sauce:**
>
> 250 ml white wine vinegar
>
> 2 egg yolks
>
> 100 g melted butter
>
> Seasoning

a) Which **two** ingredients would not mix easily?

_____ [2]

b) What is the function of the seasoning? What might the seasoning be?

_____

_____ [2]

c) Explain the function of the egg yolk in the sauce.

_____

_____

_____ [3]

3 This question is about the function of ingredients in pastry made with half fat to flour.

Choose the correct words from the boxes to complete the following sentences.

| steam | dextrinisation | gluten | binds | shorten |

a) Water _____ the ingredients together.   [1]

b) When pastry is cooked _____ of starch gives colour.   [1]

c) Fat is used to _____ pastry.   [1]

d) Water creates _____ to help pastry rise.   [1]

e) Rubbing in fat stops the development of long strands of _____.   [1]

Total Marks _____ / 13

1 Why is water an effective raising agent? Tick (✓) **one** answer.

a) It turns to steam. ☐   b) It does not add calories. ☐

c) It makes mixtures runny. ☐   d) It makes mixtures moist. ☐   [1]

2 Fill in the table by naming **two** chemical raising agents and giving an example of their use in food preparation.

Names of Chemical Raising Agent	Example of Use
.... [1]	.... [1]
.... [1]	.... [1]

3 Name the gas produced by chemical raising agents.

.... [1]

4 This question is about the function of ingredients in choux pastry.

a) When making choux paste, state **two** ingredients that help the pastry rise and puff.

I: ....   II: ....   [2]

b) Explain how these ingredients work during baking.

....

....

.... [3]

c) Why is it important to fully cook small choux buns, e.g. profiteroles?

....

....

.... [3]

5 Tick (✓) the correct answer. Raising agents can be classified as:

a) biological, microbial and physical. ☐   b) chemical, enzymic and biological. ☐

c) physical, globular and pathogenic. ☐   d) chemical, physical and biological. ☐   [1]

Total Marks .... / 15

1 Identify the conditions that food spoilage organisms need to grow.

_____

_____

_____ [6]

2 What are three different signs of food spoilage?

_____

_____

_____ [3]

3 Suggest **two** ways to store dry food such as flour in order to prevent it from spoiling.

I: _____

_____

II: _____

_____ [2]

4 Circle the correct option in each of the following sentences.

a) Moulds grow into a(n) **visible** / **invisible** plant. [1]

b) Moulds like **alkali** / **acid** conditions. [1]

c) Moulds are destroyed at temperatures above **50 °C** / **70 °C**. [1]

d) Moulds **can** / **can't** survive in the refrigerator. [1]

e) Moulds **can** / **can't** survive in a freezer. [1]

5 Tick (✓) **one** answer. Bacteria grow best at a pH level of: [1]

a) between 1.6 and 4.5 ☐

b) between 6.6 and 7.5 ☐

c) between 3.5 and 8.5 ☐

d) between 8 and 9 ☐ [1]

Total Marks _____ / 18

1 Choose the correct words from the options given below to complete the text that follows.

probiotic	harmful	digestion	single	rapidly

cheese	food poisoning

Bacteria are _____ – celled organisms that are able to reproduce

_____. Some are _____ and cause _____

_____ or even death. Some bacteria are harmless and are used in

_____ making. _____ bacteria help _____. **[7]**

2 The process of fermentation is used in the production of which food product? Tick (✓) **one** answer.

a) Bread ☐   **b)** Cheese ☐

c) Yoghurt ☐   **d)** Biscuits ☐   **[1]**

3 Tick (✓) **one** answer. When producing blue cheese, it is treated with:

a) a starter culture. ☐

b) bacteria. ☐

c) mould. ☐

d) brine. ☐   **[1]**

4 Explain how yeast makes bread rise.

_____

_____

_____

_____

_____

_____

_____   **[3]**

Total Marks _____ / 12

Bacterial Contamination

1. Complete this table relating to food poisoning.

Name of Bacteria	One Food Source	One Way to Prevent Food Poisoning
a) Salmonella	.... [1]	.... [1]
b) Campylobacter	.... [1]	.... [1]
c) Bacillus Cereus	.... [1]	.... [1]

2. Name **one** symptom of food poisoning.

.... [1]

3. State **two** conditions that bacteria need in order to reproduce.

I: ....

II: .... [2]

Total Marks .... / 9

Buying and Storing Food

1 Sally's mother often shops for food during her lunch break.

Describe how she can ensure her food shopping remains at a safe temperature and in good condition until she gets home.

_____

_____

_____

_____

_____

_____

_____

[6]

2 Explain the food hygiene rules that should be followed when storing, preparing and cooking meat.

_____

_____

_____

_____

_____

_____

_____

_____

[6]

Total Marks _____ / 12

1 Explain how to reduce the risk of food poisoning when preparing, cooking and storing food in the home.

....

....

....

....

....

....

....

.... [6]

2 State **four** food hygiene rules to be followed when preparing and cooking high-risk foods.

I: ....

II: ....

III: ....

IV: .... [4]

3 List the hygiene and safety rules you would follow when preparing and cooking food.

....

....

....

....

....

....

....

.... [8]

Total Marks .... / 18

Food Preservation

1 Name the **four** main types of food preservation.

I: .... II: ....

III: .... IV: .... [4]

2 You have been growing your own fruit and have a large crop of apples. How can you preserve them? Explain your method, and the shelf life of your chosen method.

Method ....

Shelf life ....

....

.... [2]

3 What is the main advantage of low-temperature storage when considering the nutritional value of food?

.... [1]

4 Often meats or fish are 'smoked'. What does this mean?

....

.... [2]

5 Years ago, before electricity, there were no fridges and freezers, so how did people preserve the produce from gardens to last through the seasons?

....

....

....

.... [4]

6 Roll mops are a traditional fish dish. What method of preservation do they use?

.... [1]

7 How is bacon preserved?

.... [2]

Total Marks .... / 16

Food Provenance and Production Methods

1 Why is traceability important?

_____

_____

_____

_____

_____ [4]

2 Explain the differences between the hens that lay battery, free range, barn and organic eggs.

Battery _____

_____ [2]

Free-range _____

_____ [2]

Barn _____

_____ [2]

Organic _____

_____ [2]

3 What concerns are there about GM (Genetically Modified) food production? Tick (✓) the correct answers.

a) It is more expensive. ☐

b) There is a possibility of new strains of microorganisms developing. ☐

c) It is altering and playing with nature. ☐

d) It is less resistant to plant disease. ☐

e) It is not monitored. ☐ [2]

Total Marks _____ / 14

1 Choose the correct words from the boxes below to complete the following sentences.

| transport | process | dispose | energy | carbon footprint | carbon dioxide |

At each stage of a product's lifecycle .... is needed to

...., ... and .... of the product;

.... is produced as a by-product of energy use. The .... is

the calculation of the carbon dioxide produced throughout a product's life. [6]

2 Choose the correct words from the boxes below to complete the following sentences.

| livestock | soil erosion | pasture | wasteland | plantations | deforestation |

.... occurs when trees are cut down. Cleared land is used as

.... for .... and .... of commodities

and settlements. Deforested regions typically suffer .... and frequently

degrade into .... [6]

3 When you throw away food, you waste not only the food but also the resources, such as energy, fuel and water, that went into growing, harvesting, transporting and storing the food. Discarded food then goes on to produce methane in landfill sites. Explain what every person can do to prevent this food waste.

....

....

....

....

....

....

....

[6]

4 Name **two** dishes that make use of leftover food.

I: ....   II: ....   [2]

Total Marks .... / 20

Food Provenance: Sustainability of Food

1 If large areas of rainforest are cut down, which gas will build up?

.... [1]

2 Write about **three** different things that can be done to tackle the sustainability of a food source.

I: ....

II: ....

III: .... [3]

3

a) What does this logo mean?

....

.... [2]

b) Give **two** examples of foods that could display this logo.

.... [1]

4 What are the advantages of buying a pack of chicken that displays the Red Tractor logo?

....

....

....

....

....

....

.... [8]

5 Beef burgers are a very popular takeaway food and use beef, which means that more cattle are reared to supply the fast food industry. Explain what effect this demand for beef supply is having on our climate.

....

....

.... [2]

Total Marks .... / 17

1 Tick (✓) **one** answer. 'Cuisine' relates to:

a) the way in which food is cooked in a kitchen. ☐

b) the range of dishes and foods of a particular country or region. ☐

c) the information listed on a food label. ☐

[1]

2 Which of the following is the name of a British cheese? Circle **one** answer.

Gouda   **Wensleydale**   **Brie**   [1]

3 Traditional dishes and foods are important in any society as they originate from the foods grown in that country or region, the local climate and local traditions.

Write the foods in the boxes below next to the correct countries in the table.

| tortilla | Cornish pasty | dhal | minestrone | bouillabaisse | hot pot |

| focaccia | Peking duck | paella | Quiche Lorraine | chow mein | pakora |

Country	Dishes	
a) England		[2]
b) France		[2]
c) Spain		[2]
d) China		[2]
e) India		[2]
f) Italy		[2]

4 Select the cuisine of a country you have studied and complete the table below.

Country Name	Cuisine		
Three main meal dishes	[1]	[1]	[1]
Three vegetables found in recipes	[1]	[1]	[1]

Total Marks _____ / 20

Food Manufacturing

1 Name two examples of primary foods. [2]

I: .... II: ....

2 Complete the following statements using the words in the boxes below. [5]

| ingredient | primary | change | food | secondary |

.... processing is when you .... or

adapt a .... food into an .... to make

a new .... product.

3 Name two different secondary products that could be made from milk. [2]

I: .... II: ....

4 'Natural' is one of the three groups of additives. Name the other **two**. [2]

I: .... II: ....

5 List **two** advantages of adding preservatives to foods during processing. [2]

Advantage I: ....

Advantage II: ....

6 Give **two** reasons why food manufacturers add flavour intensifiers to food products. [2]

Reason I: ....

Reason II: ....

7 Explain why some people may refuse to buy food products that contain additives. [4]

....

....

....

Total Marks .... / 19

1 Which of the following words is another name for aroma? (Circle) the correct answer.

feel   smell   touch   taste

[1]

2 How many samples of food would be needed to carry out a 'paired preference test'?
Tick (✓) **one** answer.

a) Two ☐

b) Three ☐

c) Four ☐

d) Five ☐

[1]

3 a) Describe how to set up a tasting area to trial your practical work in the food room.

_____

_____

_____

_____

_____

_____

_____

[6]

b) What do you understand by a triangle test?

_____

_____

_____

_____

[4]

c) Give **one** example of how you could carry out triangle testing when developing healthier recipes using minced beef.

Name of product: _____ [1]

Samples to trial: _____

_____ [2]

Total Marks _____ / 15

1 In which of these months are British strawberries at their best and in season? Tick (✓) **one** answer.

a) May/June ☐   b) June/July ☐

c) July/August ☐   d) August/September ☐   [1]

2 Tick (✓) **one** answer. The best strategy to eat a healthy and varied diet is to:

a) buy what is on offer. ☐

b) make a shopping list. ☐

c) plan a shopping diary, make a shopping list, and keep to it. ☐

d) eat lots of fruit and vegetables. ☐   [1]

3 a) Explain the benefits for young people of being active for at least 60 minutes every day.

....

....

....

....   [4]

b) To maintain a healthy weight, what eating model does the UK Government suggest that people use?

....   [1]

c) What factors will make a meal more enjoyable to eat?

....

....

....   [3]

d) Explain **four** factors that affect the eating patterns within a household.

....

....

....

....

....   [4]

Total Marks .... / 14

1 Which food label indicates that the food should no longer be offered for sale in a shop? Tick (✓) **one** answer.

a) Use by ☐

b) Display until ☐

c) Sell by ☐

d) Best before ☐

[1]

2 Which of the following foods is **not** classed as an allergen? Tick (✓) **one** answer.

a) Mustard ☐

b) Pumpkin seeds ☐

c) Celery ☐

d) Peanuts ☐

[1]

3 a) What does RI stand for?

.... [1]

b) Legally, the name of the product must be printed on food packaging. Explain six other items of information that also must be given by law.

....

....

....

....

....

.... [6]

4 Which of the following items does **not** need to be included on a nutrition label on pre-packed foods? Tick (✓) **one** answer.

a) Protein ☐

b) Carbohydrate ☐

c) Salt ☐

d) Sugars ☐

[1]

Total Marks .... / 10

Knife Skills

1 Which type of knife is shown in the picture? Tick (✓) **one** answer.

a) Paring knife ☐   b) Cook's knife ☐

c) Filleting knife ☐   d) Palette knife ☐   [1]

2 When boning a chicken, what colour board should you use? Tick (✓) **one** answer.

a) Blue ☐   b) Red ☐

c) Green ☐   d) Brown ☐   [1]

3 A chef or professional cook has their own set of knives that are really the 'tools of the trade' and they learn to use them and look after them when training.

Name and describe the **two** main methods of cutting that are the basis of a cook's knife handling skills.   [4]

	Knife Hold: ....
	Explanation: ....
	Knife Hold: ....
	Explanation: ....

4 Explain **four** safety rules to observe when working with knives in the kitchen.

I: ....

II: ....

III: ....

IV: .... [4]

Total Marks .... / 10

Prepare, Combine and Shape

1 Which glaze would be most suitable for a batch of Chelsea buns? Tick (✓) **one** answer.

a) Egg wash ☐   b) Arrowroot ☐

c) Sugar and water ☐   d) Egg yolk ☐   [1]

2 What type of binding agent is generally used in a sausage mixture? Tick (✓) **one** answer.

a) Breadcrumbs ☐   b) Flour ☐

c) Egg ☐   d) Water ☐   [1]

3 In baking, what is the difference between stirring and whisking?

....

....

.... [2]

4 In baking, what are the advantages of using cutters and a rolling pin when making a batch of biscuits?

....

.... [2]

5 Explain which mixing and shaping skills can be used when making a decorated Victoria sandwich cake to give a quality finish.

....

....

....

....

....

.... [8]

6 How would you make sure that a batch of burgers are all exactly the same size and shape?

....

.... [2]

Total Marks .... / 16

Dough

1. What is gluten? Tick (✓) **one** answer.

   a) A leavening agent ☐

   b) A sweetener ☐

   c) A protein found in flour ☐

   d) A muscle ☐ [1]

2. What is enriched dough? Tick (✓) **one** answer.

   a) A dough that contains organic ingredients. ☐

   b) A dough that has additional sugar and butter added. ☐

   c) A dough that has extra ingredients added, such as herbs or cheese. ☐

   d) A dough that contains expensive ingredients. ☐ [1]

3. What is the name of the method used to make shortcrust pastry?

   .... [1]

4. What is the function of water in a shortcrust pastry?

   .... [1]

5. Use the words in the boxes to complete the stages in the choux pastry method.

   | cool | accurately | rolling boil | heavy dropping |

   | fat | flour | water | paste |

   Weigh all the ingredients ....

   Place .... and .... in a pan and bring

   to a ....

   Add sieved .... immediately and mix well to form a

   ....

   .... then add beaten eggs gradually to a

   .... consistency. Cook in a hot oven. [8]

6. What are the names of the **two** proteins found in strong plain flour used in making bread?

   I: ....   II: .... [2]

   Total Marks .... / 14

Collins

GCSE
FOOD PREPARATION
and NUTRITION

Practice Exam Paper 1

COMPONENT 1
PRINCIPLES OF FOOD PREPARATION AND NUTRITION

1 HOUR 45 MINUTES

INSTRUCTIONS TO CANDIDATES

Answer ALL the questions.

Write your answers in the spaces provided.

Use black ink or black ball-point pen.

Do not use gel pen or pencil.

Do not use corrector fluid.

INFORMATION FOR CANDIDATES

The number of marks is given in brackets at the end of each question or part-question. You are advised to divide your time according to the marks available.

The total number of marks available is 100.

Section A Visual Stimuli

Using Shortcrust Pastry

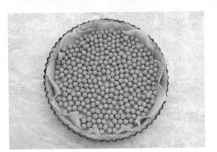

Answer all questions

1 **a)** Tick (✓) the box next to each statement to show if it is **True** or **False**. [3]

Shortcrust Pastry	True	False
(i) Wholemeal flour can be used when making shortcrust pastry.		
(ii) Melted fat is combined with the flour.		
(iii) The shortcrust pastry must be kneaded for 5 minutes after a dough has been formed.		

b) List two rules for making shortcrust pastry. [2]

(i) ....

....

(ii) ....

....

c) List two important steps to complete when rolling out shortcrust pastry and lining a flan dish. Explain why the steps are important. [4]

Step 1: ....

Explanation: ....

....

Step 2: ....

Explanation: ....

....

d) Greaseproof paper and baking beans are put into the pastry case before blind baking. Explain why this stage is important. [2]

....

....

....

e) Explain the scientific changes that take place when baking shortcrust pastry in the oven. [4]

....

....

....

....

....

....

....

Section B

Answer all questions

2 The table below shows some nutritional information for eggs, which have been cooked using two different methods.

Nutritional information	Boiled egg	Fried egg
Energy	147 kcal	232 kcal
Protein	12.3g	14.1g
Fat	10.9g	19.5g
Carbohydrates	0g	0g
Calcium	52mg	64mg
Iron	2.0mg	2.5mg

a) Identify the egg with the highest calcium value. [1]

b) Explain why the fried egg has a higher fat value when compared to the boiled egg. [2]

c) Suggest an alternative, healthier method of cooking eggs instead of frying. [1]

d) Food poisoning is caused by bacteria multiplying in or on food. Name the bacteria associated with raw eggs and state two symptoms of this type of food poisoning. [3]

e) List two ways of preventing contamination in the kitchen. [2]

(i): ....

(ii): ....

f) Explain why it is important to use colour-coded equipment when handling and preparing different foods. [3]

....

....

....

....

3 **a)** One of the most common medical procedures for primary school children is dental extraction.

Dentists are increasingly concerned that this problem is growing.

Explain in detail how sugar can cause tooth decay and suggest how children's sugar consumption can be reduced. [8]

....

....

....

....

....

....

....

....

....

....

....

....

b) Name two other diseases that can be caused by a high intake of sugar. Discuss how too much sugar causes these diseases. [6]

....

....

....

....

....

....

....

4 **a)** The table below shows two dishes that use flour as an ingredient. For each dish give one function of the flour and one description of the function. [6]

Name of Dish	Function	Description
Choux pastry		
Bread		

b) Fresh milk is processed into several different types of milk. Name **two** different types and explain how they are different from each other. [4]

c) Secondary processing of milk produces a whole variety of milk based products. Give an example of a milk based product and describe how it is made. [3]

Practice Exam Paper 1

5 a) The table below shows some problems seen when food is prepared. Complete the table to show **two** different causes of each problem. [4]

Problem	Causes
Victoria sandwich not rising	Cause 1
	Cause 2
Lumpy cheese sauce	Cause 1
	Cause 2

b) The following recipe is for a pastry based savoury flan.

Pastry case	Filling
150g plain flour	100ml full fat milk
75g butter	100ml double cream
½ teaspoon salt	2 large eggs
6 teaspoons cold water	75g full fat cheddar cheese
	1 large thinly sliced fried onion

(i) Suggest two ways in which the recipe could be adapted to reduce the fat content.   [2]

I:...

II:..

(ii) Suggest one modification that could be made to the recipe to increase the dietary fibre content.

....   [1]

(iii) The filling of the savoury flan contains eggs and cheese. Explain in detail the function of each ingredient. [6]

....

....

....

....

....

....

....

6 **a)** **(i)** Carbohydrates are a macronutrient; they provide the body with energy. Name an alternative macronutrient that could provide the body with energy. [1]

....

(ii) Carbohydrates are classified into three groups according to their structure. Monosaccharides, which are simple sugars and include glucose, are an example of one of them.

State the names of the other two groups; give a definition of each one and include an example. [8]

....

....

....

....

....

....

7. The local health centre is producing a leaflet to give to teenagers to encourage them to eat well and have a healthy lifestyle. Discuss the information that the health centre should include in the leaflet. [12]

8 **a)** There are two main groups of vitamins. State the name of each group. [2]

....

....

b) Vitamins can be lost or destroyed during the preparing and cooking of fresh vegetables such as cabbage. Explain what steps you could take to avoid vitamin loss. [10]

....

....

....

....

....

....

....

....

....

....

....

....

....

....

....

....

....

....

Practice Exam Paper 1

BLANK PAGE

Name: ....

Collins

GCSE
FOOD PREPARATION and NUTRITION

Practice Exam Paper 2

COMPONENT 1
PRINCIPLES OF FOOD PREPARATION AND NUTRITION

1 HOUR 45 MINUTES

INSTRUCTIONS TO CANDIDATES

Answer ALL the questions.

Write your answers in the spaces provided.

Use black ink or black ball-point pen.

Do not use gel pen or pencil.

Do not use corrector fluid.

INFORMATION FOR CANDIDATES

The number of marks is given in brackets at the end of each question or part-question.
You are advised to divide your time according to the marks available.

The total number of marks available is 100.

Section A Visual Stimuli

Making a Bread Dough

 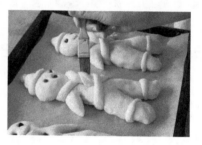

Answer all questions

1 **a)** Tick (✓) the box next to each statement to show if it is **True** or **False**. [3]

Making a bread dough		True	False
(i)	Salt is not required when making bread dough.		
(ii)	Strong flour is used to make bread as it has a higher protein content.		
(iii)	Tapping bread to see if it sounds hollow can tell you if bread is cooked.		

b) Give two reasons for glazing the bread dough before baking. [2]

(i) ....

....

(ii) ....

....

c) Name one method of heat transference that occurs during the baking of the bread and explain how the heat is transferred. [2]

....

....

....

d) Bread making includes many different stages. Describe the two bread making stages named below and explain the importance of them. [8]

Kneading: ....

....

....

....

....

....

Proving: ....

....

....

....

....

....

....

Section B

Answer all questions

2 The table below shows some nutritional information for two different types of burgers: raw beef burger and frozen chicken quarter pounder in a prefried rice coating.

Nutritional information	Raw beef burger	Frozen chicken quarter pounder in a prefried rice coating
Energy	206 kcal	326 kcal
Protein	21.5g	14.0g
Fat	11.7g	21.0g
Saturates	5.0g	2.1g
Carbohydrates	3.9g	20.0g
Sugars	0.4g	0.5g
Salt	0.8g	1.1g

a) Identify the burger with the highest salt value. [1]

....

b) Give one reason why the frozen chicken quarter pounder has a higher carbohydrate value when compared to the raw beef burger. [1]

....

....

c) During the making of the raw beef burgers they would be shaped and then stored in a refrigerator. Identify two safety points that should be followed to ensure the burgers are stored correctly. [2]

....

....

....

....

d) The information provided on the packaging of the raw beef burgers recommends frying as a cooking method. Suggest an alternative healthier method of cooking the burgers and explain why it would be healthier. [4]

....

....

....

....

e) When cooking the raw beef burgers, many changes would take place. Describe the changes that would occur as a result of cooking the meat. [6]

....

....

....

....

....

....

....

....

3 **a)** Describe and explain three functions of fat in the body. [6]

....

....

....

....

....

....

b) Sam is a teenager. He has a fried breakfast every day: two economy sausages, streaky bacon rashers, fried egg and fried wholemeal bread with a hot chocolate drink made with whole milk.

Explain how the macronutrient content of the breakfast provides Sam with energy. [6]

....

....

....

....

....

....

....

....

....

....

....

....

4 **a)** Fats and oils have different chemical compositions.

Describe the different make-up of the following types of fat, giving two examples of each type. [8]

Saturated:

....

....

....

....

....

....

Unsaturated:

....

....

....

....

....

....

b) In the UK, diets high in saturated fats are directly linked to several serious health problems.

Assess the various factors that contribute to high fat intake and explain how high fat diets in childhood and teenage years may put future health at risk. [12]

5 **a)** The information below shows a recipe for shortbread.

150 g plain flour
Grated lemon zest
100 g butter
Ground cinnamon
50 g caster sugar

Explain why this recipe is not suitable for a coeliac. [2]

....

....

b) Explain why this recipe is not suitable for someone who needs to reduce saturates in their diet. [2]

....

....

c) Explain the changes that occur during baking the shortbread. [3]

....

....

....

6 **a)** Farmers' markets are very popular these days. Discuss the advantages of buying
from farmers' markets. [6]

....

....

....

....

....

....

....

....

b) Many farmers' markets sell fresh farm eggs, but these can be laid by hens in a variety of housing conditions. Describe three different ways of egg farming. [6]

....

....

....

....

....

....

....

c) How can you ensure you are buying a quality product when buying fresh eggs? [2]

....

....

....

7 **a)** Some groups of people have a higher need for protein. Name two different groups of people who have a higher need for protein and explain why. [4]

....

....

....

....

b) Different protein foods 'complement' each other. Explain why it can be beneficial to include a mixture of protein foods in the diet. [6]

....

....

....

....

....

....

....

....

....

....

....

....

....

....

....

....

8 It is widely recognised that for a healthy balanced diet fish should be included. The Eatwell Guide suggests two portions of sustainably sourced fish per week, one of which is oily fish. Explain why we should include more fish in our diet. [8]

Answers

Page 148: Bread, Cereals, Flour and Oats

1. **One from:** Pitta bread; Naan bread; Tortilla; Chapatti **[1]**
2. The texture of the bread can become very dry **[1]** and it can change the flavour of the bread **[1]**.
3. b) **[1]**   c) **[1]**
4. It has a high protein content, **[1]** which enables gluten to be produced when water is added. **[1]** This results in an elastic, stretchy dough, **[1]** which is essential to help bread to rise during proving and baking. **[1]**
5. Extraction rate means how much of the wholegrain of wheat has been used in the milling of the flour. **[1]** White flour has an extraction rate of 70–75%. **[1]**
6. a) Slow release energy. **[1]**
   b) **Three from:** Oats are high in carbohydrates/starch; They can make a person feel fuller for longer/prevent snacking; They are high in fibre; They can help reduce cholesterol levels in the blood; which can help prevent heart disease. **[3]**

Page 149: Rice, Potatoes and Pasta

1. **Two from:** Short grain; Long grain; Brown; Wild; Jasmine; Arborio; Basmati **[2]**
2. A thick outer husk.
3. **Two from:** Boiling; Steaming; Baking **[2]**
4. **One from:** Vitamin C group; Vitamin B group **[1]**
5. King **[1]** Edward **[1]** staple **[1]** main **[1]**
6. They can turn green **[1]** and become toxic **[1]** (contain a harmful substance).
7. **Two from:** Spaghetti; Tagliatelle; Lasagne; Penne; Tortellini; Cannelloni; Ravioli; Fusilli; Any other suitable answer **[2]**
8. Egg **[1]**

Page 150: Fruit and Vegetables

1. Limes **[1]** Grapefruits **[1]**
2. Apples **[1]** Pears **[1]** **Any other suitable answer**
3. a) 5–7 portions **[1]**
   b) **Two from:** Fruits and vegetables will provide us with a range of different vitamins and minerals, e.g. Vitamin C and A; They are a very good source of dietary fibre; They are low in fat. **[2]**
4. **One from:** Potassium; Magnesium **[1]**
5. Refrigerator/fridge **[1]**
6. Asparagus **[1]** Celery **[1]**.
7. They can be grown above the ground **[1]** or below the ground **[1]**.
8. **Type of storage:** Chilled/fridge/refrigerator storage **[1]**
   Explanation: To help reduce the loss of nutrients. **[1]** The longer they are stored, the more their nutritional value lessens **[1]**.

Page 151: Milk, Cheese and Yoghurt

1. **Two from:** Whole milk (full cream); Skimmed; Semi-skimmed; Goats milk; Soy milk; Lacto free milk; Almond milk; Coconut milk; Rice milk; 1% fat milk; Gold jersey full cream; Flora pro-activ milk; Protein milk **[2]**
2. HBV **[1]**
3. Carbohydrates are in the form of lactose, **[1]** which is a milk sugar. **[1]**
4. **Two from:** Soy milk; Lacto free milk; Almond milk; Coconut milk; Rice milk **[2]**
5. Homogenised milk has been forced through tiny holes in a machine. **[1]** This breaks up the fat and disperses it – it does not reform as a layer. **[1]**
6. Calcium **[1]**
7. a) **One from:** Camembert; Brie; Goats cheese **[1]**
   b) **One from:** Stilton; Danish blue; Dolcelatte; Roquefort; Gorgonzola **[1]**
8. **Three from:** Some cheeses can have a high fat content; and they can be in the form of saturated fat; High intakes of this type of fat can lead to heart related problems; Some cheeses can have a high salt content; A diet high in salt can lead to high blood pressure; which can lead to strokes and heart disease **[3]**.
9. Yoghurt **[1]** is made from milk **[1]** which has a friendly **[1]** bacteria culture **[1]** added to it.

Page 152: Meat

1. d) **[1]**
2. c) **[1]**
3. Meat is a muscle **[1]** composed of cells consisting of fibres **[1]**, held together by connective tissue **[1]**.
4. **One of:** Leg; Shoulder **[1]**.
5. **Two from:** Stewing; Braising; Casserole; Pot-roasting **[2]**.
6. The browning **[1]** of meat is caused by a reaction with natural sugars **[1]** and proteins to produce a dark colour. This occurrence is called the Maillard **[1]** reaction or non-enzymic browning. As the meat cooks the proteins coagulate **[1]** and produce a firm texture. Collagen is broken down into gelatine **[1]**.

Page 153: Fish

1. c) **[1]**
2. a) **[1]**
3. Enrobing **[1]**; Coating **[1]**
4. Fish cooks quickly because the muscle **[1]** is short and the connective tissue **[1]** is thin.
   The connective tissue is made up of collagen **[1]** and will change into gelatine **[1]** and coagulate **[1]** at 60 °C **[1]**.

5. **Classification of fish:** round
   One example of fish: One of: Cod; Haddock; Whiting; Pollock; Coley **[1]**. Chef is cutting into the top of the fish on one side of the tail to detach the backbone from the head to the tail **[1]**; Chef has left the head on the fish **[1]**.

Page 154: Eggs and Poultry

1. **Three from:** Boiling; Poaching; Frying; Scrambling; Baking **[3]**
2. **Two from:** Hens; Quails; Ducks; Geese **[2]**
3. a) **Product: Examples:** Pies; Sausage roll; Bread product, e.g. rolls, loaf type product **[1]**
   b) **Explain:** The glaze would give the product a golden brown colour **[1]** and a sheen/shiny coating to make the product look attractive. **[1]**
4. **Four from the following. The answer must be developed/extended not just bullet points:** Free range hens can walk around outside; Therefore their living environment is more natural; They can scratch and peck the ground for food; which can mean a better diet and more flavoursome eggs; The hens can also lay their eggs in nests; Enriched cage farm hens can be fed a diet that can have an impact on the flavour of the egg and colour of the egg yolk; Some people will not buy the eggs as they are kept in small cages inside sheds where they are cramped and stacked on top of each other which some people feel is cruel and unfair on the animal. **[4]**
5. enrich **[1]** colour **[1]** yellow **[1]** flavour **[1]** increase **[1]** nutritional **[1]**.
6. The shell has tiny holes which allow air and moisture to pass through. **[1]** Strong flavours will be absorbed by the shell. **[1]**

Page 155: Soya, Tofu, Beans, Nuts and Seeds

1. Flour **[1]**
2. Bean curd **[1]**
3. tofu **[1]** protein **[1]** alternative **[1]** meat **[1]**
4. Miso is a fermented soya bean paste. **[1]** It is used in Asian cuisine to provide flavouring. **[1]**
5. **Two from:** Butter beans; Haricot beans; Black-eyed beans; Kidney beans; Cannellini beans; Any other suitable answer **[2]**
6. Beans are an excellent source of protein **[1]** (for a person who does not consume any meat or fish). They will also provide some B group vitamins and iron **[1]** which can be key nutrients that a vegetarian can lack **[1]**.

7. **Two from, for example:** Chestnuts; Cashews; Hazelnuts; Walnuts; Pecans; Pistachios; Brazil nuts; Peanuts; Pine nuts [2]
8. **Two from:** They can be eaten on their own as a snack or combined with dried fruits; They can be used in the cooking of savoury foods, e.g. nut roast, curries, chestnut, mushroom and shallot pie; They can be added to sweet baked goods, e.g. cakes, cookies. [2]
9. **One from:** Sunflower seed; Rapeseed; Grapeseed; Pumpkin seed [1]

Page 156: Butters, Oils, Margarines, Sugar and Syrup

1. dairy [1]
2. It has a high saturated fat value/it is high in fat. [1]
3. It goes rancid [1]
4. Butter is made by churning or stirring cream or milk [1] until the butterfat sticks together [1] and separates from the buttermilk. [1]
5. **One from:** Walnut; Peanut; Almond; Hazelnut [1]
6. Vitamin A [1] Vitamin D [1]
7. Sugar traps air when creamed with butter or margarine, [1] which helps to aerate/raise the cake when it is baked.[1]
8. **Three correct points:** It can lead to dental cavities and tooth decay; Sugar does not provide any nutrients; Sugar is pure carbohydrates/empty calories; If we eat too much sugar/too many sugary foods and we do not use up or burn off the energy it will be stored as fat; in the adipose tissue under the skin; This can lead to weight gain and possibly obesity. [3]
9. Golden syrup [1] Black treacle [1]

Page 157: Protein and Fat

1. growth [1]; repair [1]
2. **Possible answers, two from:** Cheese; Milk; Eggs; Pulse vegetables; Soya; TVP; Mycoprotein (Quorn); Nuts [2]
3. **Possible answers, three from:** Meat; Fish; Cheese; Eggs; Milk; Soya [3]
4. Lentil soup and bread [1]
5. c) [1]
6. **Possible answers, one of:** Any type of oil, e.g. groundnut oil; Vegetable oil; Olive oil; Sunflower oil; Any solid fat that has been melted [1]
7. Provides concentrated energy. [1]; Provides body with vitamins A, D, E and K. [1]
8. Fatty Acids [1]; Glycerol [1]
9. Hydrogenation is the name given to the process that makes solid fat from a liquid oil [1].

Page 158: Carbohydrates

1. Sugars [1]; Starches [1]; Non-Starch Polysaccharide (dietary fibre) [1]
2. **One of:** Glucose; Galactose; Fructose [1].
3. digested [1]; energy [1]
4. a) **One of:** Wholemeal bread; Granary bread [1].

b) **One of:** Branflakes; All Bran; Fruit and fibre, etc. [1].
c) Jacket potatoes [1]
5. Dental decay [1]
6. **Two from:** The body will start to use protein and fat as an energy source; Weight loss; Lack of energy; Poor digestive health [2].
7. Starches [1] have to be digested into sugars [1] before absorption – this is slow [1] energy [1] release.
8. Constipation [1]

Page 159: Vitamins

1. **Two from:** Liver; Whole milk; Cheese; Green leafy vegetables; Carrots [2].
2. The water soluble group of vitamins [1]
3. Weak bones in children, that bend under body weight [1]; Associated with a vitamin D deficiency [1]
4. Skin cracking around the mouth [1]
5. Antioxidants protect us from pollutants in the environment [1].
6. A type of vitamin D [1] formed by action of sunlight on the skin [1]
7. b) [1]

Page 160: Minerals and Water

1. d) [1]
2. **One of:** Strong bones; Strong teeth; To enable clotting of blood; For nerves and muscles; Works with Vitamin D; Prevents rickets/brittle bones/osteoporosis [1].
3. **One of:** High blood pressure; Heart disease; Strokes [1].
4. Flavour [1]
5. A lack of iron in the diet can cause iron deficiency anaemia [1] and symptoms include tiredness [1].
6. Between six and eight glasses [1]
7. Fluoride is important for strengthening teeth against decay [1]
8. a) [1]

Page 161: Making Informed Choices

1. Fruit and vegetables [1]; Potatoes, bread, rice, pasta and other starchy carbohydrates [1]; Beans, pulses, fish, eggs, meat and other proteins [1]; Dairy (and alternatives) [1]; Oils and Spreads [1]
2. Human milk [1] provides babies with all their nutritional requirements, except for iron [1]. Babies are born with a supply of this stored in their liver [1].
3. A mother's first milk is called colostrum and it is full of antibodies [1].
4. For the development of the neural tube of the foetus [1]. This can prevent the condition spina bifida [1].
5. c) [1]
6. The Eatwell Guide [1] shows the proportions of food groups that should be eaten daily for a well-balanced [1] diet.
7. Eat plenty of fibre-rich foods [1]; for example, **any one of:** wholegrain cereals/wholemeal bread/wholegrain

breakfast cereals/wholemeal pasta/wholemeal flour/fruit/vegetables/dried fruit/nuts/seeds/beans, peas/lentils [1].

Page 162: Diet, Nutrition and Health

1. Coronary Heart Disease [1] is linked to diets high in saturated [1] fats, which make cholesterol [1] in the blood.
2. c) [1]
3. Five to seven portions (**allow** 5 portions) [1]
4. **Three from:** Weight gain/obesity; Can produce high/bad cholesterol; Can block arteries; Angina; Coronary Heart Disease (CHD)/heart disease/heart attack; Higher consumption of trans fats/higher risk of cancer [3].
5. In Type 2 diabetes, too little or no insulin [1] is produced resulting in high levels of sugar [1] in the blood [1].
6. b) [1]
7. Age [1]; Gender [1]; Body size [1]

Page 163: Food Choices

1. Vegetarians eat fish. False [1]; Buddhists eat pork. False [1]; Sikhs don't eat beef. True [1]
2. c) [1]
3. c) [1]
4. **Three from:** For health reasons; For religious reasons; Ethics – against cruelty to animals; Ethics – against over-using the Earth's resources; Don't like meat; Born into a vegetarian family [3].
5. a) Lacto-vegetarians do not eat: meat/fish/eggs/non-vegetarian cheese/gelatine (from bones) [1]; which involves killing the animal [1]; but do eat animal products such as milk/cream/yoghurt, etc. [1]
   b) Vegans do not eat anything sourced from animals [1]; such as: meat/fish/honey/gelatine/milk/milk products (cheese, butter, yoghurt, cream) [1]; but do eat plant-based foods [1]

Page 164: Cooking of Food, Heat Transfer and Selecting Appropriate Cooking Methods

1. c) [1]
2. Cooking uses heat [1]; in order to change the texture, flavour and colour of food [1]; and to improve palatability [1].
3. **Dry method, change to nutritional content:** Reduces fat [1]; **Water-based method, change to nutritional content:** vitamin C loss [1]; **Example:** Boiling potatoes/cabbage [1].
4. Cooking methods can alter the sensory [1] properties of food by adding crispness or softening. The right cooking methods can conserve [1] vitamins, or add [1] energy value. When meat needs cooking, long, slow

moist **[1]** cooking is best for tough **[1]** cuts of meat.
If the meat is tender a quick **[1]** and hot **[1]** method of cooking such as grilling can be used.

Page 165: Proteins and Enzymic Browning

1. c) **[1]**
2. a) A marinade is a liquid **[1]**; made from flavoursome and acidic ingredients that is used to soak **[1]**; foods prior **[1]** to cooking.
   b) A marinade is used to add flavour to foods from ingredients such as garlic, chillies, herbs and/or spices **[1]**; A marinade using acidic ingredients such as lemon juice, vinegar or buttermilk is used to make ingredients such as meat or fish more tender **[1]**; Marinades help to add moistness in foods that otherwise might be dry **[1]**.
   c) Chicken has a fairly bland, mild flavour **[1]**; therefore a marinade would add flavour **[1]**; The meat, chicken, would be made tender, kept juicy and not be tough **[1]**; and would cook quickly **[1]**
   d) BBQ **[1]**; Grill **[1]**
3. a) True **[1]**
   b) True **[1]**
   c) False **[1]**
   d) True **[1]**

Page 166: Carbohydrates

1. a) **[1]**
2. b) **[1]**
3. **semi-skimmed milk**: liquid for the sauce **[1]**
   wheat flour: thickener **[1]**
   margarine: fat for the roux **[1]**
   seasoning: (salt and pepper) flavour **[1]**
   Red Leicester cheese: main protein/cheese flavour **[1]**
   macaroni: pasta/carbohydrate **[1]**
4. 1 Boil the pasta **[1]**
   2 Drain the pasta **[1]**
   3 Prepare the sauce **[1]**
   4 Use the roux method or use the all-in-one method to prepare the sauce **[1]**
   5 Assemble the pasta and the sauce **[1]**
   6 Au gratin option **[1]**
5. Mix the roux (or use the all-in-one method) **[1]**; Heat thickens by starch gelatinising **[2]**; and beat – agitation ensures smoothness **[2]**

Page 167: Fats and Oils

1. b) **[1]**
2. a) The vinegar **[1]** and the melted butter **[1]** would not mix easily – they would separate on standing
   b) Seasoning makes the sauce taste better **[1]** Salt and pepper are commonly used as seasoning **[1]**
   c) The egg yolk contains lecithin **[1]** which emulsifies **[1]** the butter and vinegar to create a stable sauce **[1]**

3. a) binds **[1]**
   b) dextrinisation **[1]**
   c) shorten **[1]**
   d) steam **[1]**
   e) gluten **[1]**

Page 168: Raising Agents

1. a) **[1]**
2. **Names of chemical raising agents:**
   Bicarbonate of soda **[1]**; Baking powder **[1]**
   Examples of use, two from: Scones **[1]**; Gingerbread **[1]**; Biscuits **[1]**.
3. Carbon dioxide **[1]**
4. a) Water **[1]**; Eggs **[1]**
   b) During baking the water turns to steam **[1]**; The eggs expand **[1]** before setting/coagulating **[1]**, holding the risen shape
   c) Fully cooked buns are dry inside **[1]**; Steam has escaped **[1]**; This prevents collapse **[1]**
5. d) **[1]**

Page 169: Microorganisms and Food Spoilage

1. Warm temperature/37 °C **[1]**; Moisture **[1]**; Food **[1]**; Time **[1]**; Neutral pH **[1]**; May need oxygen **[1]**.
2. **Three from**: Mould grows; Flavour changes (souring); Bacterial contamination; Physical contamination from dirty machinery or careless food handlers; Contamination by flies, cockroaches, mice, rats, mites, domestic animals; Contamination by chemicals/radiation/pollution; Colour changes; Texture changes; Unpleasant odour **[3]**.
3. **Two from**: Cupboard should be free from vermin and pets; Wash shelves regularly/deal with spills immediately; Make sure storage containers are clean; Do not top up existing stock with new; Store dry foods in airtight containers/sealed packets; Keep a check on approximate storage times/best before dates; Store in a cool dry place **[2]**.
4. a) visible **[1]**
   b) acid **[1]**
   c) 70 °C **[1]**
   d) can **[1]**
   e) can't **[1]**
5. b) **[1]**

Page 170: Microorganisms in Food Production

1. Bacteria are single **[1]** -celled organisms that are able to reproduce rapidly **[1]**. Some are harmful **[1]** and cause food poisoning **[1]** or even death. Some bacteria are harmless and are used in cheese **[1]** making. Probiotic **[1]** bacteria help digestion **[1]**.
2. a) **[1]**
3. c) **[1]**
4. Air bubbles are trapped and distributed throughout the bread dough as it is mixed and kneaded

[1]; The yeast absorbs the starches and sugars in the flour, turning them into alcohol and carbon dioxide gas **[1]**; The gas inflates the air bubbles, causing the bread to rise **[1]**.

Page 171: Bacterial Contamination

1. a) **Food source, one of**: Raw meat, poultry/chicken; Eggs; Cooked meat; Dairy foods; Cheese; Mayonnaise; Bean sprouts. **[1]**
   Prevention, one of: Wash hands after handling raw meat, eggs etc.; Hard boil eggs/avoid lightly cooked or raw eggs; Defrost chicken before cooking; Cook meat, poultry/chicken thoroughly; Boil bean sprouts before use. **[1]**
   b) **Food source, one of**: Meat; Shellfish; Untreated water; Washing raw poultry **[1]**.
   Prevention, one of: Take measures to prevent transmission between humans; Raw meat and poultry **must not** be washed, as this spreads the bacteria **[1]**.
   c) **Food source, one of**: Cooked rice; Herbs and spices; Starchy food products **[1]**.
   Prevention, one of: Do not reheat rice dishes; Cool cooked rice immediately after cooking when making salads etc.; Do not keep herbs and spices past use-by date **[1]**.
2. **One of**: Diarrhoea; Dehydration; Headache; High/low temperature; Sickness/vomiting; Stomach ache/cramps/nausea/feeling sick **[1]**.
3. **Two from**: Food/nutrients; Moisture/damp; Oxygen/air; Time; Warmth **[2]**.

Page 172: Buying and Storing Food

1. **Six from**: Use a cool bag/cool box/polystyrene material to insulate the cold food from room temperature **[1]**; Keep the food covered in the boot of the car, if transporting home by car **[1]**; Ensure all refrigerated food is kept together in the same bag **[1]**; Do not buy frozen foods if you can't get them home quickly as they will defrost **[1]**; Use a collection service to get refrigerated food home as quickly as possible **[1]**; Use a home delivery service to get refrigerated food straight from refrigerated transport into your fridge **[1]**; Take the quickest route home so that refrigerated food is out of the fridge for as short a time as possible **[1]**; Store refrigerated food in a fridge, if available, at work **[1]**; Buy food with good packaging to keep it in shape, avoid squashing etc., e.g. eggs **[1]**; Park car in a shaded cool spot/not sunny area to keep the internal temperature of the car down so that temperature gain in refrigerated food is kept to a minimum **[1]**.

2. **Six from**: Avoid cross contamination/ transfer from raw meat to cooked meat products by: foods touching/ blood and juices dripping/transferring by hands, work surfaces/knives or equipment [1]; Good personal hygiene of workers – hand washing/clean protective overalls [1]; Good hygiene during cooking and serving – cover and cool all cooked meat as rapidly as possible/don't prepare too far in advance/no exposure to flies etc. [1]; Use red chopping boards [1]; Avoid incorrect storage, i.e. room temperature instead of below 8 °C/not covering meat/store in bottom of refrigerator to avoid drip contamination [1]; Storage – use stock rotation/stick to use-by date [1]; Thaw meat thoroughly before cooking [1]; Do not undercook meat or bacteria will not be killed in centre/ use a temperature probe to make sure that the correct temperature needed to kill bacteria has been reached [1]; Chilling – allow meat to cool before putting it into chill cabinets or the freezer/90 mins to chill below 8 °C/ use a blast chiller to cool quickly [1]; Reheat to the correct temperature for a long enough period of time (over 72 °C) [1]; Hot holding – make sure hot meat products are kept at a hot enough holding temperature (63 °C) [1]; Freezing – do not refreeze meat once it has been defrosted [1].

Page 173: Preparing and Cooking Food

1. **Three from**: Store food in the correct place [1] because this reduces the chance of cross contamination/ microorganism growth [1]; Store food at the correct temperature [1] because microorganisms require specific temperatures to grow, therefore, keeping them out of their temperature-growth zone slows bacteria growth [1]; Store food for the correct period of time [1] because storing food for longer than recommended increases the likelihood of microorganisms being present and growing in the food [1]; Defrost frozen products thoroughly [1] so that they can then be cooked to the correct temperature throughout – this ensures microorganisms in the middle of the food are killed [1]; Wear clean clothes when handling food [1] because this reduces the chances of contamination from clothing, e.g. dirt or pet hair [1]; Wash hands thoroughly and regularly, especially after using the toilet, handling rubbish or handling raw or different food products [1] because this reduces the chances of contamination from these sources [1]; Use clean equipment/clean the equipment thoroughly [1] because this reduces the chances of cross contamination

if the equipment was used for a different food item, e.g. raw and cooked meats [1]; Do not allow raw food to come into contact with cooked food [1] so that the chances of cross contamination are reduced [1]; Do not cough/sneeze over food or touch your nose/face when handling food [1] because this can spread bacteria/viruses present, leading to an increased risk of food poisoning [1]; Do not let animals or pests enter the food preparation area [1] because animals carry diseases and bacteria which can infect the food, and their hairs may also infect the food [1]; Cook food to the correct temperature [1] to ensure that microorganisms are killed to stop their growth [1]; Cook food for the correct amount of time [1] so that the food is cooked all the way through, with no cold spots – this ensures that all parts of the food have been heated to at least above the danger zone for microorganism growth [1]; Cool leftover food quickly [1] so that the time in which the food is in the danger zone is minimised, thereby reducing the chances of contamination and microorganism growth [1]; Reheat food only once [1] as food that has been cooked and cooled previously gives microorganisms more opportunity to grow [1]; Tie hair back/do not wear jewellery/false nails [1] to reduce the likelihood of these objects, or bacteria from them, falling into the food and contaminating it [1]. **(1 mark for each point made, with an additional 1 mark for explanation of each point – both must be given – up to a maximum of 6 marks.)**

2. **Four from**: Avoid cross contamination [1]; Check use-by date [1]; Use appropriately colour-coded board/ separate equipment [1]; Cook thoroughly/use a probe to check the temperature [1]; Once cooked serve immediately [1]; Use a clean knife/ chopping board/work surface for preparation [1]; Wash hands before preparing/after handling [1]; Wear protective clothing/make sure hair is tied back [1].

3. **Eight from**: Store foods according to their correct storage instructions [1]; Use correct cooking utensils for different foods [1]; Clean equipment and surfaces (with an antibacterial spray) [1]; Use within the best-before and use-by dates [1]; Clear up goods that have spilled [1]; Cook foods according to their cooking instructions [1]; Wash your hands [1]; Tie hair back [1]; Take off jewellery [1]; Remove nail varnish [1]; Wear a clean apron [1]; Take extra care with food preparation when ill [1]; Cover food [1]; Avoid coughing/sneezing over food [1]; Handle food as little as possible [1]; Cover cuts with waterproof dressing [1]; Avoid cross-contamination [1].

Page 174: Food Preservation

1. High temperature [1]; Low temperature [1]; Drying [1]; Chemical [1].

2. **Method, one of**: Freezing; Sugar; Vinegar; Oven-drying [1]. **Shelf life, corresponding one of**: Freezing – food is preserved for up to one year in temperatures between −18 °C and −29 °C [1]; Sugar – fruit is preserved with sugar, e.g. jam, for a couple of years [1]; Vinegar – vegetables can be preserved for up to two years by immersion in vinegar [1]; Oven drying – a warm oven can be used to dry foods slowly and they can then be stored in an airtight container for several months [1].

3. Low temperature does not affect nutritional value [1]

4. Meat/fish is 'cooked' by exposing it to heat from wood fires [1]; This gives it a distinctive smoky taste [1].

5. Fruit could be preserved in jars of alcohol – usually brandy [1]; Fruit could be added to sugar to make jams [1]; Vegetables could be pickled in vinegar to make pickles or chutneys and stored in jars [1]; Vegetables could be stored in jars in a brine (salt) solution [1].

6. They are pickled in vinegar with spices [1]

7. It is salted [1]; It can also be smoked [1]

Page 175: Food Provenance and Production Methods

1. When traceability is fully available, trust is built between the retailer and the consumer [1]; Other criteria in which the consumer has an interest, such as ensuring the food is organic, vegetarian, specific allergen free, Kosher or Halal can be guaranteed via traceability [1]; This ensures that consumers can have confidence in the food they purchase [1]; Where there is a risk to public health, manufacturers may need to isolate sources, so traceability is practical [1].

2. **Battery, two from**: Large numbers of hens kept in massive buildings designed to maximise growth [1]; Fed on high-nutrient feeds over a short period of time [1]; Antibiotics and growth enhancers widely used [1]. **Free range**: These hens have access to outdoor areas for part of their lives [1]; They do not live in cages [1]. **Barn, two from**: These hens live in an environment similar to intensively-reared animals but have access to natural light from windows [1]; They live in a lower density of animals per square metre [1]; They have access to environment enrichment such as fresh straw [1]. **Organic**: Hens are fed on products free from chemical or synthetic treatments that have relied on natural compost and manure for fertilisers

[1]; Often kept out of doors with complete freedom [1].
3. b); c) [2]

Page 176: Food Provenance: Food and the Environment

1. At each stage of a product's lifecycle energy [1] is needed to process [1], transport [1] and dispose [1] of the product; carbon dioxide [1] is produced as a by-product of energy use. The carbon footprint [1] is the calculation of the carbon dioxide produced throughout a product's life.
2. Deforestation [1] occurs when trees are cut down. Cleared land is used as pasture [1] for livestock [1] and plantations [1] of commodities and settlements. Deforested regions typically suffer soil erosion [1] and frequently degrade into wasteland [1].
3. Wise shopping and planning ahead reduces the amount of food bought in the first place [1]; FIFO (first-in first-out storage) reduces food wasted [1]; Only prepare the food you actually need, so nothing is needlessly thrown away [1]; Use food before it goes out of date, so that food does not have to be thrown away for safety reasons [1]; Use leftover food to make other dishes, thereby avoiding having to throw leftover food out [1]; Do home composting so that any food you have to throw out does not have to be transported to a landfill site [1].
4. **Any two suitable answers, e.g.:** Bubble and squeak; Rissoles; Soup; Corned beef hash [2].

Page 177: Food Provenance: Sustainability of Food

1. CO_2/carbon dioxide [1]
2. **Three from**: Increase crop diversity; Improve soil organics by using animal waste; Change the dependence on fossil fuels to transport foods; Tackle deforestation issues; Put in irrigation systems in drier areas; Look at crop rotation to reduce soil erosion and the general health of crops; Prevent soil erosion from winds, high rainfall and flooding [3].
3. a) **Two from**: The Fairtrade logo means that the farmer in a developing country who produced the goods gets a realistic income; Investment in the local community takes place; There are better working conditions for the producing farmer; A fair price is paid for the goods; Sustainable production methods are used [2].
   b) **Possible answers, two from**: Chocolate; Tea; Coffee; Bananas **(two answers needed for 1 mark)**.
4. The Red Tractor logo tells us that the food has been produced, processed and packed to the Red Tractor standards [1]; The flag on the Red Tractor logo shows the country of origin [1]; Red Tractor labelling assures good standards of food hygiene and safety [1]; Red Tractor labelling assures high standards of equipment used in production [1]; Red Tractor standards assure good standards of animal health and welfare [1]; Environmental issues are respected by Red Tractor suppliers [1]; Red Tractor standards ensure responsible use of pesticides [1]. Any product with the Red Tractor logo can be traced from farm to fork [1].
5. Livestock, especially cows, produce methane gas [1]; Methane gas is 20 times more harmful than CO_2 [1], (cows produce more Greenhouse Gases (GHG) than the entire world's transport.)

Page 178: British and International Cuisine

1. b) [1]
2. Wensleydale [1]
3. a) Cornish pasty [1]; hotpot [1]
   b) bouillabaisse [1]; Quiche Lorraine [1]
   c) tortilla [1]; paella [1]
   d) Peking duck [1]; chow mein [1]
   e) pakora [1]; dhal [1]
   f) minestrone [1]; focaccia [1]
4. **Answers depend on student's choice of country**

Page 179: Food Manufacturing

1. **Two from:** Untreated milk; Sugar beet; Raw potatoes; Grain of wheat; Maize; Soya beans [2]
2. Secondary [1] change [1] primary [1] ingredient [1] food [1]
3. **Two from:** Cream; Butter; Cheese; Yoghurt [2]
4. Identical [1] Artificial/synthetic [1]
5. They stop foods from spoiling. [1] They give foods a longer shelf life. [1]
6. They are used to replace flavours lost during food processing. [1] They are used to enhance the flavour of a food. [1]
7. They are aware that additives can cause allergies such as skin rashes or breathing difficulties. [1] They know that the use of some artificial colours can make children hyperactive. [1] They are aware that additives can be used to conceal the use of lower quality ingredients. [1] They are concerned that a daily consumption of foods containing additives could have an impact on their health. [1]

Page 180: Factors Affecting Food Choice: Sensory Evaluation

1. smell [1]
2. a) [1]
3. a) Quiet area [1]; Invite people to taste [1]; Provide: water to cleanse palate [1]; Coded sample of food [1]; Clean eating implements, if needed [1]; Use a recording sheet [1].
   b) Testing two similar food products [1]; Three samples are used but two the same [1]; All samples are coded differently [1]; The aim is to try to identify the 'odd one out' [1].
   c) **Name of product: any suitable name [1]**
   Samples to trial: any suitable answer, e.g. 15% fat minced beef [1]; 5% fat minced beef [1].

Page 181: Factors Affecting Food Choice

1. b) [1]
2. c) [1]
3. a) Exercise improves cardiovascular and bone health [1]; Exercise helps to maintain a healthy weight [1]; Exercise improves self-confidence/mental health [1]; Exercise develops new social skills if taken with other people, e.g. team sports, aerobics classes [1].
   b) The Eatwell Guide [1]
   c) Variety of flavours [1]; Variety of textures [1]; Variety of colours [1].
   d) **Four from**: The type of work done by people in the household will affect their appetites; The number of hours worked by people in the household will affect their appetites; The travelling (commuting) time of members of the household will affect the amount of time available for the preparation and consumption of food; The pastimes of individuals will affect their appetite and the amount of time available for shopping, preparing and cooking food; Whoever is in charge of the planning and cooking of food will influence the types of food bought and consumed; The available income for buying food will affect the types of foods eaten; If someone is vegetarian/vegan; If someone has a food allergy/intolerance; Any other suitable answer [4]

Page 182: Food Labelling

1. c) [1]
2. b) [1]
3. a) Reference Intake [1]
   b) **Six from**: Weight or volume ('e' means approximate weight); Ingredients list (from largest to smallest); Allergen information; GM (Genetically Modified) ingredients; Date mark and storage; Cooking instructions – to ensure food is safe to eat; Place of origin; Name and address of manufacturer (in case of complaint); Lot or batch mark (for traceability); Nutritional information on pre-packaged foods [6].
4. b) [1]

Page 183: Knife Skills

1. a) [1]
2. b) [1]

3. **Name of knife hold 1:** Bridge
   hold [1]
   Explanation: Form a bridge with
   thumb and index finger, hold item
   flat side down on chopping board,
   position knife under the bridge and
   cut firmly downwards. [1]
   Name of knife hold 2: Claw grip [1]
   Explanation: Place item to be cut flat
   side down on chopping board, shape
   hand into a claw, tuck thumb inside
   fingers, rest the claw on item to be
   sliced, use other hand to slice the
   item, moving clawed fingers away as
   cutting progresses. [1]
4. **Four from:** Carry knife pointing
   downwards; Handle should be grease-
   free; Don't put in washing-up bowl;
   Keep clean; Keep sharp; Do not leave
   on edge of surface; Use correct knife
   for the job to be done [4].

Page 184: Prepare, Combine and Shape

1. c) [1]
2. a) [1]
3. Whisking involves adding air into
   the mixture while mixing [1]; Stirring
   does not involve adding air into the
   mixture while mixing [1].
4. **Two from:** Consistency of depth;
   Consistency of size; Consistency of
   shape [2].
5. The following mixing skills should be
   used to ensure the smooth consistency
   of the batter: Cream [1] together the
   fat and sugar [1]; Beat [1] the eggs;
   Fold [1] in the flour. The following
   shaping skills should be used to ensure
   quality of finish: Use cake tins [1] to
   mould [1] the shape of the cake. Pipe
   [1] the cream for a good decorative
   finish [1].
6. Use a burger mould (or burger press)
   [1]; Weigh the mixture to make sure
   the same quantity is used for each
   burger [1]

Page 185: Dough

1. c) [1]
2. b) [1]
3. Rubbing in [1]
4. To bind the dough together [1]
5. Weigh all the ingredients accurately
   [1].
   Place fat [1] and water [1] in a pan
   and bring to a rolling boil [1].
   Add sieved flour [1] immediately and
   mix well to form a paste [1].
   Cool [1] then add beaten eggs
   gradually to a heavy dropping [1]
   consistency. Cook in a hot oven.
6. Glutenin [1]; Gliadin [1]

Pages 186-200: Practice Exam Paper 1

1. a) (i) True [1] (ii) False [1] (iii) False [1]
   b) **Two from:** Keep ingredients/
   equipment as cool as possible;
   Sieve the flour to remove lumps/

add air; Use fingertips only to rub
the fat in; Avoid over rubbing
in the fat; Do not add too much
water; Use a palette knife/kitchen
knife to bind the ingredients to
form a dough; Handle the mixture
lightly. [2]
   c) **Two from:** Only roll the pastry
   dough out once – to avoid tough
   pastry; Avoid turning the pastry
   over when rolling out – to avoid
   tough/heavy pastry due to more
   flour being absorbed; Roll the pastry
   out using short, sharp strokes and
   turn the dough as necessary – to
   achieve an even thickness; Roll out
   the pastry to a large circle – so that
   it is the same shape as the tin and
   will fit without any patching up;
   Make sure the pastry is rolled out to
   a big enough circle – so that it will
   fit the tin accurately; Roll the dough
   gently round the rolling pin – to
   prevent the dough from tearing;
   Gently unroll the dough over the
   tin – to avoid tearing the dough/ so
   the dough is in position to be fitted
   to the tin; Gently lower the pastry
   all the way round – so that it fits the
   tin/touches the bottom and does
   not shrink down when trimmed; Use
   a small ball of pastry to mould the
   pastry to the tin – to get an accurate
   fit/avoid squashing the pastry;
   Leave the pastry to relax/chill before
   cooking – to avoid shrinking; Prick
   the base of the pastry case with a
   fork before lining with paper and
   beans – to allow steam/air to escape
   and prevent bubbling. [4]
   d) **Two clear points needed.**
   First point must be one from:
   Greaseproof paper stops
   the pastry from browning;
   Greaseproof paper protects the
   pastry from marks from the beans;
   Greaseproof paper prevents the
   beans from sticking to the pastry;
   Greaseproof paper makes it easier
   to remove/lift the beans after
   baking. [1]
   Second point must be one from:
   The beans help to keep sides
   from collapsing; Help the pastry
   case keep its structure/shape; The
   beans stop the base of the pastry
   from rising. [1]
   e) **Award 3–4 marks for a good
   response which shows clear
   knowledge and understanding of
   the scientific changes that occur
   when baking shortcrust pastry
   in the oven. At least 2–3 clear
   changes have been identified,
   described and explained and the
   candidate has made good use of
   technical vocabulary. Award 1–2
   marks for a satisfactory response
   which shows some knowledge
   and understanding of at least 1–2
   changes that occur when baking
   shortcrust pastry in the oven.
   The candidate has attempted**

**to use technical terminology.
Award 0 marks for a response not
creditworthy or not attempted.**
Answers could include:
   - Air incorporated during the
     making stages can expand on
     heating, making the pastry rise.
   - The gluten in the flour absorbs
     water and can be stretched by any
     air present as it expands.
   - The heat of the oven sets the
     gluten network in the shape of
     the tin (e.g. flan tin).
   - The starch grains in the flour will
     burst and absorb the fat.
   - If the oven is not hot enough
     the fat will melt and run out, the
     flour will not get cooked, and
     the pastry will be heavy and very
     greasy.
   - If sugar has been added to the
     pastry it will develop colour and
     flavour through the process of
     caramelisation.
   - When the surface of the pastry
     has reached a high enough
     temperature a Maillard reaction
     will provide flavour and colour.
     If the pastry surface has been
     brushed with raw egg it will add
     to this reaction.
2. a) Fried egg [1]
   b) The egg has the shell removed and
   it is put into a pan with oil/fat. [1]
   The egg is coated/basted with oil
   as it cooks, which increases the fat
   content. [1]
   c) Poaching [1]
   d) Salmonella food poisoning. [1]
   Two symptoms from: Diarrhoea;
   Vomiting; Fever [2]
   e) **Two from:** Keep the kitchen
   clean and tidy; Clean and
   disinfect all areas, equipment
   and utensils used to prepare
   food; Keep food covered;
   Handle food as little as possible;
   Store food correctly; Cook food
   thoroughly; Remove food waste
   and rubbish. [2]
   f) **Three from:** To avoid cross
   contamination; To keep raw
   foods and cooked foods apart; To
   avoid bacteria transfer; To avoid
   a named type of food poisoning/
   bacteria.
   **To award full marks some
   examples must be included in the
   answer, e.g.** Red chopping board
   for raw meat; Yellow chopping
   board for cooked meat. [3]
3. a) **Four from:** When sugar is
   consumed it is broken down by
   the bacteria on the plaque found
   on teeth; By this process, the sugar
   turns into acid; This acid causes
   the tooth enamel to dissolve; With
   damaged or non-existent enamel,
   the tooth is weakened; As a result
   of weakened enamel, a cavity
   (hole) develops in the tooth; The
   whole tooth can become damaged
   as a result of the cavity; Pain may

result because of the damaged tooth; Fillings will have to be applied to the damaged tooth or a complete extraction will be necessary [4].

Plus, four from: Avoid sugary drinks – always check labels or use sugar apps to find out information about sugar content; Choose water instead of a sugary drink; Reduce consumption of high sugar foods, cakes, biscuits, chocolate and sweets: Do not give sweets as a reward to children; Avoid breakfast cereals coated with sugar, which are typically marketed to children; Reduce the sugar content of foods when doing home baking – use natural fruits or dried fruits as an alternative to sugar; Teach children about the dangers of overconsumption of sugar – help them to make the right decisions; Parents should teach children by example – by not eating too much sugar themselves; Check school food policy on sugar and on sugar in school dinners [4].

b) Named disease, **two from**: Diabetes (Type 2) [1]; Obesity [1]; Coronary heart disease [1].
Causes – diabetes type 2: High blood sugar [1]; Lack of insulin/no insulin to regulate sugar levels [1].
Causes – obesity, two from: Sugar is high in calories [1]; Over-consumption leads to excess fat forming [1] under skin and around internal organs [1].
Causes – coronary heart disease, any two from: High blood sugar level leads to diabetes type 2, which more than doubles the risk of developing coronary heart disease [1]; Lining of blood vessels become thick, which restricts blood flow [1]; Heart has to work harder to get oxygen around the body [1].

4. a) **Choux pastry: Function** – to give structure to the pastry [1].
Description – flour is used to thicken the pastry dough [1], the flour forms structure [1]
Bread: Function – to provide gluten [1].
Description – two from: makes the dough [1], stretchy dough lets yeast work [1], sets on cooking [1]
b) **Two from**: Pasteurised milk [1] – this extends shelf life [1]; Skimmed, pasteurised [1] – all or most of the cream is removed [1]; Semi-skimmed, pasteurised [1]; some of the cream is removed [1]; Ultra-Heat Treated (UHT), also known as long life milk [1] – has a shelf life of up to six months [1]; Sterilised, homogenised [1] – has a longer shelf life/has a slightly caramel flavour [1]; Dried [1]; Evaporating the water, leaving a fine powder [1].

Canned; evaporated [1] – Water evaporated off. Sweet and concentrated. Homogenised. Sealed in cans and sterilised [1]. Condensed [1] is evaporated milk that hasn't been sterilised; added sugar; very thick [1].
(1 mark for the name of each type of milk and 1 mark for each reason.)
c) **One from**: Butter [1] – cream is churned to make butter [2]; Cream [1] – the fat removed from milk is used [2]; Cheese [1] – this is milk in its solid form [2]; Yoghurt [1] – milk has a bacteria culture added to it [2].

5. a) **Victoria sandwich not rising, two from**: Too much sugar, causing the gluten to be over-softened so that it collapses; Too much raising agent, causing the gluten to overstretch and collapse; Undercooking, caused by the wrong temperature or cooking time; Opening the oven door before the gluten has set, so the heavy cold air makes it sink [2].
Lumpy cheese sauce, two from: Liquid and starch not blended before cooking; Insufficient stirring during the cooking; Cheese added when sauce is cooled so does not melt; Roux not cooked sufficiently; Incorrect proportion of ingredients [2].
b) (i) **Two from**: Replace the full fat milk with semi skimmed/skimmed milk; Replace cream with crème fraiche/use low-fat cream products; Replace the double cream with semi-skimmed or skimmed milk; Replace Cheddar cheese with Edam/use lower-fat cheese; Use a very strong cheese and use less; Use raw onions instead of fried onions; Change pastry type and use filo pastry for case. [2]
(ii) **One from**: Plain flour could be changed to wholemeal flour or half white/half wholemeal could be used; Add additional vegetables, e.g. mushrooms/leeks to add more fibre. [1]
(iii) **If only one ingredient is discussed only half marks can be awarded. Both ingredients must be discussed in detail for top marks to be awarded. For the function of each ingredient: Award 0–1 marks for one suggested function, Award 2 marks for two suggestions with no explanation or one suggestion with a full explanation, Award 3 marks for three suggestions, or two suggestions with detailed explanation.
Eggs – Reference could be made to:** to provide protein/

adds nutritional value/enriching, they set/coagulate/solidify the filling, eggs add colour to the flan – give the filling a yellow/golden colour, when the eggs are beaten together they trap air which gives the quiche filling a light/soufflé type texture, eggs will provide some flavour to the filling.
Cheese – Reference could be made to: to provide protein/calcium/fat, which add nutritional value/increases the value, it adds colour as the cheese will go golden brown as the quiche cooks, it can provide a subtle flavour if a mild cheese is used or a sharp/mature flavour if strong cheese is used, cheese can enhance the texture of the quiche as when melted it will be soft and moist. [6]

6. a) (i) **One from**: Protein; Fat [1]
(ii) Disaccharides [1] Double sugars/more complex sugars [1] made up of two monosaccharides, [1] e.g. sucrose. [1]
Polysaccharides [1] Made up of many monosaccharides units [1] joined together [1], e.g. starch. [1]

7. Information on 6–7 of the following points should be discussed with some explanation about why it is important for teenagers to include the nutrient suggested or follow the recommendation put forward. There should include some reference to what a poor diet/an unhealthy lifestyle can lead to.
To award 10–12 marks an excellent range of detailed nutritional and dietary recommendations must be included which also refer to examples, 3–4 healthy lifestyle points are included. To award 7–9 marks a good range of nutritional and dietary recommendations must be included, with some examples; 2–3 healthy lifestyle points are included. To award 4–6 marks a satisfactory range of nutritional and dietary recommendations must be included. 1–2 healthy lifestyle points are included. To award 1–3 marks a limited range of nutritional and dietary recommendations must be included. 1 healthy lifestyle point is included.
Nutritional/ dietary recommendation points to discuss: Following the Eatwell Guide and why, the importance of five to seven portions of fruits/vegetables a day, e.g. vitamin sources, eating a range of protein foods and why, having a diet that provides calcium and iron and why, e.g. calcium for bone and teeth formation. The importance

of energy providing foods – starchy options and having a good provision of dietary fibre/NSP and basing meals on carbohydrates rather than high fat based options. Monitoring their intake of saturated fats and keeping a check on the amounts and types of fat being consumed. The importance of eating a diet low in sugar and the consequences of having a high sugar consumption. Eating foods that do not contain too much salt – what are the problems associated with a high salt consumption? Trying to incorporate two portions of oily fish per week and why.

Healthy lifestyle points could include reference to: the importance/benefits of eating breakfast, regular exercise/keeping active/taking up sport/walking – why is this important, drinking water and the recommended number of glasses – why. Making sure they get sufficient sleep and why.

8. a) Fat soluble vitamins [1] Water soluble vitamins [1]
   b) **Ten points from:** Vitamin C/B1 is destroyed by heat; So eating cabbage raw, e.g. in coleslaw, would lessen the loss of the vitamin; Prepare the cabbage quickly and just before cooking to reduce loss; Due to exposure of oxygen; If cooking the cabbage use a small amount of boiling water to cook it; Make sure the water is boiling before putting the cabbage in to reduce the cooking time; Use the cooking liquid to make a sauce or gravy; Avoid cooking the cabbage in water; Vitamin C/B1 will dissolve into water; Try an alternative method, e.g. steam/stir fry; Cook the cabbage for as short a time as possible. **[10]**

Pages 201–214: Practice Paper 2

1. a) (i) False [1] (ii) True [1] (iii) True [1]
   b) **Two from:** To give a golden brown colour/give a brown colour; To give a shiny appearance; To give an attractive sheen; To improve the appearance of the bread **[2]**
   c) Conduction [1] – the metal tin or bread loaf tin heats up by conduction and the heat passes into the food that is on the tray/in the tin [1] OR Radiation [1] – the heat is transferred from the oven element or gas flames into the oven by radiation [1]
   d) **Both sections of the question must be answered – describing the stage and explaining its importance – to gain full marks. Kneading:** Work/manipulate the dough to make it smooth/silky [1] and to add air to give it lightness [1] Distributes the yeast for an even rise [1] Helps to develop the

gluten, which enables the dough to become stretchy/elastic. This will help hold the carbon dioxide bubbles produced. [1]
   Proving: When you give the dough rest time in a warm place for a period of time, undisturbed. [1] It allows the dough to grow/rise due to the action of the yeast. The dough rises due to the production of CO_2 fermentation of yeast. [1] This allows the volume of dough to expand due to the gases and air, and gives a uniform texture. [1] It allows the gluten to recover from the strain of shaping. [1]

2. a) Frozen chicken quarter pounder [1]
   b) It has a rice coating on the outside of the burger. Rice has a high carbohydrate value. **[1]**
   c) **Two from:** The raw burgers should be kept separate from cooked meat to avoid cross contamination; The burgers should be covered; They should be stored at the bottom of the fridge; They should be stored between 0°C and 5°C. **[2]**
   d) Oven baking [1] so no additional fat is added [1] and fats within the meat [1] will melt and drain out of the burger [1] OR Grilling/barbequing [1] so the burgers will sit on cooking bars/grid [1] enabling the fat to drain away [1] compared to frying where the burgers will sit in the fat and absorb it. [1]
   e) The red meat would turn brown. [1] This is caused by a reaction with natural sugars and proteins [1] to produce a dark colour – this is called Maillard reaction or non-enzymic browning **(only one name required).** [1] As the meat cooks, the proteins coagulate due to the heat. [1] Collagen breaks down into gelatine, [1] which makes the burgers tender. [1]

3. a) **Three from:** Energy linked to Kcal [2]; Warmth/insulation linked to body fat [2]; Protection of internal organs – kidneys [2]; Source of fat-soluble vitamins A, D, E and K linked to relevant food sources [2]; Formation of cell membranes – maintenance and good health [2].
   b) **Six from:** Three energy-giving macronutrients are identified: Carbohydrates are present within breakfast in the form of starch and sugars [1]. Specifically, they will be provided from the bread and the hot chocolate drink [1]. Energy may be released in different ways depending upon the type of food. In this particular instance there will be a slow release of energy from the wholemeal bread [1]. Fat: Present within the breakfast in the form of saturated and unsaturated fats [1]. Specifically provided from the sausages, streaky bacon, whole milk and cooking fats [1]. There is a lot

of fat in this breakfast that will deliver high energy content [1]. Protein: Protein is a secondary source of energy and is available in the egg, sausage and milk [1]. **Any other relevant and correct response can be credited.**

4. a) **Saturated fat: description of make-up – two from:** Contains the maximum amounts of hydrogen; Molecule made up of single bonds (diagram could be drawn); Solid fat; Solid animal fat. **[2]**
   Examples – two from: Butter; Lard; Ghee; Dripping; Suet; Cream; Coconut oil **[2]**
   Unsaturated fat: description of make-up – two from: Able to accept more hydrogen; More than one double bond in the molecule (diagram could be drawn); Vegetable source – oils **[2]**
   Examples – two from: Vegetable oil; Corn oil; Olive oil; Rape seed oil; Sunflower oil; Groundnut oil; Sesame oil; Some fish oils; Commercial fats, e.g. Flora products **[2]**
   b) **Any 12 from:** High fat diets linked to high cholesterol [1], which attaches to sides of arteries, narrows them, restricts blood flow, blocks arteries [1], can lead to Coronary Heart Disease (CHD) [1]. Linked to High Blood Pressure, angina and stroke [1]. High fat diets are high energy possibly leading to obesity [1], which causes both physical and psychological problems [1]. In addition to a high fat diet, there are several factors that often work together to contribute to ill health and increased future health risks. **These are some possible responses, but other relevant factors should be rewarded as appropriate:** Lack of physical activity [1]; Psychological influences – for example, may use eating as a coping mechanism for dealing with emotional problems, such as family break-up, etc. [1]; Genetics – for example, family history of overweight people due to genetic reasons [1], family history of medical conditions [1]; Socio-economic issues – for example, low income backgrounds [1], lack of time, resources, knowledge, skills [1], reliance on fast foods [1], parents working and effect of each of these on food choices [1]. Also note that there are unhealthy dietary options that do not reflect current government dietary guidelines, such as the Eatwell Guide [1].

5. a) It is made with pastry/flour which contains gluten/wheat [1]; It will give them pain, upset stomach/coeliacs are glucose intolerant. [1]